MICROSOFT
QuickBASIC

MICROSOFT
QuickBASIC

Developing
Structured
Programs
With
Microsoft's
Advanced
BASIC

Douglas Hergert

MICROSOFT
PRESS

PUBLISHED BY

Microsoft Press
A Division of Microsoft Corporation
16011 N.E. 36th Way, Box 97017, Redmond, Washington 98073-9717

Library of Congress Cataloging in Publication Data
Hergert, Douglas.
Microsoft QuickBASIC
Includes index.
1. BASIC (Computer program language)
2. Microsoft QuickBASIC (Computer program)
I. Title.
QA76.73.B3H48   1987   005.13'3   86-31198

ISBN 0-914845-99-3

Printed and bound in the United States of America.

  2 3 4 5 6 7 8 9 FGFG 8 9 0 9 8 7

Distributed to the book trade in the
United States by Harper & Row.

Distributed to the book trade in
Canada by General Publishing Company, Ltd.

Distributed to the book trade outside the
United States and Canada by Penguin Books Ltd.

Penguin Books Ltd., Harmondsworth, Middlesex, England
Penguin Books Australia Ltd., Ringwood, Victoria, Australia
Penguin Books N.Z. Ltd., 182-190 Wairau Road, Auckland 10, New Zealand

British Cataloging in Publication Data available

C O N T E N T S

INTRODUCTION

*T*he Microsoft QuickBASIC Compiler is a powerful programming environment in which to create applications for IBM personal computers and compatibles. Amateur and professional programmers will appreciate outstanding new features, such as:

- A full-screen, menu-driven editor with cut-and-paste and search-and-replace features.

- A fast and efficient compiler that produces program code that runs extremely fast.

- Compiling options that enable you to generate programs to run in memory, produce two types of Object files (*OBJ*), or create Executable program files (*EXE*) that can be run directly from DOS.

- A structured language that includes subprograms, parameter passing, local and global variables, multiline user-defined functions, and flexible multiline IF...THEN...ELSE statements.

This book is for BASIC programmers who are ready to make the transition to a professional programming environment. The aim is to teach structured programming techniques through a collection of useful application examples. Five major programs appear in the book:

Mortgage, a mortgage calculation program that teaches the use of data types.

QuickChart, a chart- and table-creating utility that exemplifies the use of loops, arrays, and graphics.

Survey, an information gathering and data analysis program that shows how to create and manipulate sequential data files.

Employee, a company database management program that demonstrates how to create and manipulate random-access files.

Twenty-one, a game program that displays the power of QuickBASIC's new decision structures.

These applications are presented as exercises—for you to explore, study, use, and revise.

How this book is structured

The first three chapters orient you to QuickBASIC's programming environment and introduce you to its new development tools and language elements. They also acquaint you with the techniques and benefits of *structured programming*.

- Chapter 1, "Getting Started: New Features in Microsoft QuickBASIC," introduces the new features and development tools of the language. The chapter summarizes the features of the compiler and surveys the menu-driven user interface.

- Chapter 2, "Modular Programming: Subprograms and User-Defined Functions," begins a continuing discussion of modular programming. The chapter especially focuses on two new features of QuickBASIC that greatly facilitate modular programming: subprograms and multiline user-defined functions.

- Chapter 3, "Combining Subroutines: $INCLUDE and User Libraries," describes two techniques for transferring subprograms, functions, and other previously created QuickBASIC routines from disk files to other programs. You can create "generic" routines to use from program to program without retyping them. Finally, this chapter introduces several subprograms and functions that appear in one or more of the book's major program examples.

The last five chapters present a diverse collection of QuickBASIC programs that serve two purposes. First, as learning exercises, they illustrate specific QuickBASIC commands and structured programming techniques. Second, they are useful applications in themselves, which you can work with and customize to your own needs. You can read these five chapters in any order. Each chapter is a self-contained tutorial on the use of a particularly useful language element, in the context of a specific programming application.

- Chapter 4, "Data Types: A Mortgage Calculation Program," reviews and illustrates the various data types that are available in QuickBASIC, including strings, numeric data, and logical expressions and Boolean values. The program computes several useful

tables of information describing a home mortgage. You also learn
a variety of operations and functions that QuickBASIC provides
for each data type.

- Chapter 5, "Loops, Arrays, and Graphics: A Chart Program,"
  focuses on structured FOR…NEXT and WHILE…WEND loops
  and on the use of static and dynamic arrays. The *QuickChart* program, this chapter's application example, contains a wide range
  of simple-to-complex examples of data storage and data handling
  using arrays and loops. *QuickChart* produces three kinds of
  charts on the computer's screen: column charts, line charts, and
  pie charts. In studying this program, you explore several powerful graphics commands, and you examine techniques for producing graphic images on text-only display hardware and on printers
  with varying graphics capabilities.

- Chapter 6, "Sequential Data Files: A Business Survey Program,"
  exemplifies effective data-file programming, which is one of the
  most important skills a programmer can develop. This chapter
  and Chapter 7 cover two essential skills: using sequential data
  files and managing random-access files. The *Survey* program in
  this chapter uses sequential data files to generate survey questionnaires and analyze the results. The program is useful for con-
  ducting surveys such as opinion polls, customer satisfaction
  surveys, and consumer attitude surveys.

- Chapter 7, "Random-access Files: A Database Management
  Program," covers the QuickBASIC commands and functions
  especially designed for creating and using random-access files.
  The chapter presents a database management program called
  Employee, which works with a database of employee profiles. The
  program illustrates the techniques for adding records to a database, locating specific records in a database, modifying the con-
  tent of a record, and printing tables of records. The program
  creates a special "index file" for the database and employs sorting
  and searching routines to manage this index.

- Chapter 8, "Structured Decisions in QuickBASIC: A Game of
  Twenty-one," focuses on one of the most important new features
  of the QuickBASIC language: the multiline IF…THEN…ELSE
  statement. The *Twenty-one* card game program contains many
  illustrations of these powerful decision structures.

Conclusion

Microsoft QuickBASIC is an extremely powerful language that can handle virtually any programming task. But like writing with a human language, the ease and elegance with which you create a program with a computer language depends on your basic skills with the "grammar" of the language. You develop human language skills by reading and writing; you develop skills with a computer language by studying programs and experimenting with the elements of the language.

The programs in this book are designed to demonstrate through "real world" examples the dynamic new features of the QuickBASIC Compiler. By studying the programs and analyzing how the various elements are put together, you gain the expertise to create useful and entertaining programs of your own.

Getting Started:
New Features
in Microsoft
QuickBASIC

We'll begin with a survey of the important new features available in the Microsoft QuickBASIC compiler. If you have written programs using the Microsoft BASICA interpreter you're probably eager to master the innovations of the QuickBASIC language and environment. Although the QuickBASIC documentation includes good hands-on tutorials and in-depth reference guides, you may want to read this chapter first since it is an overview of the entire product.

First, we'll point out some practical differences between the interpreter and the compiler and see how these differences affect program development. Then we'll take a look at the major new commands and features of the QuickBASIC language itself. We will also look at the QuickBASIC *environment*: the tools for creating, editing, saving, compiling, debugging, and running QuickBASIC programs. Finally, we'll explore the unique features of the menu-driven user interface.

Let's begin by summarizing the new features.

INTERPRETER V COMPILER

Both the BASICA interpreter and the QuickBASIC compiler translate BASIC programs into instructions the computer can understand. Despite this common goal, however, the interpreter and the compiler perform this task in different ways.

The interpreter translates and executes each line of a program in turn. If a given line is to be performed more than once (as the result of a loop or a GOTO statement, for example), the interpreter must retranslate the line before each performance. If a program contains a syntax error that the interpreter cannot translate, the program runs until the error is reached and then stops.

The compiler, on the other hand, translates the *entire* program into executable code before attempting to run it. During translation, the compiler determines ways to make the resulting code run as efficiently as possible. If the program contains an error that the compiler cannot translate, no part of the program is performed until you correct the error and repeat the compilation.

The most significant difference between a QuickBASIC program and a BASICA program is speed. A compiled QuickBASIC program performs much faster than an equivalent BASICA interpreted program. As you gain experience with QuickBASIC, you will find that this speed improves almost every kind of programming project, particularly programs that perform these general kinds of activities:

- Detailed arithmetic operations (for example, the *Mortgage* program in Chapter 4)

- Extensive repetitive tasks, performed within FOR...NEXT loops or WHILE...WEND loops (for example, the *Sort* routine in Chapters 3 and 7, and the *QuickChart* program in Chapter 5)

- Complex logical decisions (for example, the *Twenty-one* game program in Chapter 8)

Besides greater performance speed, the compiler has another important feature not available with the interpreter: the option to create programs that can be executed directly from DOS. In other words, QuickBASIC can store the code of a compiled program in a disk file. To run such a program, you enter the filename at the DOS prompt.

For example, let's suppose you use this option to compile a program named *MORTGAGE* and store the compiled code under the filename *MORTGAGE.EXE* on a disk in disk drive A. To run the program from drive A, enter the filename at the DOS prompt:

```
A>MORTGAGE
```

We'll outline the various techniques for creating such a program file later in this chapter. Meanwhile, keep in mind the contrast between this option and the requirement imposed by the BASICA interpreter: Interpreted programs can only be performed from inside the BASICA environment, never directly from DOS.

Beginning programmers tend to enjoy working with the BASICA interpreter because it creates such a responsive and immediate programming environment. In BASICA you can enter a command without a line number and immediately see the result. For example, the line:

```
PRINT 5 * 18
```

immediately calculates the result and displays the number (90) on the screen after you press Enter.

This immediate performance is not possible in QuickBASIC. No matter how short or long a program is, you always have to compile a program before you can run it. You also cannot run a QuickBASIC program containing a statement that the compiler cannot translate, even if the statement is far from the beginning of the program.

In the BASICA environment, a typical technique for finding syntax errors in a new program is simply to run the program. BASICA translates and performs each line that does not contain an error; the execution does not stop until the interpreter encounters a line that cannot be translated. In the meantime, however, you can see exactly how the program behaves up to the point of the error.

By contrast, in the QuickBASIC environment your entire program must be syntactically perfect before you can run it. This means you use a new method for finding errors. The compiler goes through the entire program and keeps track of errors. Then QuickBASIC shows you the location of those errors. You correct the errors and compile again. After a compilation successfully translates the entire program, you are ready to run it.

The compiler's approach to translating programs distinguishes between two kinds of program errors: errors discovered during the compilation process (sometimes called *compile-time errors*), and errors that occur during program execution (called *runtime errors*).

You must correct compile-time errors before you can run the program. Most compile-time errors are syntax errors. In response to such errors, the compiler supplies specific messages that describe— briefly and usually clearly—what has gone wrong. QuickBASIC only reports the first 25 errors. Here are some examples:

Error Message	*Problem*
"FOR . . . NEXT without NEXT"	A FOR . . . NEXT loop that is missing its NEXT statement
"Wrong number of arguments" or "Data type conflict"	An incorrect number or type of arguments in a built-in function call
"Missing left parenthesis"; "Missing semicolon"; "Missing comma"; and so on	A punctuation problem

Runtime errors are the result of performance problems that the compiler could not predict or for which the compiler does not check. Such errors stop the program and display the following message at the bottom of the screen:

```
Runtime error. Press any key.
```

Subsequently, QuickBASIC supplies a specific error message and points you to the apparent location of the error. The following table shows a few examples.

Error Message	Problem
"Overflow" or "Division by zero"	A calculation that results in a number that is too large to handle, or an attempted division by zero
"File not found"	An attempt to open a file that does not exist on the current disk or in the current search path
"Subscript out of range"	A reference to an array element that is outside the defined dimension of the array

Some programs contain sections in which certain kinds of run-time errors are predictable. In these cases, you can write an *error trap* for your program. An error trap is a pre-planned alternate course of action that takes place only if the error occurs. The purpose of this technique is to handle the error gracefully and to avoid termination of the program. The ON ERROR GOTO statement implements an error trap, and the RESUME statement sends control back to a specified location in the program after the error recovery. Later in this chapter we'll discuss the special compiler options you can select if you use these commands in a program. Chapter 5 contains examples of error traps.

In summary, developing a QuickBASIC program is not like developing a BASICA program. The compiler imposes a specific order of debugging steps:

1. Compile the program.

2. Correct any errors that the compiler discovers.

3. Repeat Steps 1 and 2 until the compiler finds no further errors.

4. Run the program.

5. Correct runtime errors and any conceptual problems (such as an incorrect formula) not detected by the compiler.

The rewards for mastering this new procedure are significant. First, your programs run much faster (and compile quickly, too). In addition, you can store the compiled code as executable DOS programs.

Another important advantage to programming in Microsoft QuickBASIC is the language itself. In general, QuickBASIC conforms closely to BASICA; you can compile most BASICA programs in QuickBASIC without much (or any!) rewriting. However, as you begin creating new programs in QuickBASIC, you'll discover that the language has a new face, if not a new soul.

THE QUICKBASIC LANGUAGE

Several new language features in QuickBASIC enable you to create programs that are better organized and more carefully structured than programs written with the BASICA interpreter. This means that your programs are easier to write, debug, and modify. The important new language elements are:

- Subprograms (allowing for local and global variables)
- Multiline user-defined functions
- Structured decisions
- Alphanumeric labels
- New array characteristics and functions
- Metacommands

Subprograms in QuickBASIC

The subprogram is a new organizational unit in QuickBASIC programs. You use the CALL statement to run a subprogram from within a QuickBASIC program. The only equivalent BASICA unit is the subroutine, which you access with the GOSUB statement. QuickBASIC has GOSUB, but the subprogram is superior in several ways. Here are three important reasons we use subprograms throughout this book:

- You can use the CALL statement to pass specific argument values to a subprogram.
- Variables used inside a subprogram are normally *local*—that is, available only to the subprogram itself. This means that identical variable names used both in the subprogram and in the calling

program are normally treated as two different variables. Neither variable affects the value stored in the other, even though the names are the same.

- You can pass arguments to a subprogram in two ways: by *value* or by *reference*. An argument passed by value is used exclusively by the subprogram; any changes in the argument are local to the subprogram. In contrast, passing an argument variable by reference lets the subprogram send a new value back to the calling program.

Multiline user-defined functions

All versions of BASIC contain built-in functions that may receive one or more argument values and return a value of a specified type. Examples of these in BASICA might be SIN or CHR$. As its name implies, however, a user-defined function behaves like a BASIC built-in function, but the user creates it.

In BASICA, a user-defined function can be only a one-line instruction. In QuickBASIC, a user-defined function can be a multiline instruction.

Structured decisions

QuickBASIC has an enhanced form of the IF ... THEN ... ELSE statement that lets you make multiline, block-structured decisions. This new format joins the structured loops (FOR ... NEXT loops and WHILE ... WEND loops), freeing BASIC programmers from the burden of a tenacious albatross: the GOTO statement. You can now completely eliminate GOTO from your programming vocabulary.

The IF ... THEN clause and the ELSE clause can each be followed by a block of statements; QuickBASIC performs one or the other of the blocks, depending on the result of the conditional expression that governs the decision. In addition, the structure can contain any number of ELSEIF clauses (located between the IF ... THEN clause and the ELSE clause) that express alternate conditions and contain corresponding blocks of code.

Using this new structure results in significantly clearer and simpler decision statements in QuickBASIC programs.

Alphanumeric labels

As you thumb through the program listings in this book, you'll notice the absence of line numbers. (Nevertheless, QuickBASIC can successfully compile a program that contains line numbers, and is thus compatible with BASICA.) If you need to use a line label, however, you may mix together letters and numbers to form an *alphanumeric label.*

Alphanumeric labels are names consisting of a maximum of 40 letters and digits (but no spaces) and ending with a colon. You can identify any line in a program with such a label, which can then become the destination parameter of a GOSUB or GOTO statement.

The programs in this book, however, contain neither GOTO nor GOSUB statements. Subprograms are used here instead of subroutines, and GOSUB statements are replaced with CALL. And, thanks to the new structured form of decisions in QuickBASIC, we will also abandon the GOTO statement. We will, however, use line labels to identify the location of an *error trap,* the potential destination of an ON ERROR GOTO statement. The *QuickChart* program in Chapter 5 contains two such error traps, both illustrating the use of line labels.

Arrays in QuickBASIC

QuickBASIC uses two kinds of arrays: static and dynamic. The dimensions of a static array are declared and fixed when the program is compiled. The dimensions of a dynamic array are assigned when the program is run. Furthermore, you can use the REDIM statement to assign new dimensions to a dynamic array during program execution.

You can send an array of values as an argument to a QuickBASIC subprogram or user-defined function. To find out the size of any dimension in the array, the subprogram uses two new QuickBASIC functions, LBOUND and UBOUND. The LBOUND function supplies the number of the lowest subscript in the dimension. (This value is always 0 or 1, depending on whether or not the program contains an OPTION BASE statement.) The UBOUND function supplies the number of the highest subscript.

Metacommands

A metacommand is a specific instruction to the compiler; you include such instructions in REM statements in your program. To distinguish metacommands from normal REM comment lines, each metacommand begins with a dollar-sign character ($).

QuickBASIC has three metacommands. Two of them, $STATIC and $DYNAMIC, are optional methods for declaring static or dynamic arrays. The third metacommand, $INCLUDE, appears in programs throughout this book. $INCLUDE instructs the compiler to transfer QuickBASIC source code from a disk file into the current program listing at compile time. This means you won't have to waste time typing the same routines into your programs time and time again. Use $INCLUDE as an alternative to compiling your programs with *user libraries* (we'll discuss these in Chapter 3).

Formatting conventions

Because line numbers are optional, indention helps emphasize the structure of a program. You use indention to set off the blocks of code contained in FOR...NEXT loops, WHILE...WEND loops, and IF...THEN...ELSE structures. You can also insert blank lines in the listing to visually distinguish blocks of statements.

You can type a program listing in any combination of uppercase or lowercase letters. Capitalization is not significant to the compiler. Programs in this book adhere to the following conventions for alphabetic case:

- Reserved words appear in all uppercase letters.

- Subprogram and function names contain an initial uppercase letter, usually followed by all lowercase letters. (We will occasionally use additional uppercase letters in a subprogram or function name, for example, *WaitForPrinter.*

- Variable names are in lowercase letters (again, we will sometimes include an internal uppercase letter if a variable is a combination of two words, such as *maxValue* and *sumOfTerms*).

In QuickBASIC, the length of a program line may be up to 255 characters. Although QuickBASIC's editing environment allows you to scroll horizontally and see additional characters to the right, you may want to break up your program lines with an underscore character (_). This indicates that the given statement extends over two or more lines. An example is the following PRINT statement from a subprogram we'll work with in Chapter 3:

```
PRINT FN Upper$(LEFT$(menuChoices$(i%), 1)) + ")" + _
MID$(menuChoices$(i%), 2)
```

If you enter a long statement on a single line, a printer might break the statement arbitrarily at the right margin of the page in the printed listing. The previous example might look like this:

```
PRINT FN Upper$(LEFT$(menuChoices$(i%), 1)) + ")" + MID$(menuChoi
ces$(i%), 2)
```

Using QuickBASIC's continuation character avoids unattractive and confusing line breaks.

Let's look now at the highlights of the QuickBASIC user-interface.

USING THE QUICKBASIC MENUS

QuickBASIC has a convenient full-screen environment in which you can develop and modify programs. This screen is shown in Figure 1-1. To enter QuickBASIC, insert the program disk into the current disk drive and at the DOS prompt type *QB*.

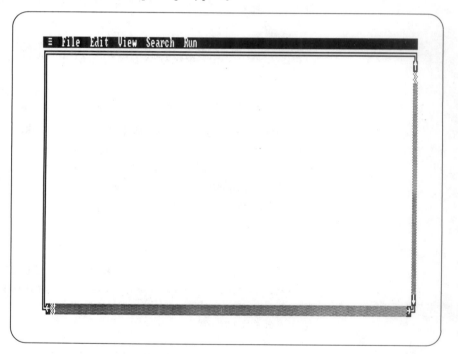

Figure 1-1. *The QuickBASIC environment.*

10

With the *QB* command you can include special parameters and options that specify certain operating conditions for a given session. For example, the following command starts QuickBASIC and immediately loads the program *MORTGAGE.BAS* into the QuickBASIC environment from a file in the current directory on the disk in drive A:

```
A>QB MORTGAGE.BAS
```

Another important QB option allows you to specify a *user library* when starting QuickBASIC. For example, the following command starts QuickBASIC, loads the program *MORTGAGE.BAS*, and includes the user library *BORDER.EXE*:

```
A>QB MORTGAGE.BAS /1 BORDER.EXE
```

We'll learn more about this option in Chapter 3.

When you load QuickBASIC and display the screen, you can begin programming immediately. Here are the steps for creating a program from within the editor:

1. Type a new program into the QuickBASIC editor, or load an existing program from disk into the editor.

2. Use the editing features necessary to make any changes in your program.

3. Save the current version of the program on disk, and/or print out the listing.

4. Compile the program, storing the compiled code in the computer's memory (the default). If the compiler finds errors, correct them and recompile. Repeat this process until the entire program compiles successfully.

5. Run the program. If the result is not exactly what you want, start again at Step 2.

6. When the program behaves exactly as you want it to, compile it again, this time selecting the option that creates an executable (*EXE*) program.

QuickBASIC has five menus that contain the tools you need to accomplish all these steps simply and efficiently.

As you can see in Figure 1-1, QuickBASIC contains a *menu line* of five menus at the top of your screen. The menus are easy to use.

You "pull down" a menu and display the command options by holding down the Alt key (located at the lower-left corner of the keyboard) and simultaneously pressing the first letter of the menu you wish to examine. For example, pressing Alt-F pulls down the File menu. To select a command from a menu that is displayed, press the first character of the command name and press Enter.

You can invoke some commands without going through a menu. For example, press Ctrl-R (hold down the Ctrl key and simultaneously press the *R* key) to invoke the Start command. This command compiles the current program in the QuickBASIC editor and then runs it if the compilation is completed without errors. (If the current program has not changed, it executes without additional compilation.)

You can find detailed information about all the menus in the documentation that comes with QuickBASIC. It describes all the menu commands and explains how to use the keyboard to access these commands. (You can also use a mouse to control the QuickBASIC menus and scroll bars. The documentation explains how to do this.)

The following sections highlight the most important QuickBASIC tools in each of the menus.

The File menu

To load a new program into the QuickBASIC editor from disk or to save the program currently in the editor to disk, you use commands in the File menu:

The New command

The New command clears the current program from the editor. If you have made changes to the current program, a dialog box appears that gives you a chance to save the revised program. (If the Auto Save option is selected, the program will be saved to disk before a new screen is opened; we will discuss Auto Save shortly.)

The Load and Save commands

The Load command reads a program file from disk, and Save stores the current program on disk. (The ellipses following the names of some menu commands mean that a dialog box appears on the screen when you select the command. For example, if you select the Load command, the screen shows a dialog box that contains a directory of filenames from which you can choose.)

When you store programs on disk from the editor, they are saved as simple text (ASCII) files, consisting of letters, digits, and punctuation marks. Programmers often refer to such a text file as the *source code* of a program, as opposed to the various forms of compiled code that the compiler can produce. (From DOS, you can use the TYPE command to view the contents of a source code file.)

Any programs that you attempt to load into the editor should also be text files. If you wish, you can use some other editor or word processor to develop a QuickBASIC program; but in doing so, be sure to create a simple text file that has no special control characters that would be meaningless to QuickBASIC. If you choose to use Microsoft Word, for example, be sure to avoid features like boldfacing and hidden text, and always save the document without formatting it.

You can also load a BASICA program into the QuickBASIC editor, as long as it has been saved as a text file. To create a text file from a BASICA program, use the *A* (ASCII) option of the SAVE command. For example:

```
SAVE "MORTGAGE.BAS", A
```

If you don't use this option, BASICA saves programs in a form that the QuickBASIC editor can't use.

The Auto Save command

The fourth command in the File menu, Auto Save, is actually a toggle. When you select it, a check mark appears to the left of the command in the menu; selecting it again removes the check. When Auto Save is toggled on, QuickBASIC saves your current program on disk before performing any operation that might result in a loss of the program. For example, if you select the New command when Auto Save is on, QuickBASIC saves the current program before clearing the editor.

The Print command

The PRINT command sends a listing to the printer. When you choose PRINT, a dialog box appears giving you the option to *Print File,* or *Print Selected Text.* If you accept the default *Print File,* the entire program listing will be printed; if you select *Print Selected Text,* only the section of the program you've highlighted with the mouse (by holding down the left button and dragging it over the section) or the direction keys (by holding down the shift key while using direction keys) will be printed.

The Shell command

The Shell command lets you leave QuickBASIC temporarily to perform one or more operations from DOS. You can subsequently return to QuickBASIC by typing *EXIT* at the DOS prompt. The screen then shows the section of the program you were working on before your temporary exit.

The Quit command

The Quit command ends the current QuickBASIC session and returns you to DOS. If Auto Save is not on, you must save the current program on disk before you choose Quit; otherwise you will lose the program.

The Edit menu

The Edit menu has four commands:

```
 Edit
┌──────────────┐
│ Undo   Sh Esc│
│ Cut      Del │
│ Copy     F2  │
│ Paste    Ins │
└──────────────┘
```

The Undo command

The Undo command restores the current program line to its contents just before the most recent editing operation. For example, if you just deleted the statement CLOSE #1, then decided you needed it after all, selecting *Undo* would return it to the program where it was deleted. (Note: This will work only if you deleted CLOSE #1 in one step; if you deleted it one character at a time, only the last character deleted is restored.)

The Cut, Copy and Paste commands

The Cut and Paste commands let you remove a block of statements from one portion of your program and copy it to another location. Copy and Paste let you copy a block of statements to another location without deleting the original. Both the cut-and-paste and copy-and-paste operations temporarily store the block in QuickBASIC's memory. This storage location is often referred to as the *Clipboard*.

The View menu

The View menu has two commands:

The Options command

The Options command displays a dialog box of options for controlling the various elements of the editor's display screen. For example, the dialog box includes check boxes and buttons that you can use to turn on and off portions of the editing screen. Furthermore, if you are using a color monitor, you can choose from a list of colors for the foreground and background of the screen.

    The Options command also lets you change the number of characters between tab stops in the QuickBASIC editor. The default tab value is eight characters. If you use a lot of indention in your programs, you may want to reduce this value. (The programs in this book use four-character indents.)

The Errors command

The Errors command is a toggle. When the compiler finds errors in a program, it displays error messages in a window at the bottom of the screen. This window appears—and the Errors command is toggled on—after any compilation that finds errors. (As you'll see shortly, the Search menu has a command that lets you jump from one error to the next in your program listing; the error window always displays a message that describes the current error.)

    After you look at all the errors found during a compilation, you may want to remove the error window from the screen. Toggle the Errors command off, and the full editing screen appears.

The Search menu

To find all occurrences of a specified string of text in the current program listing or to find a specified string and replace it with another string, select one of the first five commands from the Search menu:

```
┌─────────┐
│ Search  │
├─────────────────────────┐
│ Find...                 │
│ Selected Text      ^F   │
│ Repeat Last Find   F3   │
│ Change...               │
├─────────────────────────┤
│ Label                   │
├─────────────────────────┤
│ Next Error         F6   │
└─────────────────────────┘
```

The Find command

The Find command displays a dialog box in which you enter the text you wish to find and specify how you want the search to be conducted. You can specify to match characters alone or within longer words and to match case or disregard case.

After you enter the text, the editor scrolls forward from the current cursor position to the first occurrence of the text and highlights it. If the editor cannot find the text, the screen displays the message *Text Not Found*.

The Selected Text command

To use the Selected Text command, you first highlight a string of text in a program line. When you choose the command, the highlight moves to the next occurrence of the text in the listing.

The Repeat Last Find command

After you locate the specified text string with Find or Selected Text, you can find subsequent occurrences in the program listing with the Repeat Last Find command.

The Change command

To search and replace, use the Change command. Specify the target text and the replacement text in the dialog box. According to your instructions, Change works in one of two modes: the Find and Verify mode, in which you must confirm each replacement before it occurs; and the Change All mode, in which all replacements are made automatically.

The Label command

The Label command adds a colon character (:) to the end of the text you specify in the Find command and thus searches for an alphanumeric line label.

The Next Error command

The final command on the Search menu is Next Error. You use this command after a compilation has found errors in your program. When the compilation is complete, QuickBASIC is prepared to scroll to each error in turn and display an appropriate error message in a window at the bottom of the screen. Correct the error and then select the Next Error command to locate the next error in the listing. After you examine the last error, the screen shows the message *No More Errors*. To scroll through the list again, select Next Error.

QuickBASIC keeps track of a maximum of 25 errors in a single compilation. When the compiler finds the 25th error, compilation will stop.

The Run menu

The Run menu contains the three commands you use to compile and run a program.

The Start command

The Start command compiles and runs the program that's currently in the QuickBASIC editor. If the compilation process finds no errors, the program immediately runs. If errors are found, you must correct them before the program will run.

By default, the compiler stores compiled code in memory rather than on disk. Compiled code stays in memory until you change the source code. To run the current program in memory, use the Start command.

The Compile and Compile... commands

The Compile and Compile... commands both initiate the compilation process for the program that is currently in the editor. When you choose Compile, the compilation occurs according to the specific set of instructions that are selected as options in the Compile... dialog box:

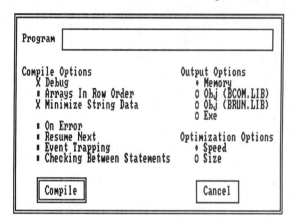

You use the Compile... command to change any of these options.

Normally, you accept the default settings as shown in the last graphic, since most of the other options are for special circumstances. The QuickBASIC documentation describes all the compilation options. Here is a summary of the most important.

The Debug option

The Debug option is a check box. By default it's selected. You will normally not want to change this setting because when Debug is on, the compiler generates the necessary code for handling runtime errors. As we have seen, runtime errors cause a program to terminate early. Two examples are: a calculation resulting in a numeric value that is too large for the compiler to handle, or an attempt to access an array element that is outside the defined dimensions of the array.

Finally, in conjunction with the TRON (*Trace On*) and TROFF (*Trace Off*) statements, the Debug option lets you run a program in a special mode in which you can see how your program works in one-line steps. When the program comes to a TRON statement, a special display on the screen shows you the source code of the current line. The rest of the screen shows the results that the program would normally produce. If you include a TROFF statement in the program after

TRON, the special display disappears, and the program resumes normal operation.

You can step through the entire program by placing TRON at the top of the program listing. Alternatively, you can position the TRON and TROFF statements so that they apply to only a portion of your program. Here is an example of such a debugging test:

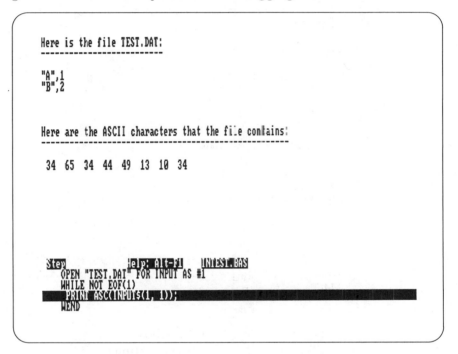

```
Here is the file TEST.DAT:
---------------------------

"A",1
"B",2


Here are the ASCII characters that the file contains:
----------------------------------------------------

 34  65  34  44  49  13  10  34
```

```
Step              Help: Alt-F1      INTEST.BAS
    OPEN "TEST.DAT" FOR INPUT AS #1
    WHILE NOT EOF(1)
       PRINT ASC(INPUT$(1, 1));
    WEND
```

The debugging mode is extremely useful if your program is not producing the exact results you want. In a long or complex program, finding the problem can be difficult. With the debugging mode you can step through a program line by line. When you find the source of the problem, you can revise the appropriate line or lines and then remove the TRON and TROFF statements before you recompile.

Other compile options

In later chapters we'll work with two other compile options: On Error and Resume Next. If you design a program that sets up an error trap using ON ERROR GOTO and RESUME NEXT, you must switch on both of these options before compiling the program. (Actually, if you switch on the Resume Next option, the On Error option is also on since you never use RESUME NEXT without an ON ERROR GOTO statement.) Chapter 5 has an example of a program using ON ERROR GOTO.

Similarly, if your program uses any of QuickBASIC's event trapping commands, you must switch on the Event Trapping option.

The Output Options menu option controls the destination of compiled code.

Using the Output Options to compile a program

You can specify that compiled code be sent to one of the following:

- Memory
- Obj (BCOM.LIB)
- Obj (BRUN.LIB)
- Exe

The default is Memory. When compiled code is stored in memory, you can run the program as often as you want during the current session. You erase the compiled code from memory if you change the source code or end the current session with QuickBASIC.

If you do either, you must recompile the entire program before running it again.

After you develop and debug a program, you may want to store the compiled code permanently. You can do this in three ways. The simplest and most common is to use Exe. When you select Exe, the compiler creates an executable program on disk, with the extension name *EXE*. For example, the compiled code for a program named *MORTGAGE.BAS* is saved as *MORTGAGE.EXE*. You can run this program directly from DOS by typing *MORTGAGE* (and the appropriate path) at the DOS prompt.

However, there is one further requirement for running a program compiled under the Exe option. A file called *BRUN20.EXE* must be in the current directory or available through the DOS PATH variable. This file is called the Microsoft QuickBASIC runtime module, and it is included on one of the disks in the QuickBASIC package. The module contains the BASIC language routines that your program requires during execution. (Without this file, the program will not even begin running.) So, for example, if both *MORTGAGE.EXE* and *BRUN20.EXE* are in the same directory on a diskette in drive A, you can run the program with this command:

```
A>MORTGAGE
```

The other output options create disk files—but not executable programs—from the compiled code. A program compiled under the Obj (BRUN.LIB) option has the extension *OBJ*; again, this is not an executable program. The Obj (BRUN.LIB) output option lets you compile subprograms to incorporate into a user library. Briefly, a user library is a file containing one or more compiled subprograms that you want to make available to a program you are currently developing. We'll discuss user libraries, and the steps required for creating and using them, in Chapter 3.

Finally, the Obj (BCOM.LIB) output option creates a third kind of compiled program file. If you compile the program *MORTGAGE.BAS* under this option, the result is a file named *MORTGAGE.OBJ*. To create an executable program from this file, you must link the program with routines contained in an alternate runtime library called *BCOM20.LIB*.

You do this linking in DOS with a program called *LINK.EXE*, included in the QuickBASIC package. There is an important difference between the resulting executable program and a program created directly from the QuickBASIC compiler using the Exe option. When you link an object file with the BCOM20.LIB library, the result is a stand-alone program. The program file itself contains all the necessary resources. You do not need the runtime module.

For example, if you have a program called *MORTGAGE.BAS* in the QuickBASIC editor and want to make it a stand-alone, executable DOS file independent of the BRUN20.EXE module, do the following:

1. Choose Compile... from the Run menu, select the Obj (BCOM.LIB), and compile the program.

2. Quit QuickBASIC and examine the directory of your work disk. You should see a file named *MORTGAGE.OBJ*.

3. Copy the files LINK.EXE and BCOM20.LIB to the work disk from the QuickBASIC disk.

4. Start the linking process with this command at the DOS prompt:

    — LINK MORTGAGE.OBJ;

The linking process may take a minute or two (partly depending on the length of the program). You could then give this program to someone who doesn't have BASIC, and they could run it from DOS.

In summary, the QuickBASIC compiler gives you four options for storing the compiled code generated from a program. Each option is useful under different circumstances:

- The Memory option stores the code in the computer's memory and is most useful while developing a program.

- The Exe option provides a simple way to create an executable program file. However, the resulting EXE file requires the presence of the BRUN20.EXE runtime module for a successful performance.

- The Obj (BRUN.LIB) option creates object files for user libraries.

- The Obj (BCOM.LIB) option creates an object file that requires linking to produce an executable program. The result is a stand-alone program that does not need the presence of a runtime module.

CONCLUSION

The advantages of programming in QuickBASIC are clear. First, compiled programs run very fast. Second, the QuickBASIC compiler offers a number of important new features that make the programmer's job easier and more enjoyable, including subprograms, multiline user-defined functions and structured decisions. Third, QuickBASIC includes a number of valuable development tools, including a good full-screen editor, and various options for compiling, debugging, running, and printing programs.

QuickBASIC is rich in features that will help you develop successful programs. To master all these features, keep the QuickBASIC documentation close at hand as you work.

Modular Programming:
Subprograms and User-Defined Functions

From a programmer's point of view, the subprogram and the multi-line user-defined function are probably the most compelling new language elements in QuickBASIC. Used appropriately, these two kinds of program modules result in clear, well-organized, and easily modified BASIC programs. The sections that follow examine the syntax and characteristics of each of these elements.

USING SUBPROGRAMS

Recall that in Chapter 1 we said that a QuickBASIC subprogram has three advantages over the traditional BASIC subroutine:

- You can pass specific values to a subprogram as values in the CALL statement's argument list.

- Variables inside a subprogram are normally *local* to it, which means that a subprogram can change the value in a variable without affecting the value of the variable in the rest of the program.

- Arguments can be passed to a subprogram by *value* or by *reference*. If passed by value, the argument is used only by the subprogram, and no changes are returned to the calling routine. In contrast, if an argument is passed by reference, any changes to the argument are returned to the calling routine. The calling routine may be a subprogram or the main program. If the calling routine is a subprogram, the returning argument only updates variables of the same name *within that subprogram*. If the calling routine is the main program, the returning argument globally updates variables of the same name throughout the program (unless the variable was declared STATIC in its assignment statement in some other subprogram).

A subprogram always begins with a SUB statement and ends with an END SUB statement. Between these two statements are any number of QuickBASIC commands, which together accomplish the designed task of the subprogram itself:

SUB *SubName (parameterList)* **STATIC**
     [the statements of the subprogram]
END SUB

The four elements in the syntax of the SUB statement appear in this order:

1. The reserved word SUB, which identifies the routine as a subprogram.

2. The designated name of the subroutine, which can be a maximum of 31 characters.

3. The list of parameter variables, which receives the argument values sent to the subprogram.

4. The reserved word STATIC, which specifies that the subprogram is not *recursive,* must appear at the end of the statement. This means that the subprogram does not call either itself or another subprogram that in turn calls it; recursion is not allowed in the current version of QuickBASIC. For example, if subprogram *Alpha* calls subprogram *Beta,* QuickBASIC does not let *Beta* then call *Alpha* in turn.

The QuickBASIC documentation distinguishes between the terms *parameter* and *argument.* This book makes the same distinction: A parameter is a variable that is listed in the SUB statement; when the subprogram is called, the parameter variable will receive a value. An argument, on the other hand, is a value that is sent directly to the program in a CALL statement.

The parameter list in the SUB statement contains one variable name or array name for each value or array of values that the subprogram is to receive. Actually, the list is optional; you can write a subprogram that takes no arguments. If present, the list is enclosed in parentheses, and the names in the list are separated by commas.

Each name in the parameter list specifies the type of value that must be sent to the subprogram. For example, the following SUB statement is for a hypothetical subprogram named *Sample:*

```
SUB Sample (strVal$, intVal%) STATIC
```

Looking at this parameter list, you see that the *Sample* subprogram expects to receive two argument values, a string and an integer. In a call to the subprogram, the values must be sent in the same order.

As with a subroutine, a program must be directed to a subprogram. This is done with a CALL statement, which takes the following syntax:

CALL SubName (argumentList)

The argument list in the CALL statement can consist of literal values (either string or numeric), variable names, or expressions (literal string and/or numeric values combined with QuickBASIC operators). Again, the argument list depends on the subprogram's parameter list; there is no list in a call to a subprogram that does not take arguments. Each element in the list corresponds, in the order given, to a name in the parameter list of the called subprogram.

A CALL statement to a subprogram can appear anywhere in the program listing that contains the subprogram itself. The exception, of course, is that a subprogram cannot call itself; as we have seen, the STATIC clause in the SUB statement indicates that subprograms are not recursive in QuickBASIC.

Let's look at three examples of CALL statements to the *Sample* subprogram discussed earlier:

```
SUB Sample (strVal$, intVal%) STATIC
```

Any call to this subprogram must send two arguments: a string value and an integer value. We know from the subprogram's SUB statement that the parameter variables *strVal$* and *intVal%* will receive these two values.

The first example sends a literal string value (enclosed in quotation marks) and a literal integer value:

```
CALL Sample("Hello", 19)
```

As a result of this call, *Hello* is stored in the parameter variable *strVal$* and *19* is stored in *intVal%*.

The next example sends the results of two expressions—a combination (or *concatenation*) of two strings—and a sum of two numbers:

```
CALL Sample (string1$ + " Wednesday", number1% + 2)
```

In this case, QuickBASIC first evaluates the expressions and then sends the result to the subprogram.

The last example sends the values currently stored in two variables, *mainStr$* and *mainInt%:*

```
CALL Sample(mainStr$, mainInt%)
```

This final example—in which both arguments are expressed as simple variables—is a special case. Variable arguments like these are normally passed to the subprogram by *reference*. This means that if the variables are assigned new values in the subprogram the values of the same variables in the calling routine will take on the new values as well. Variable names not enclosed in their own parentheses in a CALL argument are reference variables.

To see how this works, let's say that the argument variable *mainInt%* contains a value of *6* at the time of the call to the *Sample* subprogram:

```
mainInt% = 6
CALL Sample (mainStr$, mainInt%)
```

As we have seen, *Sample* receives this value in the parameter variable *intVal%*. Imagine that *Sample* doubles the value of *intVal%* before returning control to the calling program:

```
SUB Sample (strVal$, intVal%) STATIC
     [other program lines]
intVal% = 2 * intVal%
     [other program lines]
END SUB
```

Now when the execution of *Sample* is complete, the new value of *intVal%* passes back to the original argument variable, *mainInt%*. In other words, after the call to *Sample, mainInt%* contains a new value of *12*.

This feature can prove extremely useful. In many programs you might want to add a variable to the argument list of a CALL statement in order to receive a particular value from the subprogram. On other occasions, however, you may not want a variable argument to be passed by reference. Instead, you may want a variable to retain its original value, even after a subprogram call. This is called passing arguments to the subprogram by *value,* and is effected by enclosing the variable name in parentheses. For example, consider the following call to *Sample*:

```
CALL Sample (mainStr$, (mainInt%))
```

Notice the double parentheses. The outer set delimits the argument list itself. The inner set, around the variable name *mainInt%*, indicates that the variable will be sent to *Sample* by value. Now, no matter what new value *Sample* might assign to the corresponding parameter variable, *mainInt%* retains its original value.

Let's summarize what we've learned about calling subprograms and passing values to them:

● CALL statement arguments that consist of specific numbers, strings within quotes, or expressions are always passed as values to the subprogram.

- Strings or numbers can be passed either as specific values or as the contents of variables.

- If string or numeric values are passed via variables, the variables can be passed by *reference* or by *value*:

  — Reference variables return changes: Any change within the subprogram to the value of the variable is made to the variable in the calling routine.

  — Variables passed as values are enclosed within parentheses in the CALL statement's argument; the subprogram works with the value in the variable when it's passed to the sub-program, but any changes to the value affect only the sub-program: New values are not passed back to the variable in the calling routine.

A subprogram can also receive an array of values as an argument. This requires special notation in the SUB statement and in the CALL statement. For example, a subprogram named *FindAddress* is designed to accept a three-dimensional array of strings as an argument. You can write the SUB statement for this subprogram as follows:

```
SUB FindAddress (infoList$(3)) STATIC
```

As you can see, the array name, *infoList$*, is followed by the number *3* in parentheses. This indicates that the subprogram expects to receive a three-dimensional array. (The lengths of the dimensions are not specified in the parameter list.) In a call to *FindAddress*, the array argument must be followed by empty parentheses. For example:

```
CALL FindAddress(employeeList$())
```

Array arguments that represent an entire array are always passed by reference in QuickBASIC. If the called subprogram changes the values stored in the array, these changes are passed back to the calling program.

You can also send an array *element* as an argument to a sub-program. For example, suppose that your program has a three-dimensional string array *employeeList$*, and this subprogram:

```
SUB PrintAddress(address$) STATIC
```

This statement:

```
CALL PrintAddress(employeeList$(7, 2, 1))
```

sends one value from the three-dimensional string array *employeeList$* to the *address$* string variable in the subprogram.

In this case, the array element is passed by reference. If the *PrintAddress* subprogram changes the value stored in the parameter variable *address$*, that new value is passed back to the element *employeeList$(7, 2, 1)*. To prevent this, pass the array element by value, enclosing it in parentheses in the CALL statement:

```
CALL PrintAddress((employeeList$(7, 2, 1)))
```

Notice the triple parentheses in this call. The innermost set identifies the target element of *employeeList$*; the middle parentheses specify that the element is to be passed by value; and the outer parentheses enclose the argument list itself.

THE FRAME SUBPROGRAM

Thoughtful programmers always pay careful attention to the way information appears on the screen. In this book the *Frame* subprogram is used to help present screen information usefully and attractively. *Frame*, listed in Figure 2-1, simply creates a rectangular frame on the

```
'    The Frame subprogram draws a rectangular double-line frame on
'        the screen, using "text-graphics" characters from the upper
'        range of the ASCII code.

SUB Frame(leftCol%, rightCol%, topRow%, bottomRow%) STATIC
'    ---- Print the four corners.
    LOCATE topRow%, leftCol%: PRINT CHR$(201)
    LOCATE topRow%, rightCol%: PRINT CHR$(187)
    LOCATE bottomRow%, leftCol%: PRINT CHR$(200);
    LOCATE bottomRow%, rightCol%: PRINT CHR$(188);

'    ---- Print the vertical lines.
    FOR vertLine% = topRow% + 1 TO bottomRow% - 1
        LOCATE vertLine%, leftCol%: PRINT CHR$(186);
        LOCATE vertLine%, rightCol%: PRINT CHR$(186);
    NEXT vertLine%

'    ---- Print the horizontal lines.
    horizLength% = rightCol% - leftCol% - 1
    horizLine$ = STRING$(horizLength%, 205)
    LOCATE topRow%, leftCol% + 1: PRINT horizLine$
    LOCATE bottomRow%, leftCol% + 1: PRINT horizLine$;
END SUB
```

Figure 2-1. *The* Frame *subprogram.*

screen. This frame can serve a variety of purposes, such as separating different tables that appear on the same screen or drawing the user's attention to certain items.

The subprogram has four parameters, all integers:

```
SUB Frame(leftCol%, rightCol%, topRow%, bottomRow%) STATIC
```

The subprogram uses the values passed to these four variables in subsequent LOCATE statements, which move the cursor to the appropriate screen locations for the four corners of the frame. A call to the subprogram must send integer values that are within the dimensions of the text screen: The values for left and right are screen column locations from 1 to 80, where the value of *leftCol%* is smaller than the value of *rightCol%*. Likewise, the values for *topRow%* and *bottomRow%* are row numbers from 1 to 25, where *topRow%* is smaller than *bottomRow%*.

The subprogram uses six ASCII text-graphics characters from the upper range of the ASCII-code table to create the frame:

ASCII Code	*Character Produced*
201	Upper-left corner
187	Upper-right corner
200	Lower-left corner
188	Lower-right corner
186	Vertical character
205	Horizontal character

The CHR$ function supplies the actual characters corresponding to these six decimal ASCII codes.

After the screen shows four corners, a FOR ... NEXT loop draws the two vertical lines, from the top of the frame to the bottom:

```
FOR vertLine% = topRow% + 1 TO bottomRow% - 1
```

The STRING function creates the horizontal lines after the appropriate length of each line, *horizLength%*, has been calculated:

```
horizLength% = rightCol% - leftCol% - 1
horizLine$ = STRING$(horizLength%, 205)
```

For example, the following call to the subprogram draws a frame from column 15 over to column 65, and from row 5 down to row 20:

```
CALL Frame(15, 65, 5, 20)
```

Figure 2-2 shows the result.

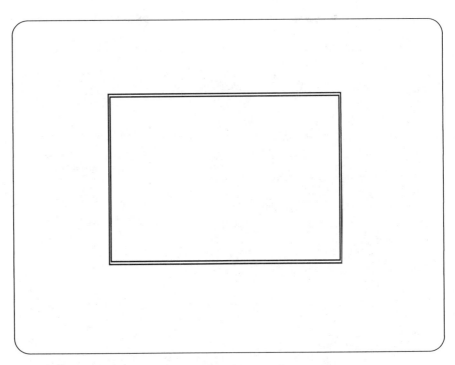

Figure 2-2. *A frame drawn by the* Frame *subprogram.*

Notice that this first subprogram example contains comments inside the listing. A few comment lines at the top of the listing tell what the subprogram does; then, inside the routine, occasional short comments identify the tasks performed by distinct blocks of code. The comment delimiter is a single quote character, rather than the reserved word REM. This is the general pattern we follow for including comment lines in programs throughout this book.

You can learn a lot about the characteristics of subprograms by comparing the *Frame* subprogram with an equivalent BASICA subroutine. Figures 2-3 and 2-4 (on the following pages) show the two programs we'll examine in this exercise. Both consist of a short controlling section at the top of the listing, followed by the *Frame* routine itself. In this book we use the term *main program* to refer to the controlling section of a BASIC program. In a well-organized program, the main program section is usually short and consists primarily of calls to routines below.

```
'    FRAMETST.BAS
'    Tests the QuickBASIC version of the Frame subprogram.

'-----------------------| Main Program Area |---------------------------

     CALL Frame(15, 65, 5, 20)

     END

'-----------------------| Subprogram Area |----------------------------

'    The Frame subprogram draws a rectangular double-line frame on
'        the screen, using "text-graphics" characters from the upper
'        range of the ASCII code.
SUB Frame(leftCol%, rightCol%, topRow%, bottomRow%) STATIC
'    ---- Print the four corners.
     LOCATE topRow%, leftCol%: PRINT CHR$(201)
     LOCATE topRow%, rightCol%: PRINT CHR$(187)
     LOCATE bottomRow%, leftCol%: PRINT CHR$(200);
     LOCATE bottomRow%, rightCol%: PRINT CHR$(188);

'    ---- Print the vertical lines.
     FOR vertLine% = topRow% + 1 TO bottomRow% - 1
         LOCATE vertLine%, leftCol%: PRINT CHR$(186);
         LOCATE vertLine%, rightCol%: PRINT CHR$(186);
     NEXT vertLine%

'    ---- Print the horizontal lines.
     horizLength% = rightCol% - leftCol% - 1
     horizLine$ = STRING$(horizLength%, 205)
     LOCATE topRow%, leftCol% + 1: PRINT horizLine$
     LOCATE bottomRow%, leftCol% + 1: PRINT horizLine$;
END SUB
```

Figure 2-3. *A QuickBASIC program using the* Frame *subroutine.*

(*Routine* is a general term that can refer to any unit of code—a QuickBASIC subprogram, a subroutine, or a user-defined function.)

In the QuickBASIC program of Figure 2-3, the main program section contains a single call to *Frame:*

```
CALL Frame(15, 65, 5, 20)
```

As we have seen, this call produces the frame shown in Figure 2-2.

In contrast, the BASICA program (Figure 2-4) implements *Frame* as a subroutine, starting at line 100 of the program. Subroutines do not allow parameter passing—in either BASICA or QuickBASIC. For this reason, the BASICA program requires some other technique for sending the four screen addresses to the subroutine. Before calling the subroutine—with a GOSUB statement—the program assigns values to

```
10 REM FRAME.BAS
20 REM This program tests the BASICA version of the Frame subroutine.
30 REM
40 REM ---- Assign values for the four corners.
50 LEFTCOL% = 15: RIGHTCOL% = 65
60 TOPROW% = 5: BOTTOMROW% = 20
70 CLS
80 GOSUB 100
90 END
100 REM The Frame subroutine draws a rectangular double-line frame on
110 REM    the screen, using "text-graphics" characters from the upper
120 REM    range of the ASCII code.
130 REM
140 REM ---- Draw the four corners.
150 LOCATE TOPROW%, LEFTCOL%: PRINT CHR$(201)
160 LOCATE TOPROW%, RIGHTCOL%: PRINT CHR$(187)
170 LOCATE BOTTOMROW%, LEFTCOL%: PRINT CHR$(200);
180 LOCATE BOTTOMROW%, RIGHTCOL%: PRINT CHR$(188);
190 REM
200 REM ---- Draw the vertical lines.
210 FOR VERTLINE% = TOPROW% + 1 TO BOTTOMROW% - 1
220     LOCATE VERTLINE%, LEFTCOL%: PRINT CHR$(186);
230     LOCATE VERTLINE%, RIGHTCOL%: PRINT CHR$(186);
240 NEXT VERTLINE%
250 REM
260 REM ---- Draw the horizontal lines.
270 HORIZLENGTH% = RIGHTCOL% - LEFTCOL% - 1
280 HORIZLINE$ = STRING$(HORIZLENGTH%, 205)
290 LOCATE TOPROW%, LEFTCOL% + 1: PRINT HORIZLINE$
300 LOCATE BOTTOMROW%, LEFTCOL% + 1: PRINT HORIZLINE$;
310 RETURN
```

Figure 2-4. *A BASICA version of the QuickBASIC
program in Figure 2-3.*

the variables LEFTCOL%, RIGHTCOL%, TOPROW%, and
BOTTOMROW%:

```
50 LEFTCOL% = 15: RIGHTCOL% = 65
60 TOPROW% = 5: BOTTOMROW% = 20
```

In BASICA programs, all variables are global. This means that
any section of the program can access variables in any other section of
the program. So, assigning values to these four variables is the program's means of communicating the values to the subroutine.

Languages such as BASICA, which do not permit parameter passing, must use global variables to share information among the various
modules of a program. But global variables can be a distinct disadvan-
tage, particularly in long and complex programs. The programmer
has to keep careful track of all the variable names in a program and

guard against unintentionally using the same name for different purposes. If a subroutine inadvertently assigns a new value to a variable that is important elsewhere in the program, unexpected and undesirable side effects will result.

Fortunately, the variables in a QuickBASIC subprogram are *local* by default, meaning that any changes to the value won't affect variables with the same name elsewhere in the program. Thanks to this characteristic you can spend less time worrying about the repetition of variable names in a program.

The following example illustrates the significance of local variables. Notice that the *Frame* subprogram contains one FOR . . . NEXT loop, which uses a variable named *vertLine%* as a loop counter:

```
FOR vertLine% = topRow% + 1 TO bottomRow% - 1
    [other program lines]
NEXT vertLine%
```

What happens if the main program section also uses the *vertLine%* variable in a FOR . . . NEXT loop that makes repeated calls to *Frame*? For example, here is a loop designed to display a diagonal series of frames from the upper-left to the lower-right corner of the screen:

```
FOR vertLine% = 1 TO 19 STEP 2
    horizLen% = vertLine% * 3
    CALL Frame(horizLen%, horizLen% + 5, vertLine%, vertLine% + 5)
NEXT vertLine%
```

In QuickBASIC, this loop produces the arrangement of ten frames shown in Figure 2-5. QuickBASIC treats the two variables named *vertLine%*—one in the main program section and the other in the subprogram—as two distinct variables. Neither interferes with the value stored in the other.

The result of using the same loop in a BASICA program is not so predictable. Like all other BASICA variables, *VERTLINE%* is global; each call to the subroutine changes the value of the loop counter in the main program. For the program to work as planned, you must modify one or more of the loop variables.

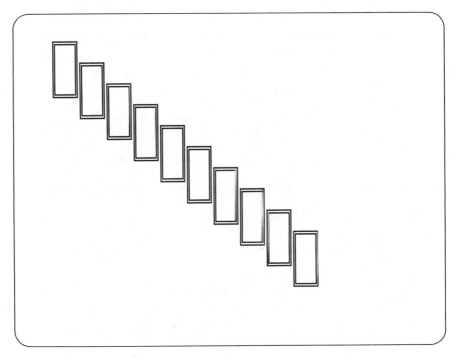

Figure 2-5. *An experiment with local variables.*

GLOBAL VARIABLES IN QUICKBASIC

Despite the clear advantages of local variables in QuickBASIC sub-programs, you may sometimes want to establish a few key variables as global in a program. If specific variables are required by most or all of the routines in a program, declaring those variables global may be clearer and more convenient than passing the variables as arguments to each routine that needs them.

QuickBASIC has several statements for declaring global variables, among them the COMMON SHARED statement. For example, the following statement declares three variables as global:

```
COMMON SHARED true%, firstName$, freeSpace
```

The values stored in these three variables are available to any routine in the program, and any routine can also change the value stored in any of these variables. The COMMON SHARED statement must appear at the top of a program, above any executable commands.

The DIM statement, used for establishing the dimensions of arrays, can also include a SHARED clause in QuickBASIC. For example:

```
DIM SHARED intArr%(5, 2), strArr$(50)
```

The SHARED clause specifies that these two arrays are global in the program. We discuss the use of global and local arrays and variables further in Chapter 5.

USER-DEFINED FUNCTIONS IN QUICKBASIC

In general, a function is a routine that has these characteristics:

- Takes one or more arguments (although some functions take no argument)

- Produces a single value of a specified type (the function's name indicates the type of value the function returns; for example, a function name that ends in $ returns a string value, and one that ends in % returns an integer value)

- Can be called in an expression that performs some further operation on the returned value

QuickBASIC has a large vocabulary of *built-in functions*. For example, SQR is an arithmetic function that takes a single numeric argument and returns the square root of the number. The statement:

```
PRINT SQR(81)
```

displays *9* as the result.

A *user-defined function* is one that you create to answer the needs of a specific program. BASICA programmers are familiar with the DEF FN statement, which establishes the specific operations performed by a user-defined function. For example:

```
10 DEF FN HYPOTENUSE(A, B) = SQR(A * A + B * B)
20 PRINT FN HYPOTENUSE(3, 4)
```

Line 10 of this program defines a function named HYPOTENUSE. This function takes two numeric arguments, represented by *A* and *B*. If *A* and *B* are the lengths of the sides of a right triangle, HYPOTENUSE performs the necessary arithmetic to compute the length of the hypotenuse:

```
SQR(A * A + B * B)
```

In the BASICA interpreted language, a user-defined function can have only a single line of code, as in line 10 of the previous example. Although QuickBASIC also allows this one-line syntax, a much more versatile structure is now available: the multiline user-defined function. This structure also uses the DEF FN statement, in the following form:

> **DEF FN** *FunctionName (parameterList)*
> > *[a block of statements that*
> > *produces the value that the function*
> > *will return]*
>
> **FN** *FunctionName* = *expression*
> **END DEF**

Notice the various elements of this structure:

- The DEF FN statement itself, which specifies the name of the function and a list of parameter variables for receiving arguments

- The body of the function, a sequence of QuickBASIC commands that produces the function's result

- The FN statement, which stores the result of the function's calculations

- The END DEF statement, which stores the actual value that the function will return

A call to a user-defined function in QuickBASIC takes the same form as in a BASICA program:

> **FN** *FunctionName (argumentList)*

Since the primary purpose of a user-defined function is to return a particular value, a function call cannot stand alone as a QuickBASIC statement. Rather, the call must be part of a statement or an expression that uses the value returned by the function.

Several important rules apply to both single-line and multiline functions in QuickBASIC. First, a DEF FN function definition may not appear inside any of the following structures: SUB...END SUB, IF...THEN...ELSE, FOR...NEXT, and WHILE...WEND. Second, the definition for a given function must appear before any calls to the function. For this reason, function definitions are typically located near the beginning of a program listing so that the functions themselves are available to subsequent routines. In this book they have been set apart in a "Function Area" in all program listings.

An important characteristic of functions in QuickBASIC is the status of variables used inside the function definition. With the exception of variables introduced in the parameter list of the DEF FN statement, all variables inside the function are global by default. The values stored in these variables are potentially available to any routine that calls the function.

As we have discussed, global variables can prove troublesome in a long program. If you inadvertently use the same global variable name for two different purposes, unexpected results may ensue. Fortunately, QuickBASIC has a statement that you can use to establish selected variables as local to a function or a subprogram—the STATIC statement. For example, the following STATIC statement, placed at the top of a function definition, establishes *i%*, *number%*, and *character$* as local variables:

```
STATIC i%, number%, character$
```

This statement appears in our first multiline function example, presented in the next section.

A multiline user-defined function: *Upper$*

The *Upper$* function, shown in Figure 2-6, receives one string argument and returns a string result. The function converts lowercase letters in a string argument to uppercase letters, which is an operation we'll use in several of the programs in this book.

```
'    UPPER.BAS
'    The Upper$ function converts alphabetic characters in a string
'        value into uppercase letters.

DEF FN Upper$(textVal$)
    STATIC i%, number%, character$

'    ---- Find the length of the string value rece_ved.
    number% = LEN(textVal$)

'    ---- Examine each character in the string, and convert as necessary.
    FOR i% = 1 to number%
        character$ = MID$(textVal$, i%, 1)
        IF (character$ >= "a" AND character$ <= "z") THEN
            MID$(textVal$, i%) = CHR$(ASC(character$) - 32)
        END IF
    NEXT i%
    FN Upper$ = textVal$
END DEF
```

Figure 2-6. *The user-defined function,* Upper$.

How the *Upper$* function works

The line *DEF FN Upper$(textVal$)* takes one string argument and stores it in the variable *textVal$*. The rest of the function converts any lower-case letters in the variable *textVal$* to uppercase. Other characters are not affected.

To avoid confusion with variables used in the calling program, the line:

```
STATIC i%, number%, character$
```

establishes the three variables as local to the function itself.

Next, the function uses QuickBASIC's built-in LEN function to determine the length (in characters) of the string stored in *textVal$*. The value is stored in the *number%* variable:

```
number% = LEN(textVal$)
```

A FOR...NEXT loop then moves character by character through *textVal$*, using the MID$ function to isolate each character in turn; the loop assigns each character to the *character$* variable:

```
FOR i% = 1 to number%
    character$ = MID$(textVal$, i%, 1)
```

An IF decision then determines if *character$* is lowercase. If it is, the loop then subtracts 32 from the lowercase character's ASCII value to

39

get its equivalent uppercase value (lowercase versions of alphabet characters on the ASCII table are the uppercase values + 32). The MID$ statement assigns a new value to a specified position in the string:

```
IF (character$ >= "a" AND character$ <= "z") THEN
    MID$(textVal$, i%) = CHR$(ASC(character$) - 32)
```

When the looping is finished, the new string stored in *textVal$* is returned as the value of the function:

```
FN Upper$ = textVal$
```

Here is an example of a call to the function:

```
PRINT FN Upper$("August 8, 1986")
```

The result of this PRINT statement is:

```
AUGUST 8, 1986
```

Notice *Upper$* changes only lowercase letters. The function has no effect on digits, punctuation characters, or letters already uppercase.

To summarize what we have learned about using subprograms and multiline functions, we'll look briefly at a demonstration program called *DEMO.BAS* that calls both the *Upper$* function and the *Frame* subprogram. The program, shown in Figure 2-7, conducts a very simple sequence of activities. It begins by asking you to enter a "message" that you want displayed on the screen. After you type your message, the screen shows it in uppercase letters. The message is centered and enclosed in a pair of frames. Figure 2-8 shows a sample of the program's output. This screen is the result of the following input dialog:

```
Enter your message here: The Microsoft QuickBASIC Compiler
```

```
'   DEMO.BAS
'   Demonstrates a function call and subprogram calls.

'------------------------| Main Program Area |--------------------------

'   ---- The string variable message$ is global.
COMMON SHARED message$
CALL GetMessage
CALL ShowMessage
CALL Frame(1, 80, 1, 25)
CALL Pause

END
```

Figure 2-7. *The DEMO.BAS program, incorporating a subprogram and user-defined function.* *(more...)*

```
'----------------------------| Function Area |----------------------------

'   The Upper$ function converts alphabetic characters in a string
'       value into uppercase letters.

DEF FN Upper$(textVal$)
    STATIC i%, number%, character$

'   ---- Find the length of the string value received.
    number% = LEN(textVal$)

'   ---- Examine each character in the string, and convert as necessary.
    FOR i% = 1 to number%
        character$ = MID$(textVal$, i%, 1)
        IF (character$ >= "a" AND character$ <= "z") THEN
            MID$(textVal$, i%) = CHR$(ASC(character$) - 32)
        END IF
    NEXT i%
    FN Upper$ = textVal$
END DEF

'----------------------------| Subprogram Area |----------------------------

'   The Frame subprogram draws a rectangular double-line frame on
'       the screen, using "text-graphics" characters from the upper
'       range of the ASCII code.

SUB Frame(leftCol%, rightCol%, topRow%, bottomRow%) STATIC
'   ---- Print the four corners.
    LOCATE topRow%, leftCol%: PRINT CHR$(201)
    LOCATE topRow%, rightCol%: PRINT CHR$(187)
    LOCATE bottomRow%, leftCol%: PRINT CHR$(200)
    LOCATE bottomRow%, rightCol%: PRINT CHR$(188);

'   ---- Print the vertical lines.
    FOR vertLine% = topRow% + 1 TO bottomRow% - 1
        LOCATE vertLine%, leftCol%: PRINT CHR$(186);
        LOCATE vertLine%, rightCol%: PRINT CHR$(186);
    NEXT vertLine%

'   ---- Print the horizontal lines.
    horizLength% = rightCol% - leftCol% - 1
    horizLine$ = STRING$(horizLength%, 205)
    LOCATE topRow%, leftCol% + 1: PRINT horizLine$
    LOCATE bottomRow%, leftCol% + 1: PRINT horizLine$;
END SUB

'   The GetMessage subprogram elicits a message string from the keyboard,
'       and converts the string to uppercase.

SUB GetMessage STATIC
'   ---- Get a message string.
    INPUT "Enter your message here:  ", message$

'   ---- Convert string to upper case.
    message$ = FN Upper$(message$)
END SUB
```

Figure 2-7. *The DEMO.BAS program (continued).*   *(more . . .)*

```
'    The ShowMessage subprogram displays the message inside a frame.

SUB ShowMessage STATIC
'    ---- Determine frame coordinates.
    leftColumn% = ((80 - LEN(message$)) \ 2) - 3
    rightColumn% = 80 - leftColumn%
    topRow% = 10
    bottomRow% = 14

'    ---- Draw the frame and print the message.
    CLS
    CALL Frame(leftColumn%, rightColumn%, topRow%, bottomRow%)
    LOCATE topRow% + 2, leftColumn% + 4: PRINT message$
END SUB


'    The Pause subprogram simply creates a pause in the action of the
'        program, until the user presses a key.

SUB Pause STATIC
    character$ = ""
    WHILE character$ = ""
        character$ = INKEY$
    WEND
END SUB
```

Figure 2-7. *The DEMO.BAS program (continued).*

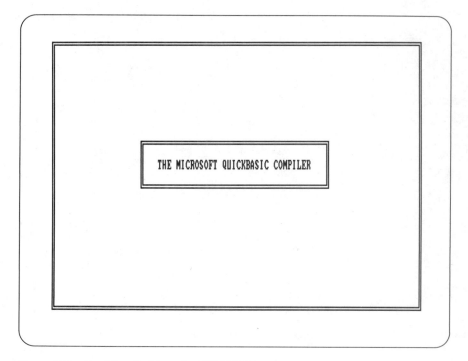

Figure 2-8. *Sample output from the DEMO.BAS program.*

The various tasks performed by this program are divided into several sections. The main program area, at the top of the listing, controls the action by calling on the subprograms below it. As you can see, the *Upper$* function appears in the function area, just after the main program area. Next comes the subprogram area, which contains four subprograms: *Frame*; *GetMessage,* which conducts the input dialog; *ShowMessage,* which produces the subsequent screen display; and *Pause,* which stops the action so you can examine the screen. Of these four subprograms, only *Frame* takes arguments.

The *GetMessage* subprogram places an input prompt on the screen and stores the resulting input value in a string variable named *message$*. Since the value in *message$* is used in several subprograms, a COMMON SHARED statement defines *message$* as a global variable.

The *GetMessage* subprogram uses the assignment statement *message$ = FNUpper$(message$)* to convert *message$* to all uppercase letters. The original value of *message$* is sent as an argument to the *Upper$* function. The result of the function is then stored in *message$* and replaces the original string.

The *ShowMessage* subprogram calls *Frame* to produce the small frame around the message, and then it displays the string value:

```
CALL Frame(leftColumn%, rightColumn%, topRow%, bottomRow%)
LOCATE topRow% + 2, leftColumn% + 4: PRINT message$
```

The four variables in this passage are the address coordinates (left, right, top, bottom) of the inner frame. The values of these coordinates are calculated from the length of the message.

The main program area simply declares the global variable *message$* and calls the four subprograms.

Simple though this program is, it illustrates a modular approach to organizing QuickBASIC programs. Each program task is isolated in an individual subprogram. If you want to change any task, you can easily locate the appropriate subprogram. Furthermore, the main program area, the function area, and the subprogram area are clearly marked, providing a broad outline of the entire program.

A *structure chart* is a tool that programmers sometimes employ to provide a picture of a program's modular organization. Figure 2-9 (on the next page) shows a structure chart of the demonstration program. The main program is represented by a round-cornered rectangle, each subprogram in the program is represented by a rectangle, and each function by a slanted rectangle. Lines extending from the rectangles represent the various subprogram calls and function calls made by the main program and various routines.

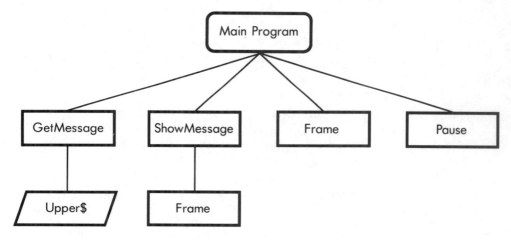

Figure 2-9. *A structure chart of the demonstration program.*

CONCLUSION

The QuickBASIC language includes elements that encourage a structured, modularized approach to programming. Among the most important of these new language features are subprograms and multiline user-defined functions. A QuickBASIC subprogram is superior to the BASIC subroutine because all variables defined inside a subprogram are local to it and because it can pass variables by value or by reference. Likewise, the QuickBASIC multiline user-defined function is more useful than its BASIC counterpart because it supports parameter passing and because it can contain many lines.

In Chapter 3 we'll examine two techniques for incorporating individual library routines into a program, and we'll continue developing our own collection of subprograms and functions.

Combining Subroutines: $INCLUDE and User Libraries

In the last chapter, we examined two general-purpose routines: the *Frame* subprogram, which draws a rectangular frame on the screen, and the *Upper$* function, which converts strings of characters to uppercase letters. These routines perform small but important tasks that are useful in a variety of application programs. In fact, calls to these two routines appear many times in the large programming projects found in this book.

To use any routine successfully, you have to know two of its characteristics: the form of the arguments required in a call to the routine, and the expected result. Once the routine is written, however, you don't need to worry about the exact sequence of program statements and commands that actually perform the action. For example, if you are working on a program that includes the following call to the *Frame* subprogram:

```
CALL Frame(30, 50, 8, 12)
```

the screen will show a rectangular frame at the specified locations. While creating your current programming project, you don't have to rethink or redevelop the procedure that produces that display.

In this chapter we add several more general-purpose routines to our collection, any one of which is available to subsequent programs. The result is a small "toolbox" of subprograms and user-defined functions, each stored in its own file on disk. For example, the *Frame* subprogram is in a file named *FRAME.BAS*.

Once you create and store these files, how do you incorporate the routines into a program? Typing each routine into the current program listing would waste time and disk space. Fortunately, Microsoft QuickBASIC has two techniques for making individual routines available to a program: the $INCLUDE metacommand and the *Buildlib* program.

The programs throughout this book employ the $INCLUDE metacommand. As discussed in Chapter 1, a metacommand is a statement that gives specific instructions to the compiler. $INCLUDE is one of three metacommands available for compiling QuickBASIC programs; its job is to incorporate a unit of source code, stored in a file on disk, into the current program.

The second technique uses the *Buildlib* program included as part of the QuickBASIC package. (The program is stored in a file named BUILDLIB.EXE.) This program builds *user libraries*. A user library is a disk file that contains one or more compiled QuickBASIC or assembly language routines. When you begin a new session with QuickBASIC, you can read any user library into memory, making all its routines available to your current program.

USING THE $INCLUDE METACOMMAND

A QuickBASIC metacommand must always appear as part of a REM statement and be preceded by a dollar-sign character. $INCLUDE metacommands appear in the following format:

REM $INCLUDE : *'filename'*

where *filename* is a filename and an extension in the current directory, or a filename and an extension preceded by a drive letter and a pathname. Notice the punctuation. The name of the file is enclosed in single quotation marks, and a colon separates the $INCLUDE command from the filename.

Here are two examples, which read the *Frame* and *Upper$* routines into the current program:

```
REM $INCLUDE : 'FRAME.BAS'
REM $INCLUDE : 'UPPER.BAS'
```

These statements cause the compiler to open each of these files in turn and compile the source code that they contain. These two routines thus become part of the current program when it's compiled.

If a source file is not on the current drive or in the current directory, you can specify a drive and directory path along with the filename in the $INCLUDE statement; for example:

```
REM $INCLUDE : 'C:\QBLIB\FRAME.BAS'
```

In response to this statement, QuickBASIC looks for the file *FRAME.BAS* in the subdirectory named *QBLIB* on drive C.

Another variation in the format of the $INCLUDE statement is the use of the single quote character (') instead of the reserved word REM. QuickBASIC always lets you use this character (in place of REM) to specify a comment line. Thus you can write a $INCLUDE statement as follows:

```
' $INCLUDE : 'FRAME.BAS'
```

In this book, however, we reserve the single quote to designate actual comment lines, and use the word REM for $INCLUDE statements.

Figure 3-1 shows a short program that demonstrates the use of
$INCLUDE. Actually, this is the same *Demo* program that we first exam-
ined in Chapter 2 (Figure 2-7). The program simply displays a message
on the screen, employing the *Upper$* function to convert the message
string into uppercase letters and the *Frame* subprogram to enclose the
message in a pair of frames. (You can review a sample of the program's
output in Figure 2-8.)

```
'    DEMO.BAS
'    Demonstrates a function call and subprogram calls.

'---------------------| Global Variable Declarations |---------------------

     COMMON SHARED message$

'--------------------------| Function Area |--------------------------

'    (Functions must be defined before being called.)

'    ---- Read in and compile BASIC user-defined function.
     REM $INCLUDE : 'UPPER.BAS'


'-------------------------| Main Program Area |-------------------------

     CALL GetMessage
     CALL ShowMessage
     CALL Frame(1, 80, 1, 25)
     CALL Pause

     END


'-------------------------| Subprogram Area |-------------------------

'    ---- Read in and compile BASIC subprogram.
     REM $INCLUDE : 'FRAME.BAS'


'    The GetMessage subprogram elicits a message string from the keyboard,
'        and converts the string to uppercase.

SUB GetMessage STATIC
'    ---- Get a message string.
     INPUT "Enter your message here:  ", message$

'    ---- Convert string to upper case.
     message$ = FN Upper$(message$)
END SUB


'    The ShowMessage subprogram displays the message inside a frame.
```

Figure 3-1. *Demonstration of the $INCLUDE
metacommand.*

(more...)

```
    SUB ShowMessage STATIC
    '    ---- Determine frame coordinates.
        leftColumn% = ((80 - LEN(message$)) \ 2) - 3
        rightColumn% = 80 - leftColumn%
        topRow% = 10
        bottomRow% = 14

    '    ---- Draw the frame and print the message.
        CLS
        CALL Frame(leftColumn%, rightColumn%, topRow%, bottomRow%)
        LOCATE topRow% + 2, leftColumn% + 4: PRINT message$
    END SUB


'   The Pause subprogram simply creates a pause in the action of the
'       program, until the user presses a key.

SUB Pause STATIC
    character$ = ""
    WHILE character$ = ""
        character$ = INKEY$
    WEND
END SUB
```

Figure 3-1. *$INCLUDE demonstration (continued).*

Recall that in the original version of the program, the *Upper$* and *Frame* routines appeared as part of the listing itself and had to be manually typed or copied-and-pasted into the listing. In contrast, the program in Figure 3-1 uses a pair of $INCLUDE statements to incorporate the two routines into the program. After being compiled, the program works just like the original.

In general, you can place $INCLUDE statements anywhere in a program listing. However, if the designated source file contains either a subprogram or a user-defined function keep in mind the following two points:

- Subprograms cannot be nested: One SUB … END SUB block cannot appear inside another. For this reason, if an included file contains a subprogram, you should not place the corresponding $INCLUDE statement inside another subprogram.

- If an included routine contains a user-defined function that will subsequently be called by the main program, the $INCLUDE statement must occur *before* the call to the function. For example, in Figure 3-1, the first $INCLUDE statement appears in the function area, just before the main program area. This $INCLUDE statement reads in the user-defined *Upper$* function, which was stored in the *UPPER.BAS* file. Since it's defined before the main program, *Upper$* can be called from the main program or any of the subprograms.

The second $INCLUDE statement appears at the top of the subprogram area. This $INCLUDE reads in the *Frame* subprogram. Since it's a subprogram, *Frame* can be called from any location in the program. In the *DEMO.BAS* program in Figure 3-1, *Frame* is called from both the main program and from the *ShowMessage* subprogram.

(Since both global variables and user-defined functions must precede the routines that call them, we'll follow the format convention used in the *DEMO.BAS* program in all the programs in the book: A global-variable declaration area will come first, followed by any function definitions, and then the main program area and the subprograms.)

The advantages of the $INCLUDE metacommand are convenience, simplicity, and clarity. $INCLUDE is easy to use and lets you incorporate any source code file into the program you are currently developing. Furthermore, the metacommand itself documents that such a file is included in the program. As you examine a program listing, the $INCLUDE statements tell you the names of the files in which you will find routines that are included in the program.

CREATING USER LIBRARIES

Another method of including subprograms in QuickBASIC programs is to use a *user library*. A user library is an executable file containing one or more compiled subprograms or assembly language routines. Although the end result of a user library is identical to that of a set of $INCLUDE metacommands, a user library is created in a significantly different way. Unlike the $INCLUDE metacommand (which compiles source code originating elsewhere on disk), a user library allows you to link together in one file all the additional routines necessary for a program to operate. This file is then specified when QuickBASIC is started (you'll learn how to do this later in the chapter). From that point on, the current program and the user library are merged. Any time the program calls a routine in the user library, the compiler simply jumps to it. Although it takes a little extra work to set up, user libraries eliminate the need for any additional program statements (like $INCLUDE).

To create a user library, first compile and save the subprograms that you want in the library as object files (with *OBJ* extension names). Then use the *Buildlib* program (*BUILDLIB.EXE*) to combine the compiled modules into one file.

As an example, we will create a user library containing two subprograms, named *Sort* and *Search*. (Later in this chapter we will work with routines that use these names.) The source code for these two subprograms is written, and the two files are stored in the current directory under the names *SORT.BAS* and *SEARCH.BAS*.

To create your user library, first start QuickBASIC. When the QuickBASIC editor appears, follow these steps:

1. Load the *Sort* subprogram into memory, using the Load command from the File menu.

2. Choose the Compile... command from the Run menu. In the Compile... dialog box, select the output option *Obj (BRUN.LIB)*. Press the Enter key to begin the compilation; if it's successful QuickBASIC will then store the compiled code in a file named *SORT.OBJ*.

3. Load the *Search* subprogram into memory, again using the Load command.

4. Choose the Compile... command from the Run menu. The *Obj (BRUN.LIB)* option will still be selected, so you need only press the Enter key to compile the routine; the resulting file will be named *SEARCH.OBJ*.

5. Choose the Quit command from the File menu to exit from QuickBASIC and return to DOS.

The two object files you created are now in the current directory as *SORT.OBJ* and *SEARCH.OBJ*.

You now have the two routines stored as object files. The next step is to incorporate them into a library file. This requires two routines that are included in the QuickBASIC package: the *Buildlib* program (*BUILDLIB.EXE*) and the library file *BRUN20.LIB*.

The procedure gets somewhat complicated at this point, since several conditions could exist, depending on the drives and pathname/directory you're using. The main issue is this: to build a user library,

QuickBASIC must know where to find *BUILDLIB.EXE* and *BRUN20.LIB*. The best method to accomplish this is to put all of the required programs into one directory. At the DOS level, either move into the current directory that contains your OBJ files so that all programs use the current path and directory or, alternatively, move the OBJ files into the directory containing *BUILDLIB.EXE* and *BRUN20.LIB*.

For example, suppose *BUILDLIB.EXE* and *BRUN20.LIB* are in the same directory as the object files you've just created. To compile *SORT.OBJ* and *SEARCH.OBJ* together in a library, you would enter:

```
BUILDLIB SORT.OBJ SEARCH.OBJ, STSCHLIB.EXE;
```

where *STSCHLIB.EXE* is the name under which you want the library file stored (for "Sort and Search library"). When you press the Enter key, the following message appears on your screen:

```
Microsoft (R) QuickBasic Library Generator  Version 1.00
Copyright (C) Microsoft Corp 1986.  All rights reserved.
```

When the DOS prompt appears on the screen, your user library is created and the current directory now contains the file *STSCHLIB.EXE*.

If you do not specify a name for your user library (that is, if you omit the final argument), when you first run the *Buildlib* program QuickBASIC gives the library the default name *USERLIB.EXE*. To create the user library for *Sort* and *Search* this way, at the DOS prompt enter:

```
BUILDLIB SORT.OBJ SEARCH.OBJ;
```

(Notice that the semicolon is still required at the end of the command.)

Although it is more convenient if all the applicable files are nicely stored in the current directory, it is not essential. Let's suppose that the object files and *BRUN20.LIB* are in the current directory, but that *BUILDLIB.EXE* is in the hard-disk directory *C:\QB\PROGS*. To create the *STSCHLIB.EXE* library with the same object files, you would have to specify a pathname to *BUILDLIB* that might look like this:

```
C:\QB\PROGS\BUILDLIB.EXE SORT.OBJ SEARCH.OBJ, STSCHLIB.EXE;
```

(You may also include the *\QB\PROGS* directory in your DOS PATH variable.) At this point, you would see the message shown in the preceding graphic.

For our final library-building scenario, let's suppose that you have overlooked the fact that *BRUN20.LIB* is *not* in the current directory. In this case, when you enter a library-building command line such as the two preceding examples, QuickBASIC displays a message telling you that it cannot find *BRUN20.LIB*, and prompts you to "enter new file spec." If, for example, *BRUN20.LIB* was in the *QB* directory on drive C, you would enter:

```
Cannot find library: BRUN20.LIB
Enter new file spec: c:\qb\brun20
```

Remember, specify the appropriate drivename (if necessary) and the pathname, but *don't* include the *EXE* extension.

Once you've linked the *Sort* and *Search* routines into the *STSCHLIB* library file, a program that uses the routines can access them directly from the *STSCHLIB* library rather than by using additional $INCLUDE statements. But since you can have a number of library files on a disk, QuickBASIC must know which one to work with for a particular program. You specify the appropriate library file by using QuickBASIC's library option when you start QuickBASIC from DOS. For example, to load *STSCHLIB* you would enter:

```
QB /L STSCHLIB.EXE
```

The */L* option of the *QB* command instructs QuickBASIC to load the routines of the user library *STSCHLIB.EXE* into memory. Any program that you write during the subsequent session can call any subprogram linked together in that library.

If the necessary linked subprograms are stored in QuickBASIC's default *USERLIB.EXE* library file (if you didn't specify a filename when you ran *BUILDLIB*), you would load the library by entering:

```
QB /L
```

If you include the */L* option without a filename, QuickBASIC looks for the user library file named *USERLIB.EXE*.

Although you can create many user library files if you wish, you can load only one library into memory when you start QuickBASIC.

Consequently, if you have a particular subprogram that you use often in your programs, you will probably want to include it in several libraries, in different combinations with other routines.

User libraries: pro and con

Before you create a user library to link to a long program, you should consider a few potential difficulties. As we have seen, the procedure itself is relatively detailed. You first compile the subprograms as object files and then use the *Buildlib* program to create the library. To make subsequent revisions in the library, you must go through the entire process again. For example, if you have the *Sort* and *Search* routines stored in *STSCHLIB* and want to add the *Frame* subprogram, you would have to compile *Frame* as an object file, then include all three of the files in the *BUILDLIB* process. Also, if you ever modify any one of the files, you will have to *BUILDLIB* all the files again.

Because of this complexity, programs that are relatively self-contained and make few calls to outside routines seem better suited for $INCLUDE metacommands than for user libraries—particularly if your library consists of a large and diverse collection of subprogram files, of which only a few will be required in some of your programs.

Furthermore, employing a user library may result in inadequately documented programs. A user library leaves no trail in the program listing of the inclusion of additional subprograms. A person examining the listing may not be aware that successful program execution relies on the presence of a user library. (To help solve this problem, you can write a comment in the program listing that names the required library file.)

Finally, user libraries can only be made up of subprograms. Although you cannot incorporate a user-defined function into a user library, you may use the $INCLUDE metacommands to include subprograms that call user-defined functions. In contrast, the $INCLUDE statement lets you introduce subprograms, user-defined functions, or any other file of code into the current program listing.

Nonetheless, a user library can be helpful for managing a small group of subprograms that you use frequently. For instance, if you have several general-purpose routines that you use in almost every program you write, you may well want to put them in a user library. The advantages are clear: Whenever you load the subprograms of a user library into memory for a particular session with QuickBASIC, the programs you write during that session require neither a listing of the

routines nor a $INCLUDE statement; rather, the routines are imme-
diately available for use. Also, because the library consists of precom-
piled code, the compilation process is much quicker.

Next we'll examine five subprograms and one user-defined function and add them to our collection of routines. All the routines are
important in the programming projects in Chapters 4 through 8. To
preview their roles, we'll look at simple demonstration programs that
show exactly what the routines do. The programs also provide further
examples of the $INCLUDE metacommand.

The first subprogram is a menu routine. It is designed to display
a menu of activity options on the screen and to elicit the user's choice
from among those options.

THE *MENU* SUBPROGRAM

We develop several menu-driven programs in this book. When running such a program, the user chooses from a recurring menu—that
is, from a list of program options that appears repeatedly on the
screen. The *Menu* subprogram, shown in Figure 3-2, performs two
useful tasks in such a program:

1.   It displays the menu attractively and clearly on the screen.

2.   It elicits an input response from the user and ensures that the
     response is appropriate in the context of the menu.

```
'    MENU.BAS
'    The Menu subprogram displays a menu on the screen, and elicits a
'        menu choice from the user.  Menu receives a string array
'        (menuChoices$) containing the menu choices, and returns an integer
'        (numChosen%) indicating the user's selection from among those
'        choices.

SUB Menu(menuChoices$(1), numChosen%) STATIC
'    ---- Find the number of choices (numOfChoices%); initialize variables.
     numOfChoices% = UBOUND(menuChoices$)
     prompt$ = " "
     okString$ = ""
     longString% = 0

'    ---- Declare true% and false% as Boolean variables. These will always
'        hold values of -1 and 0, respectively.
     true% = -1
     false% = 0
```

Figure 3-2. *The* Menu *subprogram.*   *(more...)*

```
'   ---- Prepare the prompt string (prompt$) and the string of legal input
'        characters (okString$).  Also, find the length of the longest choice
'        string (longString%).
FOR i% = 1 TO numOfChoices%
    first$ = FN Upper$(LEFT$(menuChoices$(i%), 1))
    okString$ = okString$ + first$
    prompt$ = prompt$ + first$ +"   "
    lTemp% = LEN(menuChoices$(i%))
    IF (lTemp% > longString%) THEN longString% = lTemp%
NEXT i%

longString% = longString% + 1
prompt$ = prompt$ + "-> "

'   ---- Test to see if the prompt string is longer than longString%.
IF (LEN(prompt$) >= longString%) THEN longString% = LEN(prompt$) + 1

'   ---- Given longString% and numOfChoices%, determine the dimensions of
'        the menu frame.  Draw the frame, calling on the Frame subprogram.
lc% = 37 - (longString% \ 2)
rc% = 80 - lc%
tc% = 3
bc% = 10 + numOfChoices%
CALL Frame (lc%, rc%, tc%, bc%)

'   ---- Display the menu choices.  The first letter of each choice is
'        displayed in uppercase, followed by a parenthesis character.
FOR i% = 1 to numOfChoices%
    LOCATE 6 + i%, lc% + 3
    PRINT FN Upper$(LEFT$(menuChoices$(i%), 1)) + ")" + _
    MID$(menuChoices$(i%), 2)
NEXT i%

LOCATE 4, 38: PRINT "Menu"
line$ = STRING$(longString%, 196)
LOCATE 5, lc% + 3: PRINT line$
LOCATE 7 + numOfChoices%, lc% + 3: PRINT line$

'   ---- Print the input prompt.
LOCATE 9 + numOfChoices%, lc% + 3: PRINT prompt$;

'   ---- Get a menu choice. Validate and verify the choice.
ctrlKeys$ = chr$(13) + chr$(27)
done% = false%
WHILE NOT done%
    LOCATE ,, 1
    charPos% = 0
    WHILE charPos% = 0
        ans$ = INKEY$
        IF (ans$ <> "") THEN
            ans$ = FN Upper$(ans$)
            charPos% = INSTR(okString$, ans$)
            IF (charPos% = 0) THEN BEEP
        END IF
    WEND
```

Figure 3-2. *The* Menu *subprogram (continued).* *(more...)*

```
              PRINT ans$
              LOCATE 11 + numOfChoices%, 23, 0
              PRINT "<Enter> to confirm; <Esc> to redo."
              numChosen% = charPos%

              charPos% = 0
              WHILE charPos% = 0
                  ans$ = INKEY$
                  IF (ans$ <> "") THEN
                      charPos% = INSTR(ctrlKeys$, ans$)
                      IF (charPos% = 0) THEN BEEP
                  END IF
              WEND

              IF (charPos% = 1) THEN
                  done% = true%
                  CLS
              ELSE
                  LOCATE 11 + numOfChoices%, 23: PRINT SPACE$(35)
                  LOCATE 9 + numOfChoices%, lc% + 3 + LEN(prompt$): PRINT " ";
                  LOCATE , POS(0) - 1:
              END IF
      WEND
END SUB
```

Figure 3-2. *The* Menu *subprogram (continued).*

Inside the *Menu* subprogram

A call to the *Menu* subprogram takes two arguments: a string array containing the menu choices, and an integer variable, which is used to pass back to the program the number the user chooses. Inside *Menu,* the variables corresponding to these arguments are *menuChoices$* and *numChosen%*:

```
SUB Menu(menuChoices$(1), numChosen%) STATIC
```

The routine begins by using the UBOUND function to determine the length of the array the program is passing to it via *menuChoices$*. It assigns this value to the *numOfChoices%* variable:

```
numOfChoices% = UBOUND(menuChoices$)
```

Then a FOR ... NEXT loop builds two string values: The string variable *okString$* serves as an input validation string; it contains an uppercase letter representing each of the menu's choices. The variable *prompt$* contains the prompt that appears below the menu.

An integer variable, *longString%*, stores the length of the longest string that appears in the menu, whether it is a menu choice or the prompt string. This value, together with the value in *numOfChoices%*, determines the dimensions of the frame that surrounds the menu. A FOR...NEXT loop farther down in the subprogram displays the menu choices inside this frame.

The program's interaction with the user is generated by a series of nested WHILE...WEND loops. The first of two inner loops, *WHILE charPos% = 0*, accepts a single-character menu choice and beeps if the user presses an invalid choice. The second inner loop, *WHILE charPos% = 0*, reads either the Enter key, to confirm the choice, or the Esc key, to cancel the choice. The outer loop repeats the process until the user has entered and confirmed a valid menu choice. The whole process relies on the INKEY$ function, to get a character, and on the INSTR function, to check to see if the input character is valid.

Integrating *Menu* with a main program

We have seen that *Menu* requires two arguments to be passed to it: an array of strings for *menuChoices$* and an integer variable for *numChosen%*, which is used to pass back the number that corresponds to the user's menu choice. The following is an example of a CALL statement to *Menu*:

```
CALL Menu(menuCh$(), which%)
```

The string array, *menuCh$* in this example, contains the choices that make up the menu. (*Menu* can handle a maximum of 12 menu option strings; the subprogram expects the values to be stored in array elements beginning at 1, not 0.)

The purpose of the second argument in the call to *Menu*, an integer variable, is not to pass a value to the subprogram. Instead, the variable is designed to accept a value from the subprogram when the subprogram ends. This is an example of the advantage of passing an argument by reference that we discussed in Chapter 2.

After displaying the menu and eliciting an input value, the *Menu* subprogram ultimately passes back an integer value representing the number of the user's menu choice. For example, if the user chooses the third menu option, *Menu* passes back a value of *3*. The argument is passed by reference back to the second variable argument in the call to *Menu*.

Figure 3-3 shows a program that illustrates the use of the *Menu* subprogram. The program is called *MenuTest*. It begins by creating an array named *menu$*, which contains the program's five menu options. The program reads these options into *menu$* from a series of DATA lines:

```
FOR i% = 1 to 5
    READ menu$(i%)
NEXT i%
DATA get data
DATA show statistical analysis
DATA display a column chart
DATA print a report
DATA quit
```

```
'    MENUTEST.BAS
'    The MenuTest program is designed to test the Menu subprogram.  The
'        program also uses the Upper function and the Frame subprogram.

'-----------------------| Global Variable Declarations |--------------------

'    ---- Initialize Boolean variables true% and false%.
    true% = -1
    false% = 0

'    ---- Set the lowest subscript possible for all arrays to 1.
    OPTION BASE 1

'    ---- Create the menu$ array with 5 array elements.
    DIM menu$(5)

'---------------------------| Function Area |---------------------------------

'    ---- Read in and compile BASIC user-defined function.
    REM $INCLUDE : 'UPPER.BAS'

'--------------------------| Main Program Area |------------------------------


'    ---- Initialize the menu$ array.
    FOR i% = 1 to 5
        READ menu$(i%)
    NEXT i%
```

Figure 3-3. *The* MenuTest *program.*   *(more...)*

```
'     ---- Data for the menu$ array representing the program's 5 menu options.
      DATA get data
      DATA show statistical analysis
      DATA display a column chart
      DATA print a report
      DATA quit

'     ---- ok% is 0 (false) until data is available.
      ok% = false%

'      ---- Display the menu, get the user's choice, and call the
'            appropriate subprogram.
      WHILE choice% <> 5
          LOCATE 2, 29: PRINT "Demonstration Program"
          CALL Menu(menu$(), choice%)

          IF (choice% = 1) THEN
              CALL GetData
              ok% = true%
          ELSEIF (choice% = 2 AND ok%) THEN
              CALL ShowStats
          ELSEIF (choice% = 3 AND ok%) THEN
              CALL ColChart
          ELSEIF (choice% = 4 AND ok%) THEN
              CALL Report
          END IF
      WEND

      END


'--------------------------| Subprogram Area |--------------------------

'     ---- Read in and compile external BASIC subprograms.
      REM $INCLUDE : 'FRAME.BAS'
      REM $INCLUDE : 'MENU.BAS'


'   The GetData, ShowStats, ColChart, and Report subprograms are,
'        at this point, just dummy routines.  Each displays a message
'        on the screen identifying itself.

SUB GetData STATIC
    CALL Message("This is the GetData subprogram.")
END SUB


SUB ShowStats STATIC
    CALL Message("This is the ShowStats subprogram.")
END SUB


SUB ColChart STATIC
    CALL Message("This is the ColChart subprogram.")
END SUB


SUB Report STATIC
    CALL Message("This is the Report subprogram.")
END SUB
```

Figure 3-3. *The* MenuTest *program (continued).*   (*more . . .*)

```
'   The Message subprogram receives one string argument, which it
'       displays centered on the screen inside a frame.

SUB Message (mString$) STATIC
    lc% = ((80 - LEN(mString$)) \ 2) - 3
    rc% = 80 - lc%
    tc% = 10: bc% = 14

    CALL Frame(lc%, rc%, tc%, bc%)
    LOCATE tc% + 2, lc% + 4: PRINT mString$

    CALL Pause
    CLS
END SUB


'   The Pause subprogram simply creates a pause in the action of the
'       program, until the user presses a key.

SUB Pause STATIC
    character$ = ""
    WHILE character$ = ""
        character$ = INKEY$
    WEND
END SUB
```

Figure 3-3. *The* MenuTest *program (continued).*

Subsequently, the program calls the *Menu* subprogram as follows:

```
.CALL Menu(menu$(), choice%)
```

Figure 3-4 shows the resulting screen menu. You can see that the *Menu* subprogram modifies the menu choice strings in a couple of

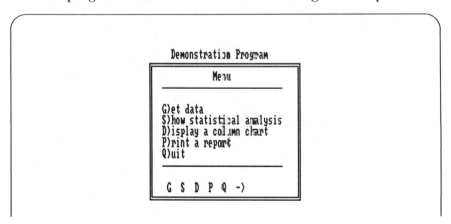

Figure 3-4. *A sample menu, created by the* MenuTest *program in Figure 3-3.*

ways: The first letter of each choice has been capitalized, and a parenthesis separates this first letter from the rest of the string. Below the choices, *Menu* displays the following input prompt:

```
G  S  D  P  Q ->
```

This line shows the valid menu responses. To choose one of the five options, press the key that corresponds to the first letter of the option itself. (Until data is entered, only the *Get data* and *Quit* options are functional, since you need to input data before you can manipulate it.)

To choose the *Get data* option, the user must press the letter *G*. Figure 3-5 shows the menu response when the user presses the appropriate key. The following message appears beneath the menu:

```
<Enter> to confirm; <Esc> to redo.
```

In other words, to confirm the menu choice the user must press the Enter key; to undo the menu choice and start again the user must press the Esc key.

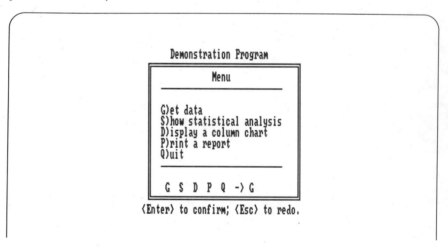

Figure 3-5. *The sample menu, after the user chooses a menu option.*

The *Menu* subprogram exerts careful control over the input process. If the user presses a key that does not represent a menu choice, the computer beeps. On the other hand, the *Menu* routine conveniently allows either uppercase or lowercase input responses.

In the array of option strings that you pass to *Menu* in a program, each string must begin with a different letter of the alphabet. (If two options begin with the same letter, the subprogram resolves the resulting ambiguity by always selecting the first of the two options.)

Let's return briefly to the *MenuTest* program to see what happens after the call to *Menu*. The subprogram passes the number of the user's menu choice to the variable *choice%* in this example. Then, in an IF ... THEN ... ELSEIF decision structure, the program calls an appropriate subprogram to respond to the user's choice. (In this demonstration program, the subprograms are just dummy routines; each simply displays a message on the screen identifying itself.) This action takes place within a WHILE...WEND loop that repeats until *choice%* equals 5:

```
WHILE choice% <> 5
```

Until the user chooses *Quit* (the fifth menu option), the menu will reappear on the screen after each activity, offering the user another choice.

Finally, notice that the *Menu* subprogram requires the use of both the *Upper$* function and the *Frame* subprogram, presented in Chapter 2. These two routines, along with *Menu* itself, are read into the program by $INCLUDE statements (one in the function area and two in the subprogram area):

```
REM $INCLUDE : 'UPPER.BAS'
REM $INCLUDE : 'FRAME.BAS'
REM $INCLUDE : 'MENU.BAS'
```

You will find this sequence of $INCLUDE statements in any program that uses the *Menu* subprogram. (Again, these subprograms must be in the current directory if a path is not specified in the $INCLUDE statement.)

The next example subprogram is a revised version of the *Frame* subprogram. This version, named *PrFrame*, creates frames that can be printed.

THE *PRFRAME* SUBPROGRAM

As you have seen, the *Frame* subprogram is designed to help produce a clear and attractive screen by drawing boxes around displayed information. Sometimes you will want similar boxes around information that you send to the printer. For example, in Chapter 5 we will look at a charting program that prepares column charts destined for printing. The program we will be looking at shortly in this chapter encloses certain elements of these charts in frames.

Unfortunately, the particular set of characters used in the *Frame* subprogram is meant to be displayed on the screen and cannot normally be printed on many printers. The *PrFrame* subprogram solves this problem by providing frames that consist of printable characters. Figure 3-6 shows a listing of the subprogram.

```
'     PRFRAME.BAS
'     The PrFrame subprogram draws a rectangular double-line frame on the
'        screen, using exclusively printable characters.

SUB PrFrame (leftCol%, rightCol%, topRow%, bottomRow%) STATIC
'     ---- Draw the four corners.
      LOCATE topRow%, leftCol%: PRINT "+"
      LOCATE topRow%, rightCol%: PRINT "+"
      LOCATE bottomRow%, leftCol%: PRINT "+";
      LOCATE bottomRow%, rightCol%: PRINT "+";

'     ---- Draw the vertical lines.
      FOR vert% = topRow% + 1 TO bottomRow% - 1
          LOCATE vert%, leftCol%: PRINT "|";
          LOCATE vert%, rightCol%: PRINT "|";
      NEXT vert%

'     ---- Draw the horizontal lines.
      horizLength% = rightCol% - leftCol% - 1
      horizLine$ = STRING$(horizLength%, "-")
      LOCATE topRow%, leftCol% + 1: PRINT horizLine$
      LOCATE bottomRow%, leftCol% + 1: PRINT horizLine$;
END SUB
```

Figure 3-6. *The* PrFrame *subprogram.*

Inside the *PrFrame* subprogram

The *PrFrame* subprogram uses the *LOCATE* command to position the cursor at specified row and column addresses on the display screen and uses the *PRINT* command to actually display the characters. Unlike the *Frame* routine, *PrFrame* uses the following characters, which most printers can produce:

+   **for corners**
| **for vertical lines**
—   **for horizontal lines**

(If your printer can't produce the vertical bar (|), you can use the uppercase letter *I*, the exclamation point (*!*), or the colon (*:*).)

    PrFrame receives the four numeric address arguments in the variables *leftCol%*, *rightCol%*, *topRow%*, and *bottomRow%*. Pairs of these numbers create a row-column screen address for the LOCATE command. For example, the following statements display a character for the upper-left corner of the box:

```
LOCATE topRow%, leftCol%: PRINT "+"
```

A FOR...NEXT loop draws the vertical sides of the box, character by character, from top to bottom:

```
FOR vert% = topRow% + 1 TO bottomRow% - 1
```

    Although the vertical lines must be drawn character by character, the routine uses QuickBASIC's built-in STRING$ function to create strings of hyphens for the top and bottom of the box. (STRING$ is a function that returns a string whose length and character type you specify in its argument.) The required length of the string is computed and stored in the variable *horizLength%*. This value becomes the first argument of the STRING$ function:

```
horizLength% = rightCol% - leftCol% - 1
horizLine$ = STRING$(horizLength%, "-")
```

    A call to the routine requires four integer arguments:

```
CALL PrFrame(left%, right%, top%, bottom%)
```

    The first two arguments give the screen column addresses of the left and right sides of the resulting frame; these should be numbers in the range 1 to 80, the dimensions of a standard, text-oriented screen. The next two arguments give the top and bottom addresses, ranging from row 1 to row 25 on the screen (these argument names may be any variable or expression in the calling program).

Figure 3-7 shows samples of the printable frames. This output was produced by substituting *PrFrame* for *Frame* in the demonstration program presented in Chapter 2 (Figure 2-7).

```
+------------------------------------------------------------------------+
|                                                                        |
|                                                                        |
|                                                                        |
|                                                                        |
|                +-------------------------------------+                 |
|                |                                     |                 |
|                |   THE MICROSOFT QUICKBASIC COMPILER |                 |
|                |                                     |                 |
|                +-------------------------------------+                 |
|                                                                        |
|                                                                        |
|                                                                        |
|                                                                        |
+------------------------------------------------------------------------+
```

Figure 3-7. *Sample printout generated by* PrFrame.

THE *SORT* AND *SEARCH* SUBPROGRAMS

The purpose of *Sort* is to alphabetize a list of string values. Given this ordered list, the *Search* subprogram is designed to locate a value in the list. Both routines actually work with a pair of arrays: a string array that contains the list of string values, and an integer array in which each number corresponds to a particular text value in the list of strings. Together these two arrays form a kind of index, as we will soon see. The *Sort* subprogram appears in Figure 3-8, and the *Search* subprogram in Figure 3-9.

```
'    SORT.BAS
'    The Sort subprogram rearranges a numeric array and a string array,
'        using the string array as the key to the sort.  This subprogram
'        implements the Shell sort algorithm.
```

Figure 3-8. *The* Sort *subprogram.* *(more...)*

```
SUB Sort (numbers%(1), names$(1)) STATIC
    true% = -1: false% = 0

    length% = UBOUND(names$)
    jump% = 1
    WHILE jump% <= length%
        jump% = jump% * 2
    WEND

    WHILE jump% > 1
        jump% = (jump% - 1) \ 2
        finished% = false%
        WHILE NOT finished%
            finished% = true%
            FOR upper% = 1 TO length% - jump%
                lower% = upper% + jump%
                IF (names$(upper%) > names$(lower%)) THEN
                    SWAP names$(upper%), names$(lower%)
                    SWAP numbers%(upper%), numbers%(lower%)
                    finished% = false%
                END IF
            NEXT upper%
        WEND
    WEND
END SUB
```

Figure 3-8. *The* Sort *subprogram (continued).*

```
'   SEARCH.BAS
'   The Search subprogram performs a binary search operation.  Specifically,
'       the routine searches for a target text value (whatText$) in a
'       sorted array of strings (names$).  If the value is located,
'       Search returns the corresponding integer (getNum%) from an
'       array of integers (numbers%).  If the value is not located,
'       getNum% is returned with a value of zero.

SUB Search (numbers%(1), getNum%, names$(1), whatText$) STATIC
    true% = -1: false% = 0
    begin% = 1
    ending% = UBOUND(names$)
    located% = false%
    getNum% = 0

    WHILE begin% <= ending% AND NOT located%
        middle% = (begin% + ending%) \ 2
        IF (whatText$ = names$(middle%)) THEN
            located% = true%
            getNum% = numbers%(middle%)
        ELSEIF (whatText$ > names$(middle%)) THEN
            begin% = middle% + 1
        ELSE
            ending% = middle% - 1
        END IF
    WEND
END SUB
```

Figure 3-9. *The* Search *subprogram.*

Inside the *Sort* routine

Sort is known as a *Shell sort routine,* named for Donald Shell, who originally developed the algorithm. The routine begins by comparing pairs of values, which are relatively far from each other in the list (by values we mean the ASCII values of characters in the list), and swapping any pair that is out of order. (The distance between compared characters is set by the *jump%* variable, discussed below.) When all of the pairs at one interval are in order, the interval is reduced for the next round of comparisons. This process continues, reducing the interval for each successive round of comparisons. By the time the routine is finally ready to compare consecutive values in the list, the array is nearly sorted.

Sort receives the list of numbers in the array *numbers%* and the list of string values in the array *names$.* *Sort* needs to know how many elements are in the *names$* string array, which it determines by using the built-in QuickBASIC function UBOUND. For a one-dimensional array, UBOUND returns the number of array elements as an integer. This value is then assigned to the *length%* variable:

```
length% = UBOUND(names$)
```

Sort assumes that the *numbers%* array is the same length as *names$* (that is, each string has a corresponding number), and that the first value in each array is stored in element 1 and not in element 0.

The routine assigns the interval between pairs of characters to sort to the variable *jump%.* A trio of nested loops then does the sort. The inner FOR ... NEXT loop compares each pair of string values at a given *jump%* interval and uses the QuickBASIC SWAP command to switch them if they're out of order. The middle WHILE...WEND loop repeats these comparisons until all of the pairs at a given interval are in order. The outer WHILE...WEND loop repeats the process through progressively smaller intervals until the final round compares consecutive values in the list.

Inside the *Search* routine

Search receives the sorted list of names—and their corresponding numbers—in the array parameters *names$* and *numbers%,* respectively. The target name—the name the routine searches for in the *names$* array—is received in the *whatText$* parameter. If the routine locates the target name, the corresponding integer in the *numbers%* array is passed back to the calling program by way of the *getNum%* parameter; otherwise, *getNum%* sends back a value of 0.

The routine uses UBOUND to find the length of the list:

```
begin% = 1
ending% = UBOUND(NAMES$)
```

The variable *located%* is given an initial value of 0 from the Boolean variable *false%*.

Next the actual search begins by comparing the ASCII value of the target string with the ASCII value of the string in the exact middle of the list. This comparison determines if the name will ultimately be in the first half or last half of the list. The routine then compares the name with the string in the middle of the appropriate half. This process continues, focusing on a quarter of the list, an eighth of the list, a sixteenth of the list, and so on until the name is either located or determined not to be in the list.

A WHILE...WEND loop conducts the search. Inside the loop, the values of *begin%* and *ending%* are constantly adjusted, allowing the routine to focus on progressively smaller portions of the list. The comparisons continue until the target value is found (and the variable *located%* becomes true) or until the value of *ending%* is smaller than the value of *begin%*, meaning that the target value is not in the list:

```
WHILE begin% <= ending% AND NOT located%
```

The *Search* algorithm is called a *binary search*. The basic idea is to locate the target name by continually reducing the search to a fractional portion of the entire list. This procedure can work successfully only if the list of names is arranged in alphabetic order. For this reason, the *Sort* and *Search* routines work together as a pair.

Putting *Sort* and *Search* together

For example, a company has five employees with the following last names:

1	Nelson
2	Barker
3	Madison
4	Carlson
5	Jones

The numbers represent the order in which the employees were hired. We will store both numbers and names as arrays—the numbers in an array called *orderHired%* and the names in an array called *lastName$*. We can then send the arrays to *Sort* to be ordered and alphabetized.

A call to the *Sort* subprogram takes two array arguments, first the integer array and then the string array. Here is how the call appears for sorting the list of employees:

```
CALL Sort(orderHired%(), lastName$())
```

When its work is complete, *Sort* passes the rearranged lists back to the same two arrays. After this call, the two lists appear in the following order in their respective arrays:

2	Barker
4	Carlson
5	Jones
3	Madison
1	Nelson

After these two lists have been arranged with the names in alphabetic order, the *Search* subprogram can locate any name in the list and supply the corresponding number from the integer list. A call to *Search* takes four arguments. The first and third arguments are the sorted integer array and the sorted string array, respectively. The fourth argument is the string value that *Search* looks for in the string array:

```
CALL Search(orderHired%(), hired%, lastName%(), "Carlson")
```

Significantly, the second argument of the call to *Search* should always appear as an integer variable. When *Search* finds the target string (as specified by the fourth argument), the subprogram uses this variable to pass back the corresponding numeric value from the integer array. In the sample call above, *Search* locates *Carlson* in the name list and returns the number 4 to the variable *hired%*, showing that Carlson was the fourth employee to be hired.

If the fourth argument represents a value that *Search* cannot locate in the string array, the routine passes a value of 0 back to the integer variable. For example, after the call:

```
CALL Search(order%(), hired%, lastname$(), "Wilson")
```

the variable *hired%* contains 0, indicating that the name *Wilson* is not in the *lastName$* array.

Of course, a list of only five names is a trivial example for the *Sort* and *Search* subprograms. The routines are designed to rearrange and search through arrays that contain hundreds, and even thousands, of values. Written in the QuickBASIC language, both subprograms work very quickly and efficiently. We will see that the routine alphabetizes a list of 100 names in seconds or less.

THE *YESNO* USER-DEFINED FUNCTION

Before we turn to the demonstration program for *Sort* and *Search,* we have one further routine to examine—a user-defined function named *YesNo.* A listing of the function is in Figure 3-10. The purpose of *YesNo* is to elicit an answer of *yes* or *no* from the the user at the keyboard in response to a question that the routine displays on the screen. As part of its defined job, the *YesNo* function actually performs an input operation.

```
'    YESNO.BAS
'    The YesNo function asks a yes-or-no question, and returns a Boolean
'        value indicating the user's response:  true for yes, false for no.

DEF FN YesNo(prompt$)
'    ---- Display the question prompt, and initialize variables.
     PRINT prompt$ " (Y or N) -> ";
     reply$ = ""
     charPos% = 0

'    ---- Get a single-letter response.
     WHILE charPos% = 0
          reply$ = INKEY$
          IF (reply$ <> "") THEN
               charPos% = INSTR("YyNn", reply$)
               IF (charPos% = 0) THEN BEEP
          END IF
     WEND

'    ---- Convert the response into an uppercase letter.
     reply$ = MID$("YYNN", charPos%, 1)
     PRINT reply$

'    ---- Convert the response into a Boolean value.
     FN YesNo = (reply$ = "Y")
END DEF
```

Figure 3-10. *The* YesNo *user-defined function.*

YesNo receives its string argument in the *prompt$* parameter and uses the following PRINT command to display the question on the screen:

```
PRINT prompt$ " (Y or N) -> ";
```

Then, inside a WHILE…WEND loop, the routine uses the INKEY$ function to monitor the response from the keyboard:

```
reply$ = INKEY$
```

Each performance of INKEY$ scans the keyboard once to see if a key has been pressed. To wait effectively for the user's input, the program must perform INKEY$ repeatedly until *reply$* actually contains a character.

After it receives a character, the program tests to see if the character is in the string of valid letters, *YyNn*:

```
IF (reply$ <> "") THEN
    charPos% = INSTR("YyNn", reply$)
```

The INSTR function returns the position of *reply$* in *"YyNn"*; if *reply$* does not contain one of these four characters, INSTR returns a value of 0. The statement *WHILE charPos% = 0* keeps the input loop idling until *charPos%* is no longer 0.

When the routine receives a valid character from the keyboard, it converts the character to uppercase and displays it on the screen:

```
reply$ = MID$("YYNN", charPos%, 1)
```

Finally, *YesNo* returns a value of true if *reply$* contains the character *Y*; otherwise, *YesNo* returns a false value:

```
FN YesNo = (reply$ = "Y")
```

Although *Y* is not a direct equivalent to true, recall that any nonzero expression will be evaluated as true by the compiler. As mentioned, a call to the function takes one string argument. This string becomes the prompt question that appears on the screen. For example:

```
continue% = FN YesNo("Do you wish to continue?")
```

The function displays the complete prompt as follows:

```
Do you wish to continue? (Y or N) ->
```

In response, *YesNo* accepts only one of four characters from the keyboard: *Y*, *y*, *N*, or *n*. (The computer sounds a beep if the user types anything else.)

After the user presses one of these keys, *YesNo* returns a value of true or false to indicate the response: true for an input of *Y* or *y*; false for an input of *N* or *n*. This returned value allows a program to use a call to the *YesNo* function in place of a conditional expression. For example:

```
WHILE FN YesNo("Do you wish to continue?")
```

In this example, the WHILE...WEND loop ends when the user presses the *N* or *n* key.

The three routines, *Sort*, *Search*, and *YesNo*, are all used in the *SortTest* demonstration program shown in Figure 3-11. To prepare a test for these routines, *SortTest* sets up two arrays of 100 elements each: *text$* is an array of random string values, and *number%* is a corresponding array of integer values, in the range of 1 to 100. Each string value in *text$* is made up of five randomly chosen uppercase letters. A sample run of *SortTest* is shown in Figure 3-12 (on page 75).

```
'   SORTTEST.BAS
'   The SortTest program is designed to test the Sort and Search routines.
'       The program also uses two user-defined functions: YesNo and Upper$.

'--------------------| Global Variable Declarations |--------------------

'   ---- Define global arrays and initialize total% variable.
    OPTION BASE 1
    COMMON SHARED total%, number%(1), text$(1), true%, false%
    total% = 100
    DIM number%(total%), text$(total%)

'   ---- Initialize Boolean variables true% and false%.
    true% = -1
    false% = 0

'--------------------------| Function Area |--------------------------

'   ---- Read in and compile BASIC user-defined functions.
    REM $INCLUDE : 'UPPER.BAS'
    REM $INCLUDE : 'YESNO.BAS'

'--------------------------| Main Program Area |--------------------------

'   ---- Call primary subprograms.
    CALL Setup
    CALL TimeSort
    CALL UserSearch
    END
```

Figure 3-11. *The* SortTest *program.*   *(more...)*

```
'--------------------------| Subprogram Area |--------------------------

'    ---- Read in and compile BASIC subprograms.
     REM $INCLUDE : 'SORT.BAS'
     REM $INCLUDE : 'SEARCH.BAS'


'    The Setup subprogram creates a numeric and a string array for the
'        demonstration.  The string array contains strings of randomly
'        selected uppercase letters.  The numeric array contains integer
'        values from 1 through total%.

SUB Setup STATIC
     RANDOMIZE(TIMER)
     PRINT
     PRINT TAB(7) "Unsorted List" TAB(38) "Sorted List"
     PRINT TAB(7) "-------- ----" TAB(38) "------ ----"

     FOR i% = 1 to total%
         number%(i%) = i%
         FOR j% = 1 to 5
             temp% = INT(RND * 26) + 65
             text$(i%) = text$(i%) + CHR$(temp%)
         NEXT j%
         IF (i% MOD 10 = 0) THEN
             LOCATE i% / 10 + 3, 5
             PRINT number%(i%) TAB(15) text$(i%)
         END IF
     NEXT i%
END SUB


'    The TimeSort subprogram sorts the arrays, using the text$ array
'        as the key to the sort.  The routine also times the operation,
'        and displays the elapsed time.

SUB TimeSort STATIC
     start! = TIMER
     CALL Sort(number%(), text$())
     done! = TIMER

'    ---- Display a selection of the values on the screen.
     LOCATE 3
     FOR i% = 1 TO 10
         LOCATE i% + 3, 35
         item% = i% * 10
         PRINT number%(item%) TAB(45) text$(item%)
     NEXT i%

     elapsedTime! = done! - start!
     PRINT
     PRINT TAB(5) "Sorting"; total%; "records took ";
     PRINT USING "###.##"; elapsedTime!;
     PRINT " seconds."
END SUB


'    The UserSearch subprogram allows the user to exercise the
'        search operation.
```

Figure 3-11. *The SortTest program (continued).*   *(more...)*

```
SUB UserSearch STATIC
    continue% = true%
    WHILE continue%
        PRINT
        PRINT TAB(15);
        INPUT "Search for what text"; target$

'   ---- Convert the user's search text to all uppercase letters
'        before searching for the value.
        target$ = FN Upper$(target$)
        CALL Search(number%(), recNum%, text$(), target$)

'   ---- Display the result of the search.
        IF (recNum% <> 0) THEN
            PRINT TAB(15) target$ " is record number" STR$(recNum%) "."
        ELSE
            PRINT TAB(15) target$ " is not in the list."
        END IF

'   ---- Find out if the user wants to search for another value.
        PRINT TAB(15);
        continue% = FN YesNo("Another search? ")
    WEND
END SUB
```

Figure 3-11. *The* SortTest *program (continued).*

```
        Unsorted List                    Sorted List
        -------- ----                    ------ ----
        10       FCQSC                   11     C[illegible]HLE
        20       RJXGK                   27     F[illegible]VEV
        30       NSKZX                   53     H[illegible]IPP
        40       GQNPF                   32     I[illegible]LHG
        50       MVNOQ                   79     M[illegible]FAJ
        60       MZITI                   94     P[illegible]NZU
        70       SFDKJ                   75     R[illegible]ISE
        80       HDIPM                   6      T[illegible]VGT
        90       HOYSO                   43     W[illegible]PAR
        100      OSTGB                   26     Z[illegible]JQF

      Sorting 100 records took   0.77 seconds.

              Search for what text? twvgt
              TWVGT is record number 6.
              Another search?  (Y or N) -> N



   Normal termination. Press any key.
```

Figure 3-12. *A sample run of the* SortTest *program.*

After creating the two arrays, the program displays a selection of their values (every tenth array element). Then it sorts the arrays by the string values and again displays a selection of values from the arrays. Finally, the program gives you a chance to perform a series of search operations.

Figure 3-12 shows the two tables of selected values from the arrays (*Unsorted List* and *Sorted List*). Just below these tables is the message *Sorting 100 records took 0.77 seconds*. The program calculates the time taken by the *Sort* routine to rearrange the two arrays; this is the result for 100 elements on a COMPAQ Portable 286 computer.

Next, the program elicits a text string to search for in the newly sorted array. (Notice that the program converts the target string value to uppercase before attempting the search process.) Upon receiving a target string value, the program makes a call to the *Search* routine, receives the result of the search, and displays a report on the screen.

If a given input string cannot be found in the array, the program displays an appropriate message. For example, if you type *edmha* as the string to search for, and this series of characters is not sorted in the *text$* array, the program responds:

```
Search for what text? edmha
EDMHA is not in the list.
```

Let's examine the subprogram calls that accomplish the sorting and searching. In the *TimeSort* subprogram, the following lines calculate the time required for the sort:

```
start! = TIMER
CALL Sort(number%(), text$())
done! = TIMER
```

The *TIMER* function reads the system clock (present on all machines) and gives the number of seconds that have elapsed since midnight of the current day. Given *start!* and *done!*, the clock values before and after the sort, the following expression calculates the number of seconds (to two decimal places) between them:

```
elapsedTime! = done! - start!
```

(By the way, the exclamation points at the end of these variable names indicate that these are single-precision variables. We discuss data types in Chapter 4.)

The *UserSearch* subprogram conducts the search dialog. An INPUT command elicits the target string. The routine then calls the *Upper$* function to convert the input string to uppercase letters and calls the *Search* subprogram to find the string:

```
INPUT "Search for what text"; target$
target$ = FN Upper$(target$)
CALL Search(number%(), recNum%, text$(), target$)
```

After this call to *Search*, the variable *recNum%* contains the numeric value that is paired with the target string. If *recNum%* is 0, the string was not located; otherwise, the program displays the number of the string:

```
IF (recNum% <> 0) THEN
    PRINT TAB(15) target$ " is record number" STR$(recNum%) "."
ELSE
    PRINT TAB(15) target$ " is not in the list."
END IF
```

Finally, the program calls the *YesNo* function to elicit instructions for continuing the program or stopping:

```
continue% = FN YesNo("Another search? ")
```

As you can see in Figure 3-12, this call places the following prompt on the screen:

```
Another search? (Y or N) ->
```

The course of the input dialog is controlled by a WHILE...WEND loop, which terminates only when *continue%* becomes false:

```
WHILE continue%
```

We will see the *Sort* and *Search* routines again in Chapter 7, where they help provide access to the records in a random-access data file. Specifically, we use them to set up an index for an employee database.

The final routine in this chapter performs a task that is just the opposite of what the *Sort* routine does. The routine, called the *Shuffle* subprogram, rearranges a list of values into a random order.

THE *SHUFFLE* SUBPROGRAM

The listing of the *Shuffle* subprogram appears in Figure 3-13. *Shuffle* receives its array variable in the *shuffledArray%* parameter. At the beginning of the routine, the TIMER function resets the "seed" of the random-number generator with a value derived from the total number of seconds that elapsed since midnight:

```
RANDOMIZE(TIMER)
```

```
'     SHUFFLE.BAS
'     The Shuffle subprogram rearranges the elements of a numeric array,
'         resulting in a random order.

SUB Shuffle (shuffledArray%(1)) STATIC
'     ---- Use the current time as the seed for RANDOMIZE, QuickBASIC's
'         built-in random-number generator.
      RANDOMIZE(TIMER)

'     ---- Find the length of the array to be shuffled.
      length% = UBOUND(shuffledArray%)

'     ---- Swap each element of the array with a randomly selected element.
      FOR card% = 1 TO length%
          randomCard% = INT(RND * length%) + 1
          SWAP shuffledArray%(card%), shuffledArray%(randomCard%)
      NEXT card%
END SUB
```

Figure 3-13. *The* Shuffle *subprogram.*

Then the routine uses the built-in UBOUND function to determine the length of the array it received:

```
length% = UBOUND(shuffledArray%)
```

The shuffling takes place inside a simple FOR ... NEXT loop. From the top to the bottom of the array, each element is exchanged with a randomly selected element elsewhere in the array:

```
FOR card% = 1 TO length%
    randomCard% = INT(RND * length%) + 1
    SWAP shuffledArray%(card%), shuffledArray%(randomCard%)
NEXT card%
```

Notice how a random selection occurs. The RND function supplies a
random number between 0 and 1, and the following expression converts this number to an integer from 1 to *length%*:

```
INT(RND * length%) + 1
```

The subsequent SWAP statement exchanges the values of the array elements numbered *card%* and *randomCard%*.

A call to the routine takes an array of integers as the single argument. For example:

```
CALL Shuffle(deck%())
```

When the routine ends, the array contains exactly the same values as
before, but the values are in a new and completely random order.

As its name suggests, the *Shuffle* subprogram is ideal for card-
game programs. If *deck%* is an array of integers in the range of 1 to 52,
where each number represents a particular card in a full deck, the
Shuffle routine shuffles the "deck" by randomizing the position of the
"cards." Chapter 8 presents a program that conducts a game of
Twenty-one, or Blackjack. The program relies on the *Shuffle* subprogram to shuffle the cards whenever necessary.

Figure 3-14 shows a demonstration program named *Cards*, which
previews several of the routines required in a card-game program.
The program sets up an array of integers to represent a deck of cards
and then shuffles the deck. To show that the *Shuffle* subprogram really
does its job, the demonstration program displays the order of cards in
the deck both before and after the shuffle. You can see a sample run
of the program in Figure 3-15 (on page 81).

```
'    CARDS.BAS
'    The Cards program is designed to test the Shuffle subprogram, and
'        to demonstrate several other routines important in card
'        game programming.

'---------------------| Global Variable Declarations |---------------------

'    ---- Initialize and prepare a deck of 52 shuffled cards.
     OPTION BASE 1
     DIM SHARED rank$(13), deck%(52)

'-------------------------| Function Area |-------------------------

'    The TransCard$ function translates a number from 1 through 52
'        into a string containing suit and rank symbols.
```

Figure 3-14. *The* Cards *program.* (more . . .)

```
DEF FN TransCard$ (number%)
    suit$ = CHR$(((number% - 1) \ 13) + 3)
    rank$ = rank$(((number% - 1) MOD 13) + 1)
    FN TransCard$ = suit$ + rank$
END DEF

'------------------------| Main Program Area |----------------------------

    CALL Initialize
    CALL StartDeck
    CALL ShuffleDeck

'    ---- Draw frames around the deck displays.
    CALL Frame(4, 34, 2, 16)
    CALL Frame(40, 70, 2, 16)
    LOCATE 17,11: PRINT "The Original Deck"
    LOCATE 17,47: PRINT "The Shuffled Deck"

    END

'------------------------| Subprogram Area |------------------------------

'    ---- Read in and compile BASIC subprograms.
    REM $INCLUDE : 'FRAME.BAS'
    REM $INCLUDE : 'SHUFFLE.BAS'


'   The Initialize subprogram creates rank$, an array containing the
'        13 card rank symbols.

SUB Initialize STATIC
    FOR card% = 1 TO 13
      READ rank$(card%)
    NEXT card%

    DATA A, 2, 3, 4, 5, 6, 7, 8, 9, 10, J, Q, K
END SUB


'   The StartDeck subprogram creates and displays the unshuffled deck.

SUB StartDeck STATIC
    FOR card% = 1 TO 52
      deck%(card%) = card%
      LOCATE (card% - 1) MOD 13 + 3, (((card% - 1) \ 13 + 1) * 8) - 2
      PRINT FN TransCard$(card%)
    NEXT card%
END SUB


'   The ShuffleDeck subprogram shuffles the deck and then displays it.

SUB ShuffleDeck STATIC
    CALL Shuffle(deck%())

    FOR card% = 1 to 52
      LOCATE ((card% - 1) MOD 13) + 3, (((card% - 1) \ 13 + 5) * 8) + 2
      PRINT FN TransCard$(deck%(card%))
    NEXT card%
END SUB
```

Figure 3-14. *The* Cards *program (continued).*

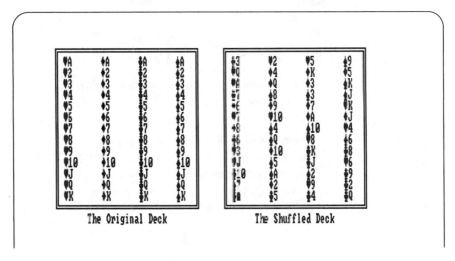

The Original Deck   The Shuffled Deck

Figure 3-15. *A sample run of the* Cards *program.*

The *Cards* program contains the source code for three subprograms—*Initialize, StartDeck,* and *ShuffleDeck,* and a user-defined function named *TransCard$. Initialize* sets up a string array called *rank$,* which contains the 13 rank symbols for the cards in the deck. Since a deck of cards contains 13 cards for each suit (2-10, Jack, Queen, King, Ace), *Initialize* sets up the *rank$* string array to contain 13 symbols for each of the four suits. *StartDeck* assigns values in the range of 1 to 52 to the *deck%* array and displays the original deck on the screen. Finally, *ShuffleDeck* calls the *Shuffle* subprogram and displays the shuffled deck on the screen. Two subprograms are read into the program at compile time via $INCLUDE statements: *Shuffle* and *Frame.*

The *TransCard$* user-defined function is perhaps the most interesting part of the demonstration program. It receives a single integer argument—a value in the range of 1 to 52—and returns a string value containing suit and rank symbols for the corresponding card. The *ShuffleDeck* routine shows a typical call to this function:

```
PRINT FN TransCard$(deck%(card%))
```

We will use the *TransCard$* function again in Chapter 8 when we examine the *Twenty-one* program.

CONCLUSION

We have seen that Microsoft QuickBASIC offers two useful techniques for introducing external subprograms into a program compilation.

The simpler of the two techniques uses the $INCLUDE metacommand. A $INCLUDE metacommand reads a source code file into the current listing at compile time. The file may contain a complete subprogram or user-defined function, or any other unit of QuickBASIC source code.

The second technique uses the *Buildlib* program to create a user-library file from a collection of compiled subprograms. This procedure is more detailed than the use of the $INCLUDE metacommand, but still is worth considering in many cases.

In this chapter and in Chapter 2 we have examined eight major subprograms and functions, all of which will reappear in the programming projects of Chapters 4 though 8. Figure 3-16 gives a summary list of these eight routines.

Name	Filename	Description
Frame	FRAME.BAS	Draws a rectangular frame on the screen.
PrFrame	PRFRAME.BAS	Draws a frame with printable characters.
Upper$	UPPER.BAS	Converts its string argument to all uppercase letters.
Menu	MENU.BAS	Displays a menu on the screen, and elicits a menu choice from the user.
Sort	SORT.BAS	Performs a Shell sort on a string array. Also rearranges a corresponding numeric array.
Search	SEARCH.BAS	Performs a binary search on a sorted string array. Finds a corresponding integer value from a numeric array.
YesNo	YESNO.BAS	Elicits a yes-or-no response from the keyboard, and returns a value of *true* (for "yes") or *false* (for "no").
Shuffle	SHUFFLE.BAS	Rearranges a numeric array in random order.

Figure 3-16. *The collection of supporting QuickBASIC routines developed in Chapters 2 and 3.*

CHAPTER 4

Data Types:
A Mortgage Calculation Program

Buying a home is probably the biggest expenditure a person ever undertakes, and the home mortgage loan that's usually involved has a big impact on the household budget. Moreover, the mathematical formulas that determine a loan's components—monthly payment, principal paid to date, interest paid to date, and total loan payment (including total interest)—intimidate most people.

This chapter's *Mortgage* program automates the complex mortgage arithmetic and generates results that allow you to compare the financial impact of various types of loans. Given the three basic loan parameters—the principal amount of the loan, the interest rate, and the term of the loan—the *Mortgage* program:

- Calculates the monthly payment

- Presents tables of monthly payments based on different principal amounts, interest rates, and terms

- Presents tables of total interest payments based on different principal amounts, interest rates, and terms

- Supplies amortization tables which, for any 12-month period, show how much principal and interest are paid for each month, as well as the loan's current balance and the total amount of principal paid to date

Actually calculating the amortization formulas is only one aspect of the *Mortgage* program. An equally important aspect is the user-interface: how the program asks the user for values and presents the user with the result. The program is designed to make these interactions smooth and convenient. As you examine the program, look closely at the input and output techniques.

Finally, the *Mortgage* program follows the modular, top-down structure that characterizes all well-written QuickBASIC programs. The program's overall organization is clear at a glance, and each individual section of the program is short and easy to understand. Consequently, the program is easy to revise. Its modular structure simplifies the task by making it easy to locate the sections you want to alter. (We consider several revisions to *Mortgage* at the end of this chapter.)

QUICKBASIC DATA TYPES

Virtually any QuickBASIC program of any complexity contains constants and variables. The values assigned to constant and variable names are collectively known as *data types*. The three categories of data types in QuickBASIC are:

- Numeric
- String
- Boolean

We will discuss each data type in the following sections.

A note on constants and variables

If you're new to programming and unfamiliar with the terms *variables* and *constants*, the distinction between them is straightforward. As we've seen in the programs so far in this book, a variable is a name that can be assigned different values during the course of a program, but which can store only one value at a time. For example, in the *GetMessage* program in Chapter 2 (Figure 2-7), this statement:

```
topRow% = 10
```

assigns a value of *10* to the *topRow%* integer variable (integers will be discussed later in this chapter). Later in the program *10* is no longer appropriate and other program lines "clear out" the *10* from *topRow%* and substitute another value.

Although a variable can change its value during a program, a constant is simply a specific value established in the program. In other words, a program can rely on a constant to have a specific value whenever it uses it. For example, the first PRINT statement that follows uses a numeric constant, and the second a string constant:

```
PRINT 10
PRINT "This is a string constant."
```

The result of the first statement is the number *10*, and the second is the phrase *This is a string constant.*

Numeric data types in QuickBASIC

QuickBASIC works with three numeric data types:

- Integers
- Single-precision numbers
- Double-precision numbers

Each data type is assigned a specific symbol that you use as a suffix when defining a numeric variable or constant name. The following table shows the three numeric data types, their corresponding symbols, and examples.

Data Type	Symbol	Example
Integers	%	term%
Single-precision numbers	!	interest! *or* interest
Double-precision numbers	#	principal#

Note the two single-precision examples. The default numeric data type in QuickBASIC is single-precision, so the *!* is optional.

It's important to note that QuickBASIC data types do not support commas (or any other nonnumeric characters). For example, the statement:

```
principal# = 80,000
```

causes the compiler to produce an *illegal syntax* error. Likewise, if you have a statement like:

```
Input "Enter the loan principal", principal#
```

in your program, and the user enters a value containing commas (or any other nonnumeric characters)—like *$80,000*—the program will display the following response:

```
?Redo from start
```

The two important aspects of each data type are *precision* and *range*. *Precision* refers to the number of accurate decimal places in a number, and *range* refers to the largest and smallest positive and negative numbers you can work with in a numeric type.

Integer numeric data types

In QuickBASIC, legal integers are whole numbers in the range of $-32,768$ to $+32,767$.

Integers require less memory and can be calculated in less time than single- or double-precision numbers. So use integer variables whenever you can, rather than variables that contain numbers of higher precision.

As mentioned, each variable name declared as an integer must be followed by the % sign. You can, however, use the DEFINT statement at the beginning of a program to specify that if variable names begin with certain letters they will be considered integers, whether or not they contain the % sign. For example, the following statement means that variable names beginning with the letters *i, j,* and *k* (both upper- and lowercase) will designate integer variables:

```
DEFINT i-k
```

Subsequently you can write a FOR...NEXT loop as:

```
FOR i = 1 TO 10
    [other program lines]
NEXT i
```

As you write a program that contains such a DEFINT statement, be careful to use the designated letters (*i, j,* and *k* in this example) only for integer variable names. Whenever you assign a noninteger value to an integer variable, QuickBASIC rounds the value to the nearest integer before carrying out the assignment statement. If you inadvertently use one of these letters for a noninteger variable, your program is likely to produce some strange and unexpected results. For example, suppose that the following assignment statement appears in the same program that contains the DEFINT *i-k* statement:

```
interest = 0.125
```

If you print the value of *interest* with the statement:

```
PRINT interest
```

the result is 0 if the integer variable *interest* is still set to 0.125.

You can override the effect of the DEFINT statement by using a different type suffix at the end of a variable name. For example, the variable named *interest!* is defined as single precision despite the previous DEFINT statement.

Single-precision numeric data types

QuickBASIC stores single-precision numbers with a maximum accuracy of seven decimal places. You can write single-precision numbers in various forms, most commonly as a number with a decimal point. For example:

123.4567

Alternatively, you can use the exponential form, in which the number is separated into a decimal value and an exponent indicating "to the power of 10." In that case the exponent is preceded by the letter *E*, and the number would be entered like this:

1.234567E2

The actual value of this number is 1.234567 times 100. (The notation *E2* signifies 10 to the second power, or 100.) A negative exponent means that the value should be divided by a power of 10. For example, the following number is equal to 0.0001234567:

1.234567E−4

You can also use the *!* suffix to specify that a constant value is single-precision, for example:

```
1.234!
```

You can declare single-precision variables by using the DEFSNG statement, the *!* symbol, or a variable name with no suffix. Unless predefined by a DEFDBL or DEFSTR statement (to be discussed later) or a DEFINT statement, a variable name that has no suffix designates a single-precision variable. For example, QuickBASIC treats the variables *rate, number,* and *subTotal* as single-precision values.

The range of single-precision positive numbers is approximately 2.9E−39 up to 1.7E+38, and for negative numbers −2.9E−39 down to −1.7E+39.

For example, the following statement creates a single-precision variable that accurately stores the number 0.125:

```
interest! = 0.125
```

Since single precision is the default numeric type, an identical statement would be:

```
interest = 0.125
```

Double-precision numeric data types

Double-precision numbers have an accuracy of up to 16 digits and have the same range as single-precision values. You can declare double-precision variables with the DEFDBL statement or with the # symbol, for example:

```
priceIncrease# = 1234567890.123456
```

Double-precision values require more memory than the other numeric data types. Also, because they must be calculated to more decimal places, they can slow down a program (though you won't usually notice the difference in speed). So, reserve double-precision numbers only for situations in which accuracy is important for more than seven digits.

For example, let's say you are working with a financial application and want to store dollar-and-cent values like $1,234.567.89. If you assigned this value to a single-precision variable, QuickBASIC would provide only seven digits and the value would be rounded to the nearest dollar:

```
priceIncrease! = 1234567.89
PRINT priceIncrease!
```

The result of this PRINT statement is 1234568. Notice that this value contains only six of the original digits; the seventh digit has been rounded from the value of the now-missing eighth digit, and the final two digits are lost. To keep the full accuracy of the number, you must provide a double-precision variable:

```
priceIncrease# = 1234567.89
PRINT priceIncrease#
```

Here the PRINT statement displays the full value of 1234567.89.

A double-precision *constant* is any literal numeric value in your program that has more than seven digits. The double-precision exponential format uses *D* (rather than *E*) to designate the exponent, for example:

1.23456789D6

Arithmetic with numeric data types

Now that we have an overview of the numeric data types, this is a good time to discuss how to manipulate them in QuickBASIC. QuickBASIC's arithmetic operations include the four basics: multiplication (which uses the asterisk, *), division (/), addition (+), and subtraction (−).

Another QuickBASIC operation is exponentiation, designated by the caret symbol (^), which yields a base number to the power of an exponent. Exponents can be integers (positive or negative) or decimal values. The following table gives three examples of exponent usage.

Statement	Result
PRINT 5 ^ 2	25
PRINT 5 ^ −2	.04
PRINT 2 ^ 0.5	1.414214

Notice the third example yields the square root of 2. This exemplifies the general rule that a fractional exponent finds the root of a number.

It is important to understand how QuickBASIC treats arithmetic expressions that contain values of mixed numeric types. Generally, the precision of the result will be that of the most precise value type in the expression. For example, compare the following statement with the third statement in the preceding list:

```
PRINT 2# ^ 0.5
```

The result is 1.414213562373095. Since the first operand in this expression is a double-precision constant, the result is also double precision.

QuickBASIC has two integer operations—integer division and the MOD operation. Integer division, symbolized by the backslash (\), yields the integer portion of a quotient. For example:

```
PRINT 7 \ 3
```

produces a result of 2.

Before performing integer division, QuickBASIC always rounds both the dividend and the divisor to the nearest integer. (After this rounding, both numbers must be within the legal range of integers, −32768 to +32767.)

Finally, the MOD operation performs Modulo arithmetic; specifically, it gives the remainder from the division of two integers. For example, the statement:

```
PRINT 7 MOD 3
```

produces a result of 1. (The game program in Chapter 8 includes some examples of both integer division and MOD.)

When an expression consists of more than one operation, QuickBASIC performs the operations in the following order:

1. Exponentiation

2. Negation (making an element negative)

3. Multiplication and division

4. Integer division

5. Modulo arithmetic (MOD)

6. Addition and subtraction

These operations are evaluated left to right in a formula. That is, when QuickBASIC comes to an arithmetic statement, it scans the line to see what operators are included. It then pairs the numbers around the operators and calculates the pairs according to the order in the preceding list. This order might not always be the one you want. For example, you might want a pair of numbers added together and then multiplied by another. You can use parentheses to force a different order of operations in an expression. For example, note the different results from the following expressions:

```
PRINT 2 * 3 + 4
```

produces a result of 10, while

```
PRINT 2 * (3 + 4)
```

returns 14.

You can also use parentheses simply to improve the readability of an expression, even if the parentheses don't change QuickBASIC's normal order of operations. For example, the following statement would yield the same result (10) without the parentheses:

```
PRINT (2 * 3) + 4
```

Numeric functions

Many of QuickBASIC's built-in functions work with or supply numeric values. Two functions that appear in the *Mortgage* program are INT and CINT. Both functions convert a number with a decimal point to an integer (the arguments of these functions must be within the legal range of integers). For positive values, INT simply eliminates the decimal portion of the number, and CINT rounds to the nearest integer. For example, the statement:

```
PRINT INT(345.6)
```

returns the integer portion of 345, while

```
PRINT CINT(345.6)
```

returns 346—the integer result after rounding.

The string data type

A QuickBASIC string can be a maximum of 32,767 alphanumeric characters. String constants are enclosed in double-quotation marks. String variables are designated by a dollar-sign ($) suffix. For example:

```
principal$ = "Principal amount . . . . "
```

assigns the string constant *Principal amount . . . .* to the string variable *principal$*.

Null strings

A *null string* (or "empty string") contains no characters. Although all QuickBASIC string variables are initialized with a null string, you may need to use one to clear the contents of a string variable at some point in a program. The following example assigns a null string value to the variable *homeAddress$*:

```
homeAddress$ = ""
```

Notice that there is no character—not even a space—between the two quotation marks in this statement.

String functions

Combining two strings is called *concatenation*, and you concatenate with the plus sign (+). Here is an example from the *Mortgage* program:

```
totalOutString$ = blankSpace$ + "Total" + outString$
```

This statement concatenates three strings—two variables and one constant—and assigns the result to *totalOutString$*.

A string variable can contain any characters from the standard ASCII character set (0-126) and the extended ASCII character set (127-255). This code assigns integers from 0 to 255 to all the characters available on IBM personal computers and compatibles. The first half of the code (0 to 126) contains the lower- and uppercase letters, the numbers, the punctuation marks, and a group of control characters that have special functions. On IBM personal computers and compatibles, the latter half of the code (127 to 255) contains letters from foreign-language alphabets and a collection of graphics characters you can use to build shapes and designs on the screen. (We saw some of these characters in the *Frame* subprogram, and we work with others in Chapter 5.)

You can generate many—but not all—of the ASCII code characters by using various key combinations. When you want characters not available from the keyboard, you can use the built-in CHR$ function to convert an ASCII code into its equivalent character. For example, consider the following three statements:

```
heart$ = CHR$(3)
escKey$ = CHR$(27)
pi$ = CHR$(227)
```

The first statement assigns the heart symbol (ASCII decimal character 3) to the string variable *heart$*. (We used this symbol, along with the three other card-suit characters, in testing the *Shuffle* subprogram in Chapter 3.) The second statement assigns the ASCII equivalent of the Esc key to the string variable *escKey$*. (The *Menu* subprogram uses this equivalent to find out whether you have pressed the Esc key on your keyboard.) Finally, the third statement assigns the Greek letter pi (ASCII decimal character 227) to the string variable *pi$*.

Two other important string functions are the type-conversion functions STR$ and VAL. The STR$ function converts a numeric value to a string, which allows you to include within a string numbers represented by numeric variables or numeric constants. In the following example, the integer variable *term%* contains the value 15. Then the statement

```
termString$ = "Term is" + STR$(term%) + " years"
```

stores the string value *Term is 15 years* in the variable *termString$*. (Note that the STR$ function adds one blank space at the beginning of the string if the argument is a positive number, which is why no space follows the *"Term is"* string constant in the statement.)

Conversely, the VAL function converts a string value into a number. For example, this string variable *value$* consists of a string of numeric characters:

```
value$ = "23456"
```

The following statement converts this string to a number and stores the result in the integer variable *number%*:

```
number% = VAL(value$)
```

Note the difference between the string value and the numeric value. The string *23456* is stored in the computer's memory as a sequence of ASCII characters, all of which happen to be numbers; the value is not a number and cannot be treated as one. On the other hand, the number

23456 is stored in memory in QuickBASIC's integer data format and therefore is available for use in numeric operations.

VAL deals with arguments containing nonnumeric characters in two ways. If the first character in the argument string is not a numeric character, VAL returns a value of 0. For example, the statement:

```
PRINT VAL("hello")
```

prints 0. If the string begins with digits but subsequently contains other characters, VAL converts only up to the first nonnumeric character. For example, the following statement prints a value of 15:

```
PRINT VAL("15 years")
```

One use of VAL is to make sure that values input by the user are numeric; this is exemplified in the *Mortgage* program.

Boolean data types

A *logical expression* contains operations that QuickBASIC can evaluate to one of two logical values: true or false. We sometimes refer to these as *Boolean values* (named after George Boole, the nineteenth-century English mathematician). A program uses these logical values to decide what actions to take; they are essential in the operation and results of many IF...THEN...ELSE structures and WHILE...WEND loops.

Relational operators

Logical expressions typically contain *relational operators* and/or *logical operators*. The six relational operators compare values, and the comparison always results in a value of true or false. Here are the relational operators and their tests:

=	is equal to
<>	is not equal to
<	is less than
>	is greater than
<=	is less than or equal to
>=	is greater than or equal to

You can use relational operators to compare numbers or strings. Consider the following numeric example:

```
sizeA% = 1234
sizeB% = 3456
IF (sizeA% >= sizeB%) THEN PRINT "bigger" ELSE PRINT "smaller"
```

In this case, the expression (*sizeA%* >= *sizeB%*) returns a value of false, since the value of *sizeA%* is smaller than the value of *sizeB%*. The IF statement performs the ELSE clause, displaying the word *smaller*.

In string comparisons, QuickBASIC actually compares the ASCII code equivalents of the strings, character by character. For example:

```
string1$ = "Tinker"
string2$ = "Tailor"
IF (string1$ > string2$) THEN SWAP string1$, string2$
```

In this sequence, the comparison (*string1$* > *string2$*) results in a value of true. (The first characters of both strings are equal, but the second characters are not: The ASCII equivalent of *i* is greater than the ASCII equivalent of *a*.) The IF statement consequently executes the SWAP statement, a typical command used in sort operations.

Logical operators

QuickBASIC also has six *logical operators* you can use to evaluate two or more logical expressions: NOT, AND, OR, XOR, IMP, and EQV. In the summary table below, assume that L1 and L2 represent logical expressions:

NOT L1	NOT reverses the value of L1. The expression is true if L1 is false, and false if L1 is true.
L1 AND L2	True only if both L1 and L2 are true. (If either L1 or L2 is false, or if both are false, the AND expression is also false.)
L1 OR L2	True if either L1 or L2 is true, or if both are true. (If both L1 and L2 are false, the OR expression is also false.)
L1 XOR L2	True if either L1 or L2 is true. (If both are true or if both are false, the XOR (exclusive or) expression is false.)
L1 IMP L2	True if both L1 and L2 are true, or if L1 is false. (If L1 is true and L2 is false, the IMP (implication) expression is false.)
L1 EQV L2	True if L1 and L2 have the same logical values—that is, if both are true or if both are false. (If they have different logical values, the EQV (equivalence) expression is false.)

When QuickBASIC evaluates a logical expression consisting of some combination of relational and logical operations, it actually associates a *numeric* value with the conditions of true or false. Specifically:

- A false expression evaluates to 0
- A true expression evaluates to −1

You don't usually need to worry about these numbers because they are, in effect, "hidden" behind the program; normally, it is only QuickBASIC that works with them. Your only concern most of the time is what the program does, depending on the outcome of a logical expression, and these values don't pertain at that level.

However, in some special circumstances you might want to use the numeric equivalents of true and false. You can, in effect, create "Boolean" variables for a program to keep track of true-or-false, yes-or-no conditions that are important to the program's performance. Such a variable—ideally established as an integer variable—will always evaluate to either true or false. When used in a conditional expression any nonzero number will evaluate to true. Only a zero will evaluate to false.

For example, let's say a program uses the Boolean variable *ready%* to keep track of a certain condition. The condition must be true before certain key routines in the program can be performed. The following statement initializes the variable to a value of false:

```
ready% = 0
```

When the proper conditions have been met, this statement sets the variable to true:

```
ready% = -1
```

Furthermore, the following statement switches the value of *ready%* to the opposite of its current value:

```
ready% = NOT ready%
```

Throughout this book we simplify the assignment of Boolean values to variables in each program by creating and initializing the global variables *true%* and *false%* in the following way:

```
COMMON SHARED true%, false%
true% = -1
false% = 0
```

Within the program, we might assign the Boolean variable *ready%* a value of true with the statement:

```
ready% = true%
```

or assign *ready%* a value of false with the statement:

```
ready% = false%
```

The program can use *ready%* as a conditional expression. For example, the variable can appear in IF structures:

```
IF ready% THEN CALL StartJob
```

The variable can also stand as the condition of a WHILE...WEND loop:

```
WHILE ready%
        [other program lines]
WEND
```

In this case, some statement inside the loop should eventually switch *ready%* to false so that the looping will stop. It is also important to note that a conditional expression will evaluate any nonzero number as true, so you have some additional flexibility in how you change your Boolean variables to true.

With this background information about data types and operations in QuickBASIC, we can now examine the *Mortgage* program.

USING THE *MORTGAGE* PROGRAM

You use the *Mortgage* program by choosing options from the main menu, shown in Figure 4-1 (on the next page). This menu is controlled by the *Menu* subprogram presented in Chapter 3. To choose an option, press the key that corresponds to the option's first letter and then press the Enter key to confirm your selection. (To cancel an option that you have selected, press the Esc key.) The main menu reappears on the screen whenever you complete a main-menu action. You can end the program anytime by choosing *Quit* from the main menu.

To run the program, choose the first option on the menu, *Enter loan information,* which lets you enter the principal amount, interest rate, and term of the mortgage (if you try to choose any other option first, except *Quit,* nothing happens). After entering this information, you can change one or more of the values by returning to the main menu and choosing the first option again.

When the program has the loan information, it can calculate results for the next four options: *monthly payment, payment comparison, interest comparison,* and *amortization over 12 months.*

To explore these four options, let's look at the real-estate transactions of the Patterson family.

The Pattersons have owned their home for slightly more than three years. They are getting ready to sell it and buy a new house in a nearby neighborhood. To make plans for the sale and subsequent purchase and to anticipate the financial implications of the two transactions, they need some information about their current mortgage and the rates available for the mortgage on the new house.

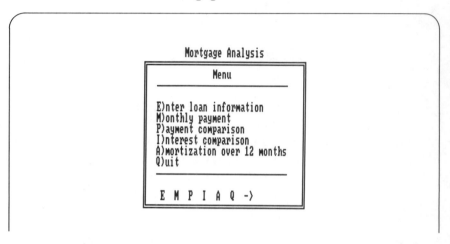

Figure 4-1. *The* Mortgage *program's main menu.*

The purchase price of their current home was $128,000. They paid 20% down and took out a 15-year mortgage at the best interest rate they could find at the time, 13.5%. In summary, the parameters of their current loan are:

Principal: $102,400 (80% of $128,000)
Interest rate: 13.5%
Term: 15 years

In January of this year they paid the 31st monthly payment on the loan. They don't expect to close on the sale of their house until the beginning of next year, so this year's final payment, in December, will be the 42nd. These two payments mark the beginning and the end of the 12-month period they need to examine. Specifically, they want to answer the following questions:

1. How much interest will they pay on the mortgage this year? (This is for tax purposes, since they can deduct the interest as an expense from their income.)

2. What will be their equity in the home at the end of the year? (Their equity is the total amount of principal they will pay on the loan over the 42-month period plus the original down payment.)

To answer these questions, they load the *Mortgage* program and then choose the first option, *Enter loan information.*

In response, the screen displays a series of loan questions (see Figure 4-2).

```
Enter the appropriate loan information after each prompt.
(Only numbers and a decimal accepted )


          Principal amount........... ? 102400
          Interest rate (percent)... ? 13.5
          Term in years.......... ... ? 15
```

Figure 4-2. *The loan information prompts.*

Notice in the figure that the Pattersons enter the principal amount as an unformatted number, without a dollar sign or commas. If they begin the entry with a dollar sign (a nonnumeric character), *Mortgage* rejects the entry, leaving the input prompt on the screen. On the other hand, they may include a percent sign at the end of the interest rate entry, and the program will accept the value.

After the input dialog, the screen shows the main menu. To be sure they entered everything correctly, the Pattersons select the second option, *Monthly payment*, and the screen displays the information box shown in Figure 4-3 (on the next page). The box redisplays the loan parameters they entered, and adds a new line of calculated information: the monthly payment. The Pattersons check all these numbers and everything appears to be correct. At the screen prompt, they press the Enter key, and the main menu appears once again.

The Pattersons also want answers to their questions about the current loan, so they choose the *Amortization over 12 months* option. The program displays the total number of payments and this question:

```
Start at which payment?
```

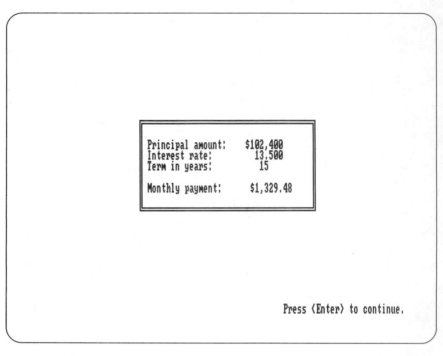

```
Principal amount:   $102,400
Interest rate:        13.500
Term in years:            15

Monthly payment:    $1,329.48




                                    Press <Enter> to continue.
```

Figure 4-3. *The* Monthly payment *display.*

The Pattersons enter 31, the number of their January payment. The program then presents the four-column table shown in Figure 4-4. For each month in the 12-month period, this table shows the interest and principal portions of the monthly payment and the new balance of the loan. At the bottom of the table, the program displays the calculated totals and averages of the columns as well as the total principal paid by the end of the 12-month period.

The Pattersons note their total interest payment on the loan for the current year: $12,783. Anticipating this hefty interest deduction helps them plan for this year's taxes.

They also notice, with some satisfaction, that they are paying an average of $264 a month toward the principal of the loan this year, an amount that becomes part of their equity. This figure is relatively high, considering that they are only three years into the term of the loan. But the Pattersons realize that this is one of the characteristics of a 15-year loan, as opposed to a 30-year loan: the shorter the term, the more accelerated the payments on principal.

```
Month    Interest      Principal      Balance
-----    --------      ---------      -------

 31      $1,081.22     $248.21        $95,860.25
 32      $1,078.43     $251.06        $95,609.20
 33      $1,075.60     $253.83        $95,355.32
 34      $1,072.75     $256.73        $95,098.59
 35      $1,069.86     $259.62        $94,838.97
 36      $1,066.94     $262.54        $94,576.43
 37      $1,063.98     $265.50        $94,310.93
 38      $1,061.00     $268.48        $94,042.45
 39      $1,057.98     $271.50        $93,770.95
 40      $1,054.92     $274.56        $93,496.39
 41      $1,051.83     $277.65        $93,218.75
 42      $1,048.71     $280.77        $92,937.98

Total    $12,783       $3,171     Principal to date:
Average  $1,065          $264     ******$9,462.02



                              Press <Enter> to continue.
```

Figure 4-4. *The* Amortization over 12 months *display.*

Finally, they look at the information displayed in the lower-right corner of the amortization table:

```
Principal to date:
 ******$9,462.02
```

This is the total amount they will have paid on the principal by the end of the year and is part of the equity they can expect to take back when they sell the house. Added to their original down payment of $25,600, this gives them a total equity of $35,062.

Since they are planning to buy another house after the sale, the Pattersons naturally want to know how much cash they will be able to put into the new purchase. Given the current market conditions, they think they can sell the house for $135,000, which is $7,000 more than they paid for it three years ago. The total proceeds from this sale then, after they pay off their current mortgage, will be *$35,062 (total current equity) + $7,000 (increase in sale price) = $42,062.* (Of course, they'll have to deduct from this amount the costs of selling their home.)

Next, the Pattersons consider the financial questions regarding the new house. The asking price of the house they want is $157,500, but they expect to negotiate for a price between $147,500 and $152,500.

While loan shopping, the Pattersons were pleased to discover that mortgage interest rates are much more favorable now than they were three years ago. The best current rate is 10.25% for a 30-year loan. But the Pattersons also know that the rates are fluctuating from month to month, usually by one-eighth of a percentage point. They hope to close on a rate of between 10% and 10.5%. They are considering a 30-year mortgage, to reduce their monthly payments, but they also want to see the payment range for a 15-year loan.

After weighing these issues, the Pattersons settle on the following parameters to enter in the *Mortgage* program:

Principal: $120,000 (80% of $150,000)
Rate: 10.25%
Term: 30 years

At the main menu they once again select the *Enter loan information* option. This time, they are greeted with a new menu (Figure 4-5) that shows the loan information currently stored in memory. This submenu gives them the option of changing any combination of the values. In this case they want to change all three parameters so they press the *C* key to *Change all values*. The program subsequently prompts them to enter the principal, interest rate, and term of the new loan, and they do so.

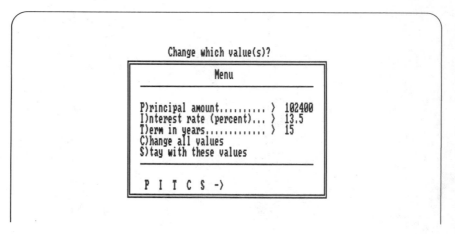

```
            Change which value(s)?

         ┌──────────────────────────────────┐
         │               Menu               │
         │ ──────────────────────────────── │
         │                                  │
         │ P)rincipal amount.......... >  102400 │
         │ I)nterest rate (percent)... >  13.5   │
         │ T)erm in years............. >  15     │
         │ C)hange all values               │
         │ S)tay with these values          │
         │ ──────────────────────────────── │
         │                                  │
         │   P  I  T  C  S  ->              │
         └──────────────────────────────────┘
```

Figure 4-5. *The submenu for the loan information.*

After they enter the last number, the program returns them to the main menu where they select the *Monthly payment* option. The program displays the box in Figure 4-6, showing a monthly payment of $1,075.32. Despite the higher principal, two factors make this payment considerably less than the payment for their current mortgage: the lower interest rate and the 30-year term.

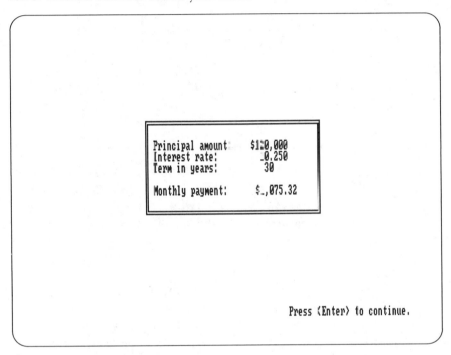

```
Principal amount:      $1_0,000
Interest rate:           _0.250
Term in years:              30

Monthly payment:        $_,075.32




                                    Press <Enter> to continue.
```

Figure 4-6. *The* Monthly payment *display.*

However, the Pattersons would also like to see what the monthly payment would be for a variety of principal amounts, interest rates, and terms. So they press the Enter key to display the main menu and choose the *Payment comparison* option. The program responds with another series of loan questions that ask for directions on how to prepare the comparison tables. The input box and the Pattersons' responses are shown in Figure 4-7 (on the next page).

Three values are asked for: an increment amount for the principal, an increment amount for the interest rate, and a comparison term for the loan. The Pattersons want to see principal amounts in increments of $1,000 and interest rates in increments of one-eighth (0.125) of a percentage point. Furthermore, they want to compare the 30-year payment amounts with 15-year payment amounts.

```
Enter the increments of your choice after each prompt.
(Only numbers and a decimal accepted.)

     Increment the principal by how much.....? 1000
     Increment the rate by how much..........? 0.125
     Use what term (years) for comparison....? 15
```

Figure 4-7. *The* Payment comparison *prompts.*

Figure 4-8 shows the comparison table that the program produces for the Pattersons. If they take a 30-year loan, their monthly payment will fall somewhere between $1,035.53 (for a principal amount of $118,000 and an interest rate of 10%) and $1,115.98 (principal of $122,000, rate of 10.5%). In contrast, they see that a 15-year loan gives them a payment between $1,268.03 and $1,348.59 for the same range of principal amounts and interest rates. Notice that the parameters they entered as an estimate for the loan ($120,000 at 10.25%) are right in the middle of the table, which allows a range of lesser and greater principal amounts and interest rates to be compared to the current parameters.

Entering the *Interest comparison* option from the main menu produces yet another table that manipulates the current loan information. Like the monthly payment table, the total interest table prompts the user for increments in principal, rate, and term values. Rather than compare monthly payments, however, this table compares the total amount of interest scheduled to be paid over the term of a mortgage. The Pattersons will want to take a good look at these figures before they make their final decision. A sample of this table that uses the increments of Figure 4-7 can be found in Figure 4-9.

```
                    Monthly Payment Comparison

   Term: 30 years

  ┌─────────────────────────────────────────────────────────────────────┐
  │   Rate..... 10.000      10.125      10.250      10.375      10.500    │
  │ Principal                                                            │
  │ $118,000   $1,035.53   $1,046.45   $1,057.40   $1,068.38   $1,079.39 │
  │ $119,000   $1,044.31   $1,055.32   $1,066.36   $1,077.43   $1,088.54 │
  │ $120,000   $1,053.09   $1,064.19   $1,075.32   $1,086.49   $1,097.69 │
  │ $121,000   $1,061.86   $1,073.06   $1,084.28   $1,095.54   $1,106.84 │
  │ $122,000   $1,070.64   $1,081.92   $1,093.24   $1,104.60   $1,115.98 │
  └─────────────────────────────────────────────────────────────────────┘


   Term: 15 years

  ┌─────────────────────────────────────────────────────────────────────┐
  │   Rate..... 10.000      10.125      10.250      10.375      10.500    │
  │ Principal                                                            │
  │ $118,000   $1,268.03   $1,277.07   $1,286.14   $1,295.24   $1,304.37 │
  │ $119,000   $1,278.78   $1,287.90   $1,297.04   $1,306.21   $1,315.43 │
  │ $120,000   $1,289.52   $1,298.72   $1,307.94   $1,317.19   $1,326.48 │
  │ $121,000   $1,300.27   $1,309.54   $1,318.84   $1,328.17   $1,337.54 │
  │ $122,000   $1,311.02   $1,320.36   $1,329.74   $1,339.14   $1,348.59 │
  └─────────────────────────────────────────────────────────────────────┘

                                        Press <Enter> to continue.
```

Figure 4-8. *Comparison table for the values shown in* Figure 4-7.

```
                    Total Interest Comparison

   Term: 30 years

  ┌────────────────────────────────────────────────────────────────────────────┐
  │   Rate..... 10.000       10.125       10.250       10.375       10.500       │
  │ Principal                                                                    │
  │ $118,000  $254,790.81  $258,721.97  $262,661.00  $266,616.81  $270,580.41   │
  │ $119,000  $256,951.63  $260,915.19  $264,883.59  $268,874.81  $272,874.41   │
  │ $120,000  $259,112.38  $263,108.38  $267,115.19  $271,136.38  $275,168.38   │
  │ $121,000  $261,269.59  $265,301.62  $269,343.81  $273,394.44  $277,462.38   │
  │ $122,000  $263,430.41  $267,491.22  $271,565.38  $275,656.00  $279,752.78   │
  └────────────────────────────────────────────────────────────────────────────┘


   Term: 15 years

  ┌────────────────────────────────────────────────────────────────────────────┐
  │   Rate..... 10.000       10.125       10.250       10.375       10.500       │
  │ Principal                                                                    │
  │ $118,000  $110,245.41  $111,872.59  $113,505.19  $115,143.19  $116,786.61   │
  │ $119,000  $111,180.41  $112,822.00  $114,457.22  $116,117.78  $117,777.41   │
  │ $120,000  $112,113.61  $113,769.59  $115,429.19  $117,094.19  $118,766.39   │
  │ $121,000  $113,048.61  $114,717.22  $116,391.19  $118,070.61  $119,757.22   │
  │ $122,000  $113,983.61  $115,664.81  $117,353.19  $119,045.19  $120,746.19   │
  └────────────────────────────────────────────────────────────────────────────┘

                                        Press <Enter> to continue.
```

Figure 4-9. *The* Interest comparison *table.*

INSIDE THE *MORTGAGE* PROGRAM

The structure chart in Figure 4-10 shows the overall organization of the *Mortgage* program, including calls to the various subprograms. The *Mortgage* program itself appears in Figure 4-11 (beginning on page 109). As you examine the main program and each of the subprograms, you will see how the program uses the QuickBASIC data types. Notice also the variety of input and output techniques.

The global variable declarations area

The global variable declarations area first establishes a small set of important global variables. These variables include all the data types we discussed earlier in the chapter: strings, integers, single- and double-precision numbers, and Boolean values.

The three numeric variables destined to store the program's current loan parameters are:

- *principal#*—a double-precision variable for the principal of the loan

- *rate*—a single-precision variable for the interest rate

- *term%*—an integer variable for the term of the loan

Since these variables are used throughout the program, they are established as global variables with the COMMON SHARED statement, making them available to any subprogram.

Several other variables are also declared global, including the string variables *principalPrompt$*, *interestPrompt$*, and *termPrompt$*, which contain input prompts for the three loan parameters. Additionally, the program dimensions three small global arrays:

```
DIM menu$(6), setOfTerms%(2), dataMenu$(5)
```

The *setOfTerms%* array holds the two term values for producing the comparison tables. The *menu$* array stores the options for the program's recurring main menu. To read values into this string array, the main program calls the *Initialize* subprogram. This routine uses a FOR ... NEXT loop to read a string element into each element of the array from a series of DATA lines.

Likewise, the *dataMenu$* array contains the options for the data-input submenu. However, since the first three option lines of this menu

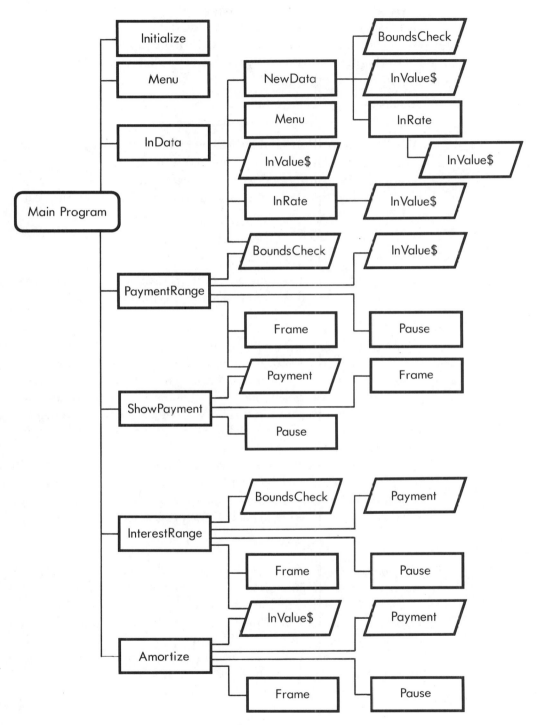

Figure 4-10. *The structure chart for the* Mortgage *program.*

also display the current loan parameter values (principal, rate, and term), which may change each time the menu appears, the *Initialize* routine assigns values only to the final two elements of *dataMenu$*, which remain constant:

```
dataMenu$(4) = "change all values"
dataMenu$(5) = "stay with these values"
```

We will see later that the first three elements of this array are always assigned concatenated string values, beginning with the input prompts, *principalPrompt$*, *interestPrompt$*, and *termPrompt$*. These three variables also receive their values in the *Initialize* subprogram:

```
principalPrompt$ = "Principal amount . . . . . . . . . "
interestPrompt$ = "Interest rate (percent) . . . "
termPrompt$ = "Term in years . . . . . . . . . . . "
```

The *Mortgage* program uses a DEFINT statement to establish variables that begin with the letters *i, j,* and *k* as integer variables:

```
DEFINT i-k
```

These three letters are used as counter variables in FOR . . . NEXT loops throughout the program. As we discussed earlier, an alternative technique for declaring them as integers is to include the % character at the end of each variable name: *i%, j%,* and *k%*. (This technique is used in all the other programs in this book.) The choice between using DEFINT or the % suffix in QuickBASIC programs is a matter of personal preference.

The last thing the global variable declaration section does is initialize the Boolean variables *true%* and *false%*. These will be used any time a Boolean variable needs to be initialized or changed. You will see this final declaration in each of the programs in this book.

The main program area

The main program area begins by calling the *Initialize* subprogram. As mentioned, *Initialize* prepares the two global menu arrays (*menu$* and *dataMenu$*), and defines the three global string variables (*principalPrompt$, interestPrompt$,* and *termPrompt$*) for use throughout the program.

Next, the main program area assigns an initial value of false to an important Boolean variable, *parametersOk%*:

```
parametersOk% = false%
```

```
'    MORTGAGE.BAS
'    Mortgage program.  Given the principal amount, the interest rate, and the
'        term (in years), this program performs any of the following tasks:
'
'        1. Calculates the monthly payment on the loan.
'        2. Presents tables of mortgage payments for a range of principals,
'           interest rates, and terms.
'        3. Presents tables of total interest payments for a range of
'           principals, interest rates, and terms.
'        4. Computes and displays a 12-month amortization of the loan, giving
'           the monthly interest and principal portions of the payment.


'---------------------| Global Variable Declarations |---------------------

    DIM menu$(6), setOfTerms%(2), dataMenu$(5)
    COMMON SHARED principal#, rate, term%, principalPrompt$, _
        interestPrompt$, termPrompt$, menu$(), setOfTerms%(), dataMenu$(), _
        true%, false%, tooBig%
    DEFINT i-k

'    ---- Initialize Boolean variables true% and false%.
    true% = -1
    false% = 0


'-------------------------| Function Area |--------------------------------


'    ---- Read in and compile BASIC user-defined function.
    REM $INCLUDE: 'UPPER.BAS'


'    The Payment function calculates the payment for a given mortgage loan.
'    It takes three arguments:
'        princ# is the principal amount of the loan.
'        rt is the annual interest rate, a percentage.
'        tm% is the term of the loan (in years).

DEF FN Payment (princ#, rt, tm%)
    monthlyRate = rt / (12 * 100)
    monthsInTerm% = tm% * 12

    factor = (monthlyRate + 1) ^ (-1 * monthsInTerm%)
    tempPayment = (princ# * monthlyRate) / (1 - factor)

    dollars% = FIX(tempPayment)
    cents = (CINT((tempPayment - dollars%) * 100)) / 100
    tempPayment = dollars% + cents

    FN Payment = tempPayment
END DEF


'    The InValue$ function accepts a numeric value from the keyboard.
'        To avoid QuickBASIC's "?Redo from start" message (which
'        is displayed in the event of an input data-type error),
'        the function reads the value as a string, and then verifies
'        that the string can be successfully converted to a
'        positive nonzero number.
```

Payment

Figure 4-11. *The* Mortgage *program.*   *(more...)*

When the *parametersOk%* variable contains a value of true, the program knows that a set of loan parameters is available in memory; the program can then safely call the subprograms that work with those parameters. However, until the user first chooses the *Enter loan information* option from the main menu, *parametersOk%* retains a Boolean value of false.

The core of the main program is a WHILE...WEND loop that repeatedly displays the main menu on the screen and elicits the user's option choice:

```
WHILE choice% <> 6
    LOCATE 2, 32: PRINT "Mortgage Analysis"
    CALL Menu(menu$(), choice%)
```

Recall that the *Menu* subprogram returns an integer indicating which menu option the user selected. The *Mortgage* program stores that integer in the integer variable *choice%*. When the user chooses the *Quit* option, *choice%* contains a value of 6, and the WHILE...WEND loop ends. A *choice%* value other than 6, however, is processed by an IF...THEN...ELSEIF structure, which calls the appropriate subprogram in response to a given menu choice.

If you refer to the main program area, you will notice how this decision structure uses the Boolean variable *parametersOk%*. The *InData* subprogram conducts the input dialog for eliciting the loan parameters and passes a value of true to *parametersOk%* when the values are available.

The other major subprograms—*ShowPayment, PaymentRange, InterestRange,* and *Amortize*—correspond to the second, third, fourth, and fifth menu options. The compound AND conditions in the ELSEIF clauses make sure that calls to these subprograms only take place if *parametersOk%* is true, for example:

```
ELSEIF (choice% = 2 AND parametersOk%) THEN
```

Consequently, if the user chooses one of these options before entering a first set of loan parameters, the WHILE...WEND loop redisplays the main menu, without calling one of the major subprograms.

The sections of the program we've looked at so far set up the variables the program works with and prompt the user for values to assign to them. Once the program has these values, it can perform the necessary calculations. Let's look first at how *Mortgage* determines the monthly payment.

```
DEF FN InValue$
'    ---- Find the current cursor position, and calculate the number
'         of spaces necessary to erase an invalid input value.
     currentX% = POS(0)
     currentY% = CSRLIN
     filledArea% = 81 - currentX%

'    ---- Begin the input-validation loop. (Note that an input value of 0
'         would not be appropriate for any of the numeric parameters in
'         this program.)
     number = 0
     WHILE number <= 0
         INPUT value$
         number = VAL(value$)
         IF (number <= 0) THEN
             LOCATE currentY%, currentX%
             PRINT SPACE$(filledArea%);
             LOCATE currentY%, currentX%
         END IF
     WEND

     FN InValue$ = value$
END DEF
```

InValue

```
'    The BoundsCheck function checks to see if a given monthly payment is
'         larger than $32,767 and thus too large for the Payment function to
'         round properly.  The function returns the Boolean variable
'         BoundsCheck, which will be false if the monthly payment is in the
'         proper range, and true if it is out of the range.

DEF FN BoundsCheck(maxPrincipal#, maxRate, maxTerm%)
'    ---- Set maxInteger to 32,767, the largest value the truncation
'         functions CINT and FIX can manipulate.
     maxInteger = 32767

'    ---- Compute the monthly payment.
     monthlyRate = maxRate / (12 * 100)
     monthsInTerm% = maxTerm% * 12
     factor = (monthlyRate + 1) ^ (-1 * monthsInTerm%)
     largestPayment = (maxPrincipal# * monthlyRate) / (1 - factor)

'    ---- If tempPayment is too large, clear the screen, print an appropriate
'         message, and return a value of true to the calling program.
     IF (largestPayment > maxInteger + 1) THEN
         CLS
         LOCATE 9, 15
         PRINT "This program cannot support a payment that large."
         LOCATE 11, 24
         PRINT "Please enter smaller loan values."
         CALL Pause
         FN BoundsCheck = true%
     ELSE
'    ---- If largestPayment is in the proper range, return a value of false.
         FN BoundsCheck = false%
     END IF
END DEF
```

BoundsCheck

Figure 4-11.   *The* Mortgage *program (continued).*   *(more . . .)*

The *Payment* function

The function area of the *Mortgage* program begins by reading in and compiling the user-defined function *UPPER.BAS* with a $INCLUDE metacommand. As we discussed in Chapter 2, the function of *Upper$* is to receive a string from some calling program, convert all of that string's lowercase characters to uppercase, and return the string to the calling program. In this program, *Upper$* is used exclusively by another external routine brought in by a $INCLUDE metacommand, *MENU.BAS*.

Directly below the function area's $INCLUDE statement is the user-defined function *Payment*. *Payment* returns the monthly payment for the loan, rounded to the nearest cent. Its name and parameter list are defined by the following statement:

```
DEF FN Payment (princ#, rt, tm%)
```

where *princ#* (a double-precision numeric value) is the principal of the loan; *rt* (a single-precision value) is the annual interest rate, expressed as a percentage; and *tm%* (an integer) is the number of years in the term of the loan.

To determine the monthly payment, the function must first compute the monthly interest rate and the number of months in the term of the loan based on the total principal amount, interest rate, and term. The first two assignment statements in the function perform these two calculations:

```
monthlyRate = rt / (12 * 100)
monthsInTerm% = tm% * 12
```

For example, if the function receives a value of 13.5 (meaning 13.5%) for the rate, the decimal value 0.01125 is the calculated monthly interest rate, *monthlyRate*. An argument of 15 (that is, 15 years) for the term generates 180 as the *monthsInTerm%*.

Given these parameters, the next two statements perform the required arithmetic for finding the monthly payment:

```
factor = (monthlyRate + 1) ^ (-1 * monthsInTerm%)
tempPayment = (princ# * monthlyRate) / (1 - factor)
```

The first statement illustrates exponentiation. A value of 1 is added to the monthly interest rate, and the sum is multiplied by itself *monthsInTerm%* times. The inverse of the result is assigned to *factor*. In the second assignment statement, the program uses the value of *factor*

```
'-------------------------| Main Program Area |----------------------------

    CALL Initialize
    parametersOk% = false%

'    ---- Display the main menu, get a choice, and respond accordingly.
    WHILE choice% <> 6
        LOCATE 2, 32: PRINT "Mortgage Analysis"
        CALL Menu(menu$(), choice%)

        IF (choice% = 1) THEN
            CALL InData(parametersOk%)
        ELSEIF (choice% = 2 AND parametersOk%) THEN
            CALL ShowPayment
        ELSEIF (choice% = 3 AND parametersOk%) THEN
            CALL PaymentRange
        ELSEIF (choice% = 4 AND parametersOk%) THEN
            CALL InterestRange
        ELSEIF (choice% = 5 AND parametersOk%) THEN
            CALL Amortize
        END IF
    WEND

    END



'-------------------------| Subprogram Area |----------------------------


'    ----Read in and compile BASIC subprograms.
    REM $INCLUDE : 'FRAME.BAS'
    REM $INCLUDE : 'MENU.BAS'


'    The Initialize subprogram sets the values of the two global menu
'        arrays (menu$ and dataMenu$), along with three global string
'        variables that provide input prompts in the program.

SUB Initialize STATIC
    FOR i = 1 TO 6
        READ menu$(i)
    NEXT i

    DATA enter loan information
    DATA monthly payment
    DATA payment comparison
    DATA interest comparison
    DATA amortization over 12 months
    DATA quit

    principalPrompt$ = "Principal amount.......... "
    interestPrompt$ = "Interest rate (percent)... "
    termPrompt$ = "Term in years............. "

    dataMenu$(4) = "change all values"
    dataMenu$(5) = "stay with these values"
END SUB
```

Initialize

Figure 4-11. *The* Mortgage *program (continued).*   (more...)

to calculate the payment and stores the result in *tempPayment*. Notice the careful placement of parentheses to establish the correct order of operations in both these statements.

Unfortunately, *tempPayment* may contain a monthly payment value that is too accurate for the subsequent amortization calculations. In practice, a fixed monthly payment is always in dollars and cents; it cannot include fractions of a cent, even if those fractions would make the mortgage calculations more precise. If you carry out a loan to the very last payment, you will normally find a small discrepancy in the ending balance, due to precision limitations with the dollar-and-cent money system.

Since the value calculated for *tempPayment* is a single-precision number, it will contain up to seven digits of precision. For example, if the first *tempPayment* statement calculates a monthly payment of \$1,329.476, a rounded monthly payment of \$1,329.48 is produced. If the program used the initial unrounded value in the amortization calculations, the resulting table (Figure 4-4) would appear to contain inaccuracies. In some months, the sum of the interest and the principal portions displayed for a payment would not exactly equal the payment total. For this reason, the *Payment* function rounds the payment to the nearest cent.

The rounding process uses QuickBASIC's FIX function to truncate *tempPayment* and produce the dollar portion of the payment, and it uses the CINT function to round the remaining decimal portion to the nearest cent:

```
dollars% = FIX(tempPayment)
cents = (CINT((tempPayment - dollars%) * 100)) / 100
```

The FIX function is the only truncation function in QuickBASIC that simply drops any fractional part of a number. QuickBASIC's other truncation functions perform some rounding: INT returns the largest integer less than or equal to the number specified and CINT rounds the specified number to the next greater integer. In this case we just want to remove the fractional part of *tempPayment*.

The rounded payment is the sum of *dollars%* and *cents*:

```
tempPayment = dollars% + cents
```

After being rounded, *tempPayment* is returned as the value of the *Payment* function:

```
FN Payment = tempPayment
```

```
'   The InData subprogram controls the input process for the required
'       loan parameters. It accepts one Boolean argument: true if a
'       set of parameters currently exists, false if not.

SUB InData(dataExists%) STATIC
'   ---- If this is the first input session, accept a new value for each
'       loan parameter.
    notValid% = true%
    WHILE notValid%
        IF NOT dataExists% THEN
            CALL NewData

'   ---- Otherwise, if a set of parameters already exists, give the user
'       the option to change one, two, or all three of the values.
        ELSE
            selection% = 0
            WHILE NOT(selection% = 4 OR selection% = 5)
                dataMenu$(1) = principalPrompt$ + "> " + STR$(principal#)
                dataMenu$(2) = interestPrompt$ + "> " + STR$(rate)
                dataMenu$(3) = termPrompt$ + "> " + STR$(term%)

                LOCATE 2, 28
                PRINT "Change which value(s)?"
                CALL Menu(dataMenu$(), selection%)
                LOCATE 11, 20

                IF (selection% = 1) THEN
                    PRINT principalPrompt$;
                    principal# = VAL(FN InValue$)
                ELSEIF (selection% = 2) THEN
                    CALL InRate
                ELSEIF (selection% = 3) THEN
                    PRINT termPrompt$;
                    term% = VAL(FN InValue$)
                ELSEIF (selection% = 4) THEN
                    CALL NewData
                END IF

                CLS
            WEND
        END IF
'   ---- Determine if the monthly payment is in the proper range.
        notValid% = FN BoundsCheck(principal#, rate, term%)
        CLS
    WEND
'   ---- Return a value of true in dataExists%, to tell the main program
'       that a data set now exists and clear the screen.
    dataExists% = true%
END SUB


'   The NewData subprogram actually conducts the input dialog for
'       accepting three new loan parameters.

SUB NewData STATIC
    LOCATE 6, 5
    PRINT "Enter the appropriate loan information after each prompt."
    LOCATE 7, 5
    PRINT "(Only numbers and a decimal accepted.)"
```

InData

NewData

Figure 4-11. *The* Mortgage *program (continued).*   *(more...)*

There is one additional problem that you should be aware of during the rounding process, however. None of QuickBASIC's truncating functions can process numbers greater than 32,767. This means that if we use FIX and CINT to round a monthly payment of $32,768 or greater, a runtime error will occur. As the program currently stands, payments of this size cannot be processed (you may want to try this as an exercise).

The *BoundsCheck* function

To stop the error from occurring and inform the user of the dilemma, the *BoundsCheck* user-defined Boolean function is called every time the user enters any new loan information or requests a table that compares different ranges of loan information (the *NewData, PaymentRange,* and *InterestRange* subprograms).

The operation of *BoundsCheck* is very simple: First, the integer variable *maxInteger%* is initialized to 32,767. Next, the monthly payment is calculated with the parameter list received from the calling routine. (The formula for this calculation is identical to the one found in the *Payment* function.) If the value of *largestPayment* is greater than $32,768, an appropriate message is printed and *BoundsCheck* returns a value of *true%* to the calling routine. To continue using the *Mortgage* program, the user will have to reduce the size of one or all of the loan parameters. If the *largestPayment* value is not larger than $32,768, a value of *false%* is returned.

```
IF (largestPayment > maxInteger + 1) THEN
    CLS
    LOCATE 9, 15
    PRINT "This program cannot support a payment that large."
    LOCATE 11, 24
    PRINT "Please enter smaller loan values."
    CALL Pause
    FN BoundsCheck = true%
ELSE
    FN BoundsCheck = false%
END IF
```

```
      LOCATE 10, 20: PRINT principalPrompt$;
      principal# = VAL(FN InValue$)

      CALL InRate

      LOCATE 12, 20: PRINT termPrompt$;
      term% = VAL(FN InValue$)
END SUB


'   The InRate subprogram performs a special input check on the rate value.
'       The rate should be entered as a percentage, that is, a value
'       that is greater than 1.

SUB InRate STATIC
      rate = 0
      WHILE rate < 1
          LOCATE 11, 20: PRINT interestPrompt$;
          rate = VAL(FN InValue$)
          IF (rate < 1) THEN
              LOCATE 11, 20: PRINT SPACE$(50)
              LOCATE 15, 5
              PRINT "Enter the interest rate as a percentage, for example"
              LOCATE 16, 5
              PRINT "type 20 or 20% rather than 0.20."
          END IF
      WEND
END SUB


'   The ShowPayment subprogram displays the loan parameters on the screen,
'       along with the calculated monthly payment on the loan.

SUB ShowPayment STATIC
      columnPosition1% = 25
      columnPosition2% = 43

      LOCATE 10, columnPosition1%
      PRINT "Principal amount:" TAB(columnPosition2%);
      PRINT USING "$$#,######"; principal#

      LOCATE 11, columnPosition1%
      PRINT "Interest rate:" TAB(columnPosition2%);
      PRINT USING "      ##.###"; rate

      LOCATE 12, columnPosition1%
      PRINT "Term in years:" TAB(columnPosition2%);
      PRINT USING "      ###"; term%

      LOCATE 14, columnPosition1%
      PRINT "Monthly payment:" TAB(columnPosition2%);
      PRINT USING "$$#,######.##"; FN Payment(principal#, rate, term%)

      CALL Frame (23, 60, 8, 16)
      CALL Pause
END SUB
```

InRate

ShowPayment

Figure 4-11. *The* Mortgage *program (continued).*   *(more . . .)*

Unlike the majority of user-defined functions, which simply return a value, *BoundsCheck* displays additional information based on what it discovers about the proposed payment size.

Input routines in the *Mortgage* program

Several subprograms in the *Mortgage* program elicit information from the user. The *InData* subprogram is the major input routine and is called whenever the user chooses the *Enter loan information* option from the main menu.

The *InData* subprogram

InData receives a value of true or false from the main program, to indicate whether or not a set of loan parameters is currently in memory. This value is received in the Boolean variable *dataExists%*:

```
SUB InData(dataExists%) STATIC
```

When the user first chooses the *Enter loan information* option, *dataExists%* is false (nothing has been entered yet). So, *InData* calls the *NewData* subprogram, which displays the initial input box shown in Figure 4-2:

```
IF NOT dataExists% THEN
    CALL NewData
```

The logical operator NOT in the expression reverses the value of *dataExists%*: The expression evaluates as true if *dataExists%* is false, or false if *dataExists%* is true. Therefore, if *dataExists%* is false, the program calls *NewData* to get the user's initial input. If *dataExists%* is true, the program instead presents a submenu displaying the existing mortgage parameters. The submenu appears in Figure 4-5; the statements that set up this menu are:

```
dataMenu$(1) = principalPrompt$ + "> " + STR$(principal#)
dataMenu$(2) = interestPrompt$ + "> " + STR$(rate)
dataMenu$(3) = termPrompt$ + "> " + STR$(term%)
LOCATE 2, 28
PRINT "Change which value(s)?"
CALL Menu(dataMenu$(), selection%)
```

```
'    The Pause subprogram simply creates a pause in the action of the
'        program, until the user presses a key.

SUB Pause STATIC
    LOCATE 25, 54
    PRINT "Press <Enter> to continue.";
    character$ = ""
    WHILE character$ = ""
        character$ = INKEY$
    WEND
    CLS
END SUB
```

Pause

```
'    The PaymentRange subprogram computes and displays two tables of
'        comparison mortgage payment values.

SUB PaymentRange STATIC
'    ---- Begin by eliciting the increment values (for the principal
'        and the interest rate).
    LOCATE 6, 5
    PRINT "Enter the increments of your choice after each prompt."
    LOCATE 7, 5
    PRINT "(Only numbers and a decimal accepted.)"

    LOCATE 10, 10
    PRINT "Increment the principal by how much.....";
    principalIncrement# = VAL(FN InValue$)

    LOCATE 11, 10
    PRINT "Increment the rate by how much..........";
    rateIncrement = VAL(FN InValue$)

'    ---- The term of the first table will be the current value
'        of term%. Elicit a term value for the second table.
    setOfTerms%(1) = term%
    LOCATE 12, 10
    PRINT "Use what term (years) for comparison....";
    setOfTerms%(2) = VAL(FN InValue$)

'    ---- Determine if the monthly payment is out of range.
    maxPrincipal# = principal# + (2 * principalIncrement)
    maxRate = rate + (2 * rateIncrement)
    IF (setOfTerms%(1) < setOfTerms%(2)) THEN maxTerm% = setOfTerms%(1) _
        ELSE maxTerm% = setOfTerms%(2)
    tooBig% = FN BoundsCheck(maxPrincipal#, maxRate, maxTerm%)

'    ---- If the payment is not too large, plot the payment information.
    IF NOT tooBig% THEN

'    ---- Print the title of the comparison chart.
        CLS
        LOCATE 1, 26
        PRINT "Monthly Payment Comparison";

'    ---- Print chart labels.
        LOCATE 5, 7: PRINT "Rate.....";
        LOCATE 6, 4: PRINT "Principal";
        LOCATE 17, 7: PRINT "Rate.....";
        LOCATE 18, 4: PRINT "Principal";
```

PaymentRange

Figure 4-11. *The* Mortgage *program (continued).*   *(more...)*

Each of the first three elements of the *dataMenu$* array receives a concatenated string value that consists of an input prompt (*principalPrompt$*, *interestPrompt$*, or *termPrompt$*, the global variables that received prompt strings in the *Initialize* subprogram), a pointer symbol ("> "), and the string equivalent of the corresponding numeric loan parameter currently stored in memory: *principal#*, *rate*, or *term%*. The program uses the built-in STR$ function to supply the string equivalents of these three numbers.

The *Menu* subprogram returns the user's menu choice back to the integer variable *selection%*. So, if the user presses a key corresponding to any of the first three menu choices, the *InData* subprogram conducts an input dialog to elicit a new value for the selected parameter. If the user presses C for *Change all data*, the *InData* subprogram calls the *NewData* subprogram again to get new values for the entire data set:

```
IF (selection% = 1) THEN
    PRINT principalPrompt$;
    principal# = VAL(FN InValue$)
ELSEIF (selection% = 2) THEN
    CALL InRate
ELSEIF (selection% = 3) THEN
    PRINT termPrompt$;
    term% = VAL(FN InValue$)
ELSEIF (selection% = 4) THEN
    CALL NewData
END IF
```

This passage calls on two routines that are the heart of *Mortgage's* input process:

- A general-purpose user-defined function named *InValue$*, which elicits a single input value and verifies that the value is a valid positive number.

- A special-purpose subprogram named *InRate*, which only accepts a value for the rate parameter if it is greater than 1.

The *InValue$* function

The *InValue$* function solves a special problem that can occur whenever you use QuickBASIC's INPUT statement to accept numeric data

```
'    ---- Finally, display the two tables.
     FOR i = 1 to 2
         top% = 4 + (i - 1) * 12
         LOCATE top% - 1, 5
         PRINT "Term:" setOfTerms%(i) "years"
         CALL Frame(2, 79, top%, top% + 8)
         tempPrincipal# = principal# - (2 * principalIncrement#)

'    ---- Calculate the temporary rate and print the rate and principal
'         headings for each respective column and row.
         FOR j = 1 TO 5
             tempRate = rate - (2 * rateIncrement)
             LOCATE 5 + (i - 1) * 12, 13 * j + 4
             PRINT USING "##.###"; tempRate + (j - 1) * rateIncrement
             verticalPos% = 6 + (i - 1) * 12 + j
             LOCATE verticalPos%,3
             PRINT USING "$$###,###"; tempPrincipal#

'    ---- Use the Payment function to calculate the monthly payment.
             FOR k = 1 TO 5
                 LOCATE verticalPos%, 13 * k
                 pmt = FN Payment(tempPrincipal#, tempRate, setOfTerms%(i))
                 PRINT USING "$$###,###.##"; pmt
                 tempRate = tempRate + rateIncrement
             NEXT k
             tempPrincipal# = tempPrincipal# + principalIncrement#
         NEXT j
     NEXT i

     CALL Pause
    END IF
END SUB


'   The InterestRange subprogram computes and displays two tables of
'       comparison mortgage interest values.

SUB InterestRange STATIC
'   ---- Begin by eliciting the increment values (for the principal
'        and the interest rate).
    LOCATE 6, 5
    PRINT "Enter the increments of your choice after each prompt."
    LOCATE 7, 5
    PRINT "(Only numbers and a decimal accepted.)"

    LOCATE 10, 10
    PRINT "Increment the principal by how much.....";
    principalIncrement# = VAL(FN InValue$)

    LOCATE 11, 10
    PRINT "Increment the rate by how much.........";
    rateIncrement = VAL(FN InValue$)

'   ---- The term of the first table will be the current value
'        of term%. Elicit a term value for the second table.
    setOfTerms%(1) = term%
    LOCATE 12, 10
    PRINT "Use what term (years) for comparison....";
    setOfTerms%(2) = VAL(FN InValue$)
```

InterestRange

Figure 4-11. *The Mortgage program (continued).*   *(more...)*

from the keyboard. For example, let's say you have written a program that contains the following statement:

```
INPUT "Please enter a number > ", number
```

When the program runs, this statement produces a prompt on the screen and waits for the user to enter a value from the keyboard.

QuickBASIC attempts to store the user's input value in *number,* a single-precision numeric variable. If the user mistakenly enters a value that begins with a nonnumeric character, such as a dollar sign ($), QuickBASIC rejects the input and displays an error message to elicit a new value:

```
?Redo from start
```

This simple error message may work well in some contexts. However, when you strive to create an attractive input screen, the *?Redo from start* message is likely to spoil the visual effect. The *InValue$* function is designed to avoid this problem.

InValue$ takes no argument; as its name indicates, the function returns a string value:

```
DEF FN InValue$
```

The function uses the INPUT statement to read a given input value from the keyboard as a string and then checks to see if the string can be successfully converted to a positive, nonzero number. If not, *InValue$* simply erases the input value from the screen, repositions the flashing cursor at its original location, and waits for another input value. When it can convert the number, the string is returned to the calling program as the value of *InValue$*.

Before reading a value from the keyboard, the function determines the current screen position of the cursor:

```
currentX% = POS(0)
currentY% = CSRLIN
```

The POS function gives the screen column position (an integer from 1 to 80), and CSRLIN gives the row position (an integer from 1 to 25). *InValue$* then calculates the number of spaces from the current cursor position to the right side of the screen:

```
filledArea% = 81 - currentX%
```

```
'    ---- Determine if the monthly payment is out of range.
     maxPrincipal# = principal# + (2 * principalIncrement)
     maxRate = rate + (2 * rateIncrement)
     IF (setOfTerms%(1) < setOfTerms%(2)) THEN maxTerm% = setOfTerms%(1) _
         ELSE maxTerm% = setOfTerms%(2)
     tooBig% = FN BoundsCheck(maxPrincipal#, maxRate, maxTerm%)

'    ---- If the payment is not too large, plot the payment information.
     IF NOT tooBig% THEN

'    ---- Print the title of the comparison chart.
         CLS
         LOCATE 1, 27
         PRINT "Total Interest Comparison";

'    ---- Print chart labels.
         LOCATE 5, 7: PRINT "Rate.....";
         LOCATE 6, 4: PRINT "Principal";
         LOCATE 17, 7: PRINT "Rate.....";
         LOCATE 18, 4: PRINT "Principal";

'    ---- Finally, display the two tables.
         FOR i = 1 to 2
             top% = 4 + (i - 1) * 12
             LOCATE top% - 1, 5
             PRINT "Term:" setOfTerms%(i) "years"
             CALL Frame(2, 79, top%, top% + 3)
             tempPrincipal# = principal# - (2 * principalIncrement#)

'    ---- Calculate the temporary rate and print the rate and principal
'         headings for each respective column and row.
             FOR j = 1 TO 5
                 tempRate = rate - (2 * rateIncrement)
                 LOCATE 5 + (i - 1) * 12, 13 * j + 4
                 PRINT USING "##.###"; tempRate + (j - 1) * rateIncrement
                 verticalPos% = 6 + (i - 1) * 12 + j
                 LOCATE verticalPos%, 3
                 PRINT USING "$$###,###"; tempPrincipal#

'    ---- Use the Payment function to calculate the monthly payment for each
'         column.  Multiply this by the number of months in the term and
'         subtract the principal to get the total interest due.
                 FOR k = 1 TO 5
                     LOCATE verticalPos%, 13 * k
                     pmt = FN Payment(tempPrincipal#, tempRate, _
                         setOfTerms%(i))
                     totalPayment = pmt * 12 * setOfTerms%(i)
                     totalInterest = totalPayment - tempPrincipal#
                     PRINT USING "$$###,###.##"; totalInterest
                     tempRate = tempRate + rateIncrement
                 NEXT k
                 tempPrincipal# = tempPrincipal# + principalIncrement#
             NEXT j
         NEXT i

         CALL Pause
     END IF
END SUB
```

Figure 4-11. *The* Mortgage *program (continued).*   *(more...)*

The function uses the string variable *value$* to store the input string and uses the variable *number* to test the value. After *number* is initialized to 0, a WHILE…WEND loop takes control of the input process:

```
number = 0
WHILE number <= 0
    INPUT value$
    number = VAL(value$)
```

The VAL function supplies the numeric equivalent of *value$*, which is stored in *number,* and the looping continues until *number* contains a positive, nonzero value. If the user enters a string value that cannot be converted to a number, the VAL function returns a value of 0; if the user enters a negative number or 0, the input is rejected by the *WHILE number <= 0* statement. (None of the loan parameters used in the *Mortgage* program may be a negative value or 0.)

If the input value is not valid, the following lines overwrite the value with a string of blank characters and return the cursor to its original position:

```
IF (number <= 0) THEN
    LOCATE currentY%, currentX%
    PRINT SPACE$(filledArea%);
    LOCATE currentY%, currentX%
END IF
```

When *value$* contains a string that QuickBASIC can successfully convert to a positive, nonzero number, the looping stops. The string is returned as the result of the *InValue$* function:

```
FN InValue$ = value$
```

Whenever the *Mortgage* program calls this function, VAL converts the returned value to a number. The converted number then becomes a double-precision, single-precision, or integer value, depending on the type of variable that receives it. For example:

```
principal# = VAL(InValue$)
```

converts the result of the *InValue$* function to a double-precision number and assigns it to the variable *principal#*.

The *InRate* input subprogram

The final input routine in the *Mortgage* program is the *InRate* subprogram, which ensures that the user inputs the interest rate in the

```
'   The Amortize subprogram computes and displays a 12-month
'       amortization table for the current loan parameters.

SUB Amortize STATIC
'   ---- Print an introductory message and find the starting point for
'       the amortization period.
    totalPayments% = term% * 12
    LOCATE 9, 15
    PRINT "There are"; totalPayments% "payments in your loan."

    LOCATE 11, 15
    PRINT "Which payment would you like to start at";
    startMonth% = VAL(FN InValue$)

'   ---- Determine if startMonth% is bigger than the total number of payments
'       in the loan.
    maxStart% = (term% * 12) - 11
    IF (startMonth% > maxStart%) THEN startMonth% = maxStart%

'   ---- Initialize variables needed later in the subprogram.
    pmt = FN Payment(principal#, rate, term%)
    balance# = principal#
    totalInterest = 0
    totalPrincipal = 0

'   ---- Clear the screen, prepare output formatting strings for the
'       amortization values, and display table labels.
    CLS
    PRINT: PRINT: PRINT
    blankSpace$ = SPACE$(12)

    outString$ = blankSpace$ + "###    $$#,######.##   $$#,######.##      "
    outString$ = outString$ + "$$#,#######.##"

    PRINT blankSpace$ " Month       Interest         Principal        ";
    PRINT " Balance"
    PRINT blankSpace$ " -----       --------         ---------        ";
    PRINT " -------"
    PRINT

'   ---- Compute and display the table.
    FOR i = 1 TO startMonth% + 11
        monthlyInterest = balance# * (rate / 1200)
        monthlyPrincipal = pmt - monthlyInterest
        balance# = balance# - monthlyPrincipal
        IF (i >= startMonth%) THEN
            PRINT USING outString$; i, monthlyInterest, _
                monthlyPrincipal, balance#
            totalInterest = totalInterest + monthlyInterest
            totalPrincipal = totalPrincipal + monthlyPrincipal
        END IF
    NEXT i
    PRINT
```

Amortize

Figure 4-11. *The* Mortgage *program (continued).*   *(more...)*

proper format. For example, a user working with an interest rate of 12% might try to enter the number as 0.12, a decimal value, but the program expects to receive the value as 12. Using techniques similar to those in the *InValue$* function, the *InRate* subprogram rejects any rate value that is less than 1 and prints a message describing the correct input format.

Once the user enters valid values for the principal amount, interest rate, and term, the *Mortgage* program can call any of the remaining four major subprograms: *ShowPayment*, *PaymentRange*, *InterestRange*, and *Amortize*.

The *ShowPayment* subprogram

ShowPayment creates the box shown in Figure 4-3, which displays the three parameter values and the monthly payment calculated from those values. The subprogram begins by storing two screen column addresses in variables named *columnPosition1%*, for the left-margin position of the labels, and *columnPosition2%*, for the first-character position in the amounts column:

```
columnPosition1% = 25
columnPosition2% = 43
```

Given these two addresses, the routine uses LOCATE, PRINT, TAB, and PRINT USING statements to create each line of the display, for example:

```
LOCATE 10, columnPosition1%
PRINT "Principal amount:" TAB(columnPosition2%);
PRINT USING "$$#,#######"; principal#
```

PRINT USING is an extremely useful statement that specifies how a number appears on the screen. In this example, the $$ symbols become a "floating" dollar sign, which appears just to the left of the number. The # symbol marks the place for a single digit, and the comma specifies that a comma appears after every third digit to the left of the decimal point. For example, if *principal#* contains the number 1234567, the value is displayed as $1,234,567.

ShowPayment calls the *Payment* function to produce the monthly payment for the loan:

```
PRINT USING "$$#,######.##"; FN Payment(principal#, rate, term%)
```

```
     ---- Provide statistics summarizing the loan's status.
     outString$ = "$$#,######      $$#,######"
     totalOutString$ = blankSpace$ + "Total    " + outString$
     averageOutString$ = blankSpace$ + "Average  " + outString$

     PRINT USING totalOutString$; totalInterest, totalPrincipal
     PRINT USING averageOutString$; totalInterest / 12, totalPrincipal / 12
     LOCATE 20, 52: PRINT "Principal to date:"
     LOCATE 21, 53: PRINT USING "**$#,#######.##"; principal# - balance#

     CALL Frame (9, 71, 3, 22)
     CALL Pause
END SUB
```

Figure 4-11. *The* Mortgage *program (continued)*

Finally, when all the numbers are on the screen, the program calls the
Frame subprogram to draw a frame around the display and calls the
Pause subprogram to create a pause in the action:

```
CALL Frame (23, 60, 8, 16)
CALL Pause
```

Pause places the message *Press <Enter> to continue* at the lower-
right corner of the screen and then waits for the user to press Enter.

The *PaymentRange* subprogram

PaymentRange creates the table in Figure 4-8, showing a range of mortgage payment figures based on incremented principal amounts and
interest rates. The subprogram begins by displaying the dialog box
shown in Figure 4-7, which prompts the user to input the increment
amounts and the comparison loan term. Given these numbers, the
routine calculates and displays the table.

The subprogram uses the *InValue$* function to elicit and validate
the input values. For example, the following sequence gets an increment value for the principal and stores the value in the variable
principalIncrement#:

```
LOCATE 10, 10
PRINT "Increment the principal by how much....";
principalIncrement# = VAL(FN InValue$)
```

The global array *setOfTerms%* receives the two comparison loan terms;
the first is the current value of *term%*, and the second value is elicited
from the user:

```
setOfTerms%(1) = term%
LOCATE 12,10
PRINT "Use what term (years) for comparison....";
setOfTerms%(2) = VAL(FN InValue$)
```

127

After the input dialog, the *BoundsCheck* function determines if any of the monthly payments in the table will be out of range (recall the payment function can only handle monthly payments less than $32,768). Finding these error-producing payments is a simple matter. The tables are set up with 5 rows and 5 columns, with the initial parameter in the center of each row and the center of each column. The largest value is simply the initial parameter plus two times the parameter increment entered by the user. The three parameters are determined like this:

```
maxPrincipal# = principal# + (2 * principalIncrement)
maxRate = rate + (2 * rateIncrement)
IF (setOfTerms%(1) < setOfTerm%(2)) THEN
    maxTerm% = setOfTerms%(1) _
    ELSE maxTerm% = setOfTerms%(2)
tooBig% = FN BoundsCheck(maxPrincipal#, maxRate, maxTerm%)
```

If the *BoundsCheck* function determines that the set of loan information will cause a runtime error in the payment function, *BoundsCheck* returns a value of true and program flow is channeled back to the main program. If *BoundsCheck* returns a value of false, subprogram execution continues with the labeling and printing of the payment range table.

A trio of nested FOR...NEXT loops (using the integer loop counters *i*, *j*, and *k*) creates the two tables. The payment amounts are ordered in rows following the principal amounts in the left column, and each cycle of the innermost loop displays the next payment amount in a row:

```
FOR k = 1 TO 5
    LOCATE verticalPos%, 13 * k
    pmt = FN Payment(tempPrincipal#, tempRate, setOfTerms%(i))
    PRINT USING "$$###,###.##"; pmt
```

The middle loop displays the values in *tempPrincipal#* as row headings and the values in *tempRate* as column headings. The outer loop repeats the entire process twice, once for each of the two comparison terms stored in the array *setOfTerms%*. The most difficult part of the process is keeping track of screen locations; a series of LOCATE and PRINT USING statements places each value on the screen.

When the tables are complete, *PaymentRange* calls the *Pause* subprogram to give the user time to study the information.

The *InterestRange* subprogram

The *InterestRange* subprogram is similar to the *PaymentRange* subprogram. In fact, except for a minor difference in labels, the code for these two routines is identical until the final FOR ... NEXT loop because both routines do the same thing: display loan payment information for a range of principals, rates, and terms. Rather than display a monthly mortgage payment, however, *InterestRange* displays the total interest payment over the term of a loan. Since the formula for total interest paid over the term of a loan is:

(Monthly Payment * 12 * Term Years) - Principal

the additional code for the final FOR ... NEXT loop is simply:

```
totalPayment = pmt * 12 * setOfTerms%(i)
totalInterest = totalPayment - tempPrincipal#
```

The *Amortize* subprogram

The *Amortize* subprogram generates a 12-month amortization table like the one in Figure 4-4. After an introductory message, the routine first prompts the user for the month number of the first payment in the table; this number is stored in the integer variable *start%*:

```
LOCATE 11, 15
PRINT "which payment would you like to start at";
startMonth% = VAL(FN InValue$)
```

Since *Amortize* always shows the interest and principal payments for a full 12-month period, the largest workable value for *startMonth%* is the first payment in the final year of the loan. The program calculates this number and stores it in the variable *maxStart%*. If the user enters a starting number that is larger than *maxStart%*, the program sets the *startMonth%* variable to *maxStart%*:

```
maxStart% = (term% * 12) - 11
IF (startMonth% > maxStart%) THEN startMonth% = maxStart%
```

The program next initializes four variables required for the amortization calculations: *pmt* is the calculated monthly payment on the loan; *balance#* is the balance of the principal on the loan after each payment; *totalInterest* is the total interest paid during the 12-month period; and *totalPrincipal* is the total principal paid during the period.

The starting value of *balance#* is the total principal, *principal#*. The variables *totalInterest* and *totalPrincipal* both begin with values of 0:

```
pmt = FN Payment(principal#, rate, term%)
balance# = principal#
totalInterest = 0
totalPrincipal = 0
```

The routine employs a series of PRINT USING statements to specify how the numbers are displayed. The PRINT USING statements work with various concatenated string values. For example, these statements display the *Total* label and the following two amounts near the bottom of the amortization table:

```
blankSpace$ = SPACE$(12)
     [other program lines]
outString$ = "$$#,######          $$#,######"
totalOutString$ = blankSpace$ + "Total      " + outString$
     [other program lines]
PRINT USING totalOutString$; totalInterest, totalPrincipal
```

If you look back at Figure 4-4, you will see an example of the output line produced by this sequence:

```
Total          $12,783             $3,171
```

The program computes and displays the entire table from within a FOR ... NEXT loop. No matter what the value of *startMonth%* is, the calculations must always begin with the first payment of the loan:

```
FOR i = 1 TO startMonth% + 11
```

Inside the loop, three assignment statements calculate the required values for each month of the loan. First, the interest payment for the current month is the product of the monthly interest rate and the current balance:

```
monthlyInterest = balance# * (rate / 1200)
```

The principal payment is simply the difference between the total monthly payment and the interest amount:

```
monthlyPrincipal = pmt - monthlyInterest
```

Finally, the new balance is calculated as the old balance minus the principal portion of the current monthly payment:

```
balance# = balance# - monthlyPrincipal
```

The program starts printing these values only when the loop counter, *i*, reaches the value of *startMonth%*:

```
IF (i >= startMonth%) THEN
    PRINT USING outString$; i, monthlyInterest, _
        monthlyPrincipal, balance#
```

For the months that are actually printed, the program also accumulates the total interest and principal portions of the payments:

```
totalInterest = totalInterest + monthlyInterest
totalPrincipal = totalPrincipal + monthlyPrincipal
```

As we have seen, the program displays these two values at the bottom of the table, after the FOR ... NEXT loop has completed the calculations for the entire 12-month period.

Finally, the program uses an empty two-line space in the lower-right corner of the table to display the total principal paid on the loan at the end of the target 12-month period. This value is calculated simply as the original principal of the loan minus the balance at the end of the period:

```
LOCATE 20, 52: PRINT "Principal to date:"
LOCATE 21, 53: PRINT USING "**$#.########.##"; _
    principal# - balance#
```

Notice the two asterisks at the beginning of the PRINT USING statement. These characters display a sequence of asterisks that will precede the dollar sign; for example:

```
******$9,462.02
```

CONCLUSION

If you are interested in additional work with the *Mortgage* program, here are a few suggestions for further programming exercises you can try:

1. Include the sale price of the home and the down payment (a percent of the sale price) as parameters that the user will enter from the keyboard. The program will then calculate the principal of the loan from these two values. The owner's total current equity (down payment plus total principal payments) could then appear as part of the amortization table.

2. Write a new subprogram that will create a five-year summary table, detailing the total annual interest and principal payments for the first five years of the loan. (This kind of information is often interesting to people who are anticipating entering into their first mortgage; such a table shows the tax advantage of the mortgage for the first five years.)

3. Create new variables (and input routines) that will allow the program to hold two complete sets of loan parameters at a time. Devise tables that will compare the characteristics of these two loans: this will enable a person to understand the differences between two available mortgage plans. For example, five-year summary tables could be produced for the two loans, and then they could be displayed side by side on the same screen.

These three exercises will provide you with ample opportunities to practice using QuickBASIC's numeric data types and operations.

Loops, Arrays, and Graphics:
A Chart Program

*I*n business presentations, tables of numbers tend to be dry and static and therefore are easy to ignore. Charts, on the other hand, are dramatic and attractive—and they command attention. A well-designed chart provides a clear picture of numeric data by revealing trends, showing the relative contribution cf individual parts to the whole, illustrating high points and low points of a particular data category over time, and generally making the numbers easier to grasp. Consequently, many integrated software packages developed in recent years include charting capabilities: Users can create charts quickly and efficiently from stored tables of numbers.

QuickBASIC contains the programming tools necessary to create presentation-quality charts that accurately represent sets of numeric data values. We'll try out these tools in *QuickChart*, a menu-driven chart program. *QuickChart* displays three styles of charts on the computer's screen: column charts, line charts, and pie charts. The program can read tables of data for the charts either directly from the keyboard or from specially formatted data files stored on disk. In addition, we will explore techniques for transferring the program's screen displays to the printer, producing paper copies of the charts.

Figures 5-1 through 5-3 (on the following pages) show the *QuickChart* program in action. The charts model this scenario: Nancy, the owner of a busy downtown restaurant, kept records of the total number of breakfasts, lunches, and dinners served in her restaurant during the first four months of the year. By analyzing this information, she hopes to respond more efficiently to levels of demand at various hours in the workday.

She stored the data (shown in Figure 5-1) on a disk. Figures 5-2 and 5-3 show two *QuickChart* charts created from the data. First, a line chart enumerates the meals served in each of the three categories during the four-month period. Second, a pie chart illustrates the ratio of each meal to the total number of meals served during March.

You can see from the figures that the *QuickChart* program is first given a set of values, which it then uses to create a graphic representation of those values. The program must also create other enhancements to the chart, such as vertical and horizontal axes, labels, and a legend describing what elements are being charted.

Doing this requires *multidimensional arrays* and *structured loops*. In addition, the *QuickChart* program contains many techniques to display graphics on monochrome screens or color screens. (Although QuickBASIC also supports the IBM Enhanced Graphics Adapter—often used with high-resolution color monitors—the *QuickChart* program does not.) These three topics—arrays, loops, and graphics—are the main focus in this chapter.

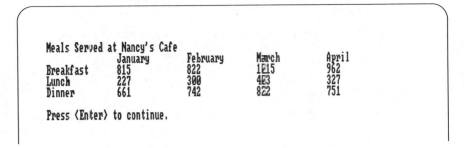

Figure 5-1. *Table of values used to create Figures 5-2 and 5-3.*

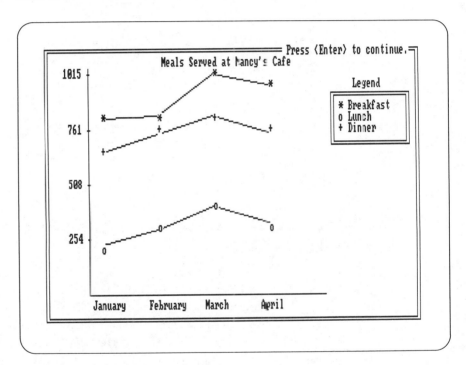

Figure 5-2. *A line chart created from the values in Figure 5-1.*

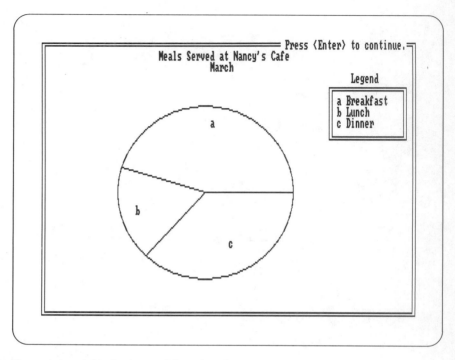

Figure 5-3. *A pie chart created from the values describing the month of March in Figure 5-1.*

STRUCTURED LOOPS IN QUICKBASIC: FOR...NEXT AND WHILE...WEND

The QuickBASIC compiler supplies two looping structures: FOR...NEXT and WHILE...WEND. Both result in the repeated performance of a delimited block of statements. However, a FOR...NEXT loop is most often used to repeat the actions specified in the block of statements between the FOR part and the NEXT part a *specific* number of times; the intervening statements change the program actions, so each time through the loop produces a different result. A WHILE...WEND loop, on the other hand, is used with a *conditional* expression. The looping continues as long as the condition is true and stops when the condition becomes false.

FOR...NEXT loops

The most important structural difference between FOR...NEXT and
WHILE...WEND is the mechanism that determines the number of rep-
etitions (or *iterations*) that will occur before the looping stops. In a
FOR...NEXT loop, you must establish a *counter variable* and specify the
range of values that the variable will take on during the loop. At the
beginning of each iteration, the counter variable receives a new value,
and the block of statements is performed once. The looping ends
when the counter has gone through the entire range of values from
start number to *end number*.

A FOR...NEXT loop in QuickBASIC has the following format:

```
FOR counterVariable = start TO end STEP increment
    [block of statements]
NEXT counterVariable
```

Keep in mind the following characteristics of FOR...NEXT loops:

- The block of statements is delimited by a FOR statement at the top
  of the structure and by a NEXT statement at the bottom of the
  structure.

- The FOR statement names the counter variable and specifies the
  starting and ending values in the counter's range. You can express the starting and ending values as:

  — Constants
  — Variables whose values are derived sometime before the
    start of the loop
  — Arithmetic expressions that compute a range of values
    for the counter variable

The STEP clause

The FOR...NEXT statement also lets you use an optional STEP clause,
which gives the amount by which the counter variable is incremented
or decremented after each iteration. If this number is positive, the
value of the counter increments with each iteration; if it is negative,
the counter decrements. (You can supply a constant, a variable, or an
expression as the value for STEP; the value can be an integer or a decimal number.) If the STEP clause is missing, the default increment is 1.

For example, the following loop steps backward from 22 to 3.

```
FOR i% = 22 TO 3 STEP -1
     [other program lines]
NEXT i%
```

No matter how you define the range of values for the counter variable, QuickBASIC always performs the block of statements at least once. (The test for terminating the looping occurs at the end of each iteration, when QuickBASIC encounters the NEXT statement.)

The WHILE...WEND loop

We just saw that in a FOR...NEXT loop you supply a FOR statement that precisely specifies the number of loops. In a WHILE...WEND loop you supply a conditional expression, which ultimately determines the number of iterations. QuickBASIC evaluates the condition before each iteration. Each time the condition evaluates to true, the block of statements is performed once. As soon as the condition becomes false, the looping ends.

A WHILE...WEND loop in QuickBASIC has the following format:

```
WHILE condition
     [block of statements]
WEND
```

Here are the important characteristics of the WHILE...WEND loop structure:

- The block of statements is delimited by a WHILE statement at the top of the structure and by a WEND statement at the bottom.

- The WHILE...WEND statement contains the conditional expression that determines the extent of the looping. This may be any expression that QuickBASIC can evaluate to true or false. Typically, such an expression is built with one or more of the six relational operators (= , <>, <, <=, >, >=). You can write compound expressions using one or more of the six logical operators (AND, OR, NOT, XOR, IMP, EQV) available in QuickBASIC.

- QuickBASIC actually evaluates conditional expressions to one of two numeric values: -1 for true, or 0 for false. You can, therefore, create "Boolean" variables for your program to keep track of the current state of important conditions. A Boolean variable is simply a numeric variable that always contains a value of either -1 or 0. It's often useful to include such a variable as the controlling condition in a WHILE loop, as we did in the *Mortgage* program in the last chapter.

- If the WHILE condition is false when QuickBASIC first encounters the loop, no iteration is performed. In other words, unlike a FOR...NEXT loop, a WHILE...WEND loop may result in no action at all.

We will study examples of these looping characteristics as we examine the *QuickChart* program.

Nested loops

Although a single loop can perform some quite powerful operations, its utility is often greatly increased by including still other loops within the main, or "outer," loop. We refer to these as *nested loops*, and *QuickChart* demonstrates the power and versatility of nested loops.

ARRAYS IN QUICKBASIC

So far when we've worked with variables we've assigned only one value to a single variable. But often you need to store several values, and assigning each value to a specific variable can be unwieldy. QuickBASIC lets you set up an *array*, which organizes one or more values under one *array variable* name. An array can be organized as:

- A list of values (a one-dimensional array).

- A table of values (a two-dimensional array).

- Some other multidimensional arrangement of values (the QuickBASIC compiler allows a maximum of 63 dimensions).

Each value in such an arrangement is called an *element* of the array. A program accesses elements by using numeric *subscripts* that identify the position of a given value in the array.

The DIM statement

The DIM statement declares the name, size, and type of an array with the following syntax:

DIM *arrayName(subscripts)*

where *arrayName* is a legal variable name and *subscripts* is a list of numeric subscripts (starting with the first dimension) separated by commas for each dimension in the array.

The following DIM statement defines a two-dimensional string array named *table$*, with three elements in the first dimension and four elements in the second:

```
DIM table$(2, 3)
```

By default, subscripts range from 0 to the maximum value indicated in the DIM statement (0 to 2 and 0 to 3 in the *table$* example). We can thus think of the *table$* array as a three-column by four-row arrangement of values.

table$(0, 0)	table$(1, 0)	table$(2, 0)
table$(0, 1)	table$(1, 1)	table$(2, 1)
table$(0, 2)	table$(1, 2)	table$(2, 2)
table$(0, 3)	table$(1, 3)	table$(2, 3)

Array names can include the same type-declaration characters that are used for simple variable names: $ for strings; % for integers; ! for single-precision numbers; and # for double-precision numbers. An array that does not have a type character is then assumed to be single-precision numeric.

The OPTION BASE statement

If you prefer counting from 1 rather than 0 you can start all subscripts at 1 by including an OPTION BASE statement at the beginning of your program:

```
OPTION BASE 1
```

This means that all arrays defined in the program have subscripts that begin with 1. For example, the *table$* array would have 2 columns, 3 rows, and 6 elements instead of 12 elements:

table$(1, 1)	table$(2, 1)
table$(1, 2)	table$(2, 2)
table$(1, 3)	table$(2, 3)

As you will see, the *QuickChart* program uses the "zeroth" elements in its most important array; for this reason, the program simply omits the OPTION BASE statement. If an OPTION BASE statement is not included in a program, QuickBASIC assumes that all arrays start with the zeroth element.

Static and dynamic arrays

In QuickBASIC, you can define either *static* or *dynamic* arrays. The size of a static array is fixed when you compile your program and remains unchanged when the program runs. The size of a dynamic array, however, is not defined until you actually use the array during the running of the program. Furthermore, the dimensions of a dynamic array may change one or more times during the run of a program.

Sometimes you will have a good idea of how big an array needs to be; for example, if you know there will be 26 elements in an array that has one place for each letter of the alphabet, you can then define a one-dimensional array with a subscript of 26. At other times, though, an array will vary in size according to user input or some other action of the program, for example an inventory list that grows and shrinks. QuickBASIC allows for these two possibilities by letting you declare *static* or *dynamic* arrays.

To declare an array as *static*, use positive integer *constants* as subscripts within the DIM statement. For example, the statement:

```
DIM income(3, 4, 4)
```

defines a three-dimensional array named *income* with dimension lengths of 3, 4, and 4, respectively.

If you define an array as static, you may not redimension it later in the program. You do gain a small amount of speed with static arrays, because QuickBASIC needs less memory to store them and can process them quicker.

To define an array as dynamic, use positive integer *variables* as subscripts within the DIM statement. For example, the statement:

```
DIM income(years%, grossIncome%, profits%)
```

defines a three-dimensional array named *income* with the values of the integer variables *years%, grossIncome%,* and *profits%* when the DIM statement is executed. If you define a dynamic array like this, you may redimension it later in the program with the REDIM statement. If you do, all the values of the current array will be lost. Although it takes QuickBASIC a little longer to process the elements of a dynamic array, they provide more efficient use of memory because space for the array is not allocated until it is needed.

Besides the DIM statement, QuickBASIC has two metacommands, $STATIC and $DYNAMIC, which you can use to declare the status of arrays. These metacommands override the format of the dimensions in subsequent DIM statements.

Global arrays

If you use the COMMON SHARED statement to declare a *global* array, you must carefully distinguish between static and dynamic arrays. A DIM statement defining *static* arrays must appear *before* the COMMON SHARED statement. For example:

```
DIM table$(2, 3)
COMMON SHARED table$()
```

In this case the array named in the COMMON SHARED statement is simply followed by a pair of empty parentheses.

On the other hand, a DIM statement that defines dynamic variables is said to be an *executable* statement. An executable statement is one performed at runtime. In QuickBASIC all statements are executable except the following:

- COMMON

- DATA

- DEF *type*

- DIM *(static arrays only)*

- OPTION BASE

- REM

- *All metacommands*

Since no executable statement may appear before the COMMON SHARED statement, dynamic dimensioning must occur after the global declaration. For example:

```
COMMON SHARED table$(2)
INPUT i%
INPUT j%
DIM table$(i%, j%)
```

In this case the array name in the COMMON SHARED statement must be followed by an integer (in parentheses) representing the number of dimensions in the array. The expression *table$(2)* indicates that *table$* will ultimately be defined as a two-dimensional array.

Note that the DIM statement itself also allows an optional SHARED clause. This is an alternative technique for declaring arrays as global. However, in a program that uses several global arrays and variables (*QuickChart*, for example), grouping all their names together in one COMMON SHARED statement may be a clearer approach.

The REDIM statement

We have seen that we use the DIM statement to set the size of an array. However, when we are working with dynamic arrays, the size can vary. The REDIM statement lets you change the size (but not the number of dimensions) of a dynamic array during a program's performance. REDIM has the same syntax as the DIM statement:

REDIM *arrayName(subscripts)*

where *arrayName* is a legal variable name and *subscripts* is a list of subscripts separated by commas for each dimension in the array (starting with the first dimension). For example, if you previously defined the three-dimensional dynamic array *income* with the statement:

```
DIM income(years%, grossIncome%, profits%)
```

you may redimension *income* later in the program by entering:

```
REDIM income(years% + 1, newGross%, newProfits%)
```

(You may use any subscript you like as long as it is a valid integer-variable expression. The array being redimensioned, however, must retain the same number of dimensions.) This will result in an empty array with new dimension lengths. You'll see examples of both DIM and REDIM in the *QuickChart* program.

QUICKBASIC GRAPHICS AND SYSTEM HARDWARE

Microsoft QuickBASIC includes a rich vocabulary of powerful, yet easy-to-use, graphics commands. However, the set of commands you can actually use depends on your computer system. If you have a graphics adapter board, and an appropriate monitor, you can use QuickBASIC's medium- and high-resolution graphics commands. But if your display adapter board can display only text characters, the graphics commands aren't available to you.

Accordingly, one of the first things that *QuickChart* does is check what hardware is being used. Given a graphics adapter and a graphics display, *QuickChart* can produce column, line, and pie charts. If a system can display only text, however, the program offers only the column chart. Let's first examine the technique required for creating column charts on text-only display hardware.

QuickBASIC graphics on text-only display hardware

The program uses the extended character set (ASCII decimal values 128–255) to create the column chart. We learned in Chapter 2 that the ASCII code is simply a number assigned to every character that the computer can display on the screen. The first half of the ASCII code— numbers 0 to 127—is fairly standard among all computers, being assigned to the letters of the alphabet (uppercase and lowercase), the digits (from 0 to 9), the punctuation characters, and a few control characters that represent keyboard functions.

The second half of the code—from 128 to 255—is not standard at all. On IBM personal computers, these code numbers represent a variety of useful characters, as you can see in Figure 5-4. The characters include letters from foreign-language alphabets; special mathematical and technical symbols; and—what interests us primarily in this chapter—several dozen graphics symbols.

We have already used some of these graphics characters in the *Frame* subprogram, described in Chapter 2, which builds a double-line rectangular frame on the screen using six characters corresponding to ASCII codes 186, 187, 188, 200, 201, and 205. Recall that the CHR$

127	△	143	Å	159	ƒ	175	»	191	┐	207	╧	223	▀	239	∩
128	Ç	144	É	160	á	176	░	192	└	208	╨	224	α	240	≡
129	ü	145	æ	161	í	177	▒	193	┴	209	╤	225	ß	241	±
130	é	146	Æ	162	ó	178	▓	194	┬	210	╥	226	Γ	242	≥
131	â	147	ô	163	ú	179	│	195	├	211	╙	227	π	243	≤
132	ä	148	ö	164	ñ	180	┤	196	─	212	╘	228	Σ	244	⌠
133	à	149	ò	165	Ñ	181	╡	197	┼	213	╒	229	σ	245	⌡
134	å	150	û	166	ª	182	╢	198	╞	214	╓	230	µ	246	÷
135	ç	151	ù	167	º	183	╖	199	╟	215	╫	231	τ	247	≈
136	ê	152	ÿ	168	¿	184	╕	200	╚	216	╪	232	Φ	248	°
137	ë	153	Ö	169	⌐	185	╣	201	╔	217	┘	233	Θ	249	·
138	è	154	Ü	170	¬	186	║	202	╩	218	┌	234	Ω	250	·
139	ï	155	¢	171	½	187	╗	203	╦	219	█	235	δ	251	√
140	î	156	£	172	¼	188	╝	204	╠	220	▄	236	∞	252	ⁿ
141	ì	157	¥	173	¡	189	╜	205	═	221	▌	237	φ	253	²
142	Ä	158	₧	174	«	190	╛	206	╬	222	▐	238	ε	254	■

Figure 5-4. *The IBM PC extended character set.*

function retrieves the character corresponding to the ASCII-code number given in its argument; the LOCATE command places the screen cursor at a specified row and column position; and the PRINT command displays the character. The STRING$ function provides a convenient way to build horizontal lines, but vertical lines require the control of a FOR...NEXT loop.

The *QuickChart* program uses a similar technique to build stacked column charts on a text-only display screen. Since stacked column charts usually use colors or shading to distinguish the components being compared, you can see in Figure 5-4 that ASCII codes 176, 177, 178, and 219 are ideal. These characters supply graduated shades of light and dark blocks, each of which takes up one character space. By carefully juxtaposing many such blocks, one on top of another, you can create the illusion of high-resolution graphics on a text-only display screen. (In fact, QuickBASIC's editing environment uses many of these same characters to create its "graphic" screen images, such as its scroll bars.)

Figure 5-5 (on the next page) is an example of such a column chart, created by the *QuickChart* program. You can see that each column is made up of vertical rectangles of contrasting shades; each stacked rectangular area represents one data value. As you will see when you examine the program, creating this effect requires three nested FOR...NEXT loops.

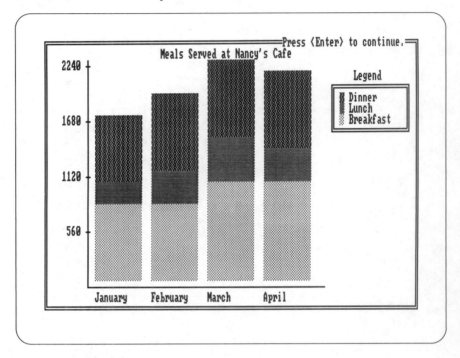

Figure 5-5. *A column chart using ASCII codes 176, 177, and 178.*

Unfortunately, printing a copy of a chart created by graphics characters in the extended character set is problematic. For example, the graphics characters in the extended character set are usually not available on a daisy-wheel printer. This is also the case with many dot-matrix and laser printers.

For these reasons, a stacked column chart created by using graphics characters for display on a text-only monitor must substitute printable characters from the first half of the ASCII-code set to produce a printed version. When this version is displayed on the screen, it can be printed as a screen dump using the Shift-PrtSc key combination. Admittedly, this version is not terribly attractive, but it does get

146

the essential information across. Figure 5-6 shows an example of this printable column chart. Another method (not used in the *QuickChart* program) would be to send information directly to the printer with a QuickBASIC statement like LPRINT. We will use this technique in Chapter 7.

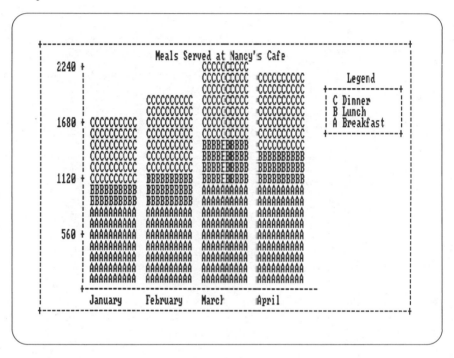

Figure 5-6. *A printable column chart available with a text-only hardware system.*

QuickBASIC graphics on graphics-display hardware

So far we have used the *QuickChart* program to explore techniques for creating graphics with QuickBASIC on a text-only hardware system. However, if your system is equipped with a graphics card and a graphics monitor, you can use *QuickChart* to create more sophisticated graphics, including line and pie charts, as well as column charts. Doing so requires using several of QuickBASIC's built-in graphics commands.

The SCREEN command

QuickBASIC's SCREEN command selects one of the display modes available for a given hardware configuration. The format of this command is:

SCREEN *mode*

where mode is an integer representing the display mode. The default display mode is SCREEN 0, the text-only mode. Consequently, this is the only mode available in a system that has a monochrome monitor and a monochrome ("text-only") display. Other modes yield graphics screens with various resolutions and color ranges. The following table provides a summary of these:

Screen Mode	Hardware Required	Resolution	Colors/Attributes
SCREEN 0	IBM Monochrome Adapter and Monochrome Display	80 columns X 25 rows	none
SCREEN 1	IBM Color Graphics Adapter and Color Display	320 pixels X 200 pixels	$^{16}/_4$
SCREEN 2	IBM Color Graphics Adapter and Color Display	640 pixels X 200 pixels	$^{16}/_2$
SCREEN 7	IBM Enhanced Graphics Adapter and Color Display	320 pixels X 200 pixels	$^{16}/_{16}$
SCREEN 8	IBM Enhanced Graphics Adapter and Color Display	640 pixels X 200 pixels	$^{16}/_{16}$
SCREEN 9	IBM Enhanced Graphics Adapter and Enhanced Color Display	640 pixels X 350 pixels	$^{16}/_4$
SCREEN 10	IBM Enhanced Graphics Adapter and Monochrome Display	640 pixels X 350 pixels	none

The resolution of a graphics screen is usually described in terms of *pixels* ("picture elements"). A pixel is the smallest screen element that you can control in any screen mode. Each pixel has a screen address, which we can represent as *(x,y)*, where *x* is the horizontal coordinate of the address and *y* is the vertical coordinate. Although all QuickBASIC graphics commands use this (x,y) coordinate system, the range of legal (x,y) numbers—and therefore the number of pixels—depends on the current screen mode. Thus, screen resolution relates to the size of the pixels: bigger screen-coordinate numbers indicate smaller pixels; smaller pixels mean more pixels per inch; more pixels per inch mean better resolution.

For the line and pie charts, the *QuickChart* program works in SCREEN 2, which has a resolution of 640 (horizontal) by 200 (vertical) pixels. By default, the upper-left corner of the screen is the beginning of the coordinate system, with an address of (0,0). The four corner coordinates of SCREEN 2 are:

upper-left	*upper-right*
(0,0)	(639,0)
lower-left	*lower-right*
(0,199)	(639,199)

As long as you remain in SCREEN 2 display mode, you will need to construct your images based on this system.

The SCREEN 2 mode, however, allows both graphic images and text characters to be displayed on the screen. To place text characters at specific locations on a graphics display, you use the LOCATE command to position the cursor before printing a character:

```
LOCATE row, column
```

When you use text-oriented commands like LOCATE in one of QuickBASIC's graphics-oriented screen modes such as SCREEN 2, however, you need to use your display's character dimensions as a frame of reference. In all screen modes, QuickBASIC defines a character-oriented screen as 80 *character* columns by 25 *character* rows. *Character* in this definition is emphasized to distinguish the measurement from the *pixel* sizes used in the graphics statements.

Printing screen images

To capture a screen of standard text characters (those with decimal ASCII values between 32 and 127) and send it to a printer, you simply press the Shift-PrtSc key combination. For example, Shift-PrtSc enables you to print a copy of the stacked column chart shown in Figure 5-6. If you have an IBM Monochrome Adapter and a monochrome display, this is all you have to do to print an image of the screen.

If you have an IBM Color Graphics Adapter (CGA) or compatible you can also print screens of standard characters by using the Shift-PrtSc key combination. However, you can take advantage of your hardware's ability to produce graphic images if you have the DOS program

GRAPHICS.COM and a suitable dot-matrix or laser printer. If you plan to capture any images in a charting session, load the *GRAPHICS* program before you start *QuickChart*. At the DOS prompt type:

```
GRAPHICS
```

to load the DOS graphics printing program. At this point you may also specify the kind of printer you have attached to your computer. For example, if you have an IBM PC Graphics Printer or compatible attached, type:

```
GRAPHICS graphics
```

From that point until you reboot your machine, the Shift-PrtSc key combination will send a graphic image to your printer. Basically, this image is sent pixel by pixel rather than character by character. If you have a CGA and a color display, you will want to use the *GRAPHICS* program to capture images created by the *QuickChart* program while it is in SCREEN 2 mode. (See your DOS manual for more information about the *GRAPHICS* program and the specific printers it supports.)

The PSET, LINE, and CIRCLE statements

If you have a CGA or an Enhanced Graphics Adapter (EGA) and a color display, the *QuickChart* program will determine it and enter SCREEN 2 graphics mode. In the SCREEN 2 graphics mode the *QuickChart* program uses the PSET and LINE statements to build line charts, and it uses the CIRCLE statement to draw pie charts. These statements offer a number of interesting options.

The PSET statement illuminates a single pixel at a specified screen address. The format for the statement is:

PSET(x,y)

For example, the following statement illuminates a pixel located at the center of the SCREEN 2 graphics screen:

```
PSET(320,100)
```

The PSET statement, then, works with individual pixels. The LINE statement, on the other hand, works with a series of pixels: It draws a line from the first pixel specified in its argument to the second pixel. The basic form of the LINE statement is:

LINE $(x1,y1) - (x2,y2)$

The result is a line drawn from the first coordinate address (*x1,y1*) to the second (*x2,y2*). An alternate form is:

```
LINE — (x2,y2)
```

In this case, QuickBASIC draws a line from the last pixel that was previously drawn on the screen to the pixel address (*x2,y2*). *QuickChart* uses this form to draw each segment of a line chart as the program processes the data set.

An additional feature used by *QuickChart* is the *box option* of the LINE statement. The following statement draws a box on the screen, using the addresses (*x1,y1*) and (*x2,y2*) as the upper-left and lower-right corners of the box:

```
LINE (x1,y1) — (x2,y2),, B
```

Notice that two commas separate the addresses from the *B* option. The second comma represents a missing optional argument, color, which normally specifies the color in which the line or box is drawn. The *QuickChart* program does not use the color argument.

As its name implies, the CIRCLE statement draws a circle. In its simplest form, the CIRCLE statement's syntax is:

```
CIRCLE (x,y), r
```

where (*x,y*) is the pixel coordinate for the center of the circle and *r* is the radius of the circle in pixels.

Since *QuickChart* represents data values as proportional wedges of a circle, the program uses a somewhat more detailed form of the CIRCLE statement:

```
CIRCLE (x,y), r,, start, end
```

In this syntax, the *start* and *end* arguments are angles expressed in *radians*; they represent the starting angle and ending angle of a given wedge. (Again, notice the missing color argument, represented by the second comma after the radius value.)

Radian values of 0 to 2π are equivalent to angles of 0 to 360 degrees. For example, $\pi/2$ is the same as 90 degrees; π is 180 degrees; and so on. In the CIRCLE statement, angles are measured from a line that extends horizontally to the right from the center of the circle.

To make the CIRCLE statement draw the radius sides of a wedge (not just the arc itself), you must supply negative values for *start* and *end*. For example, the following sequence draws the 45-degree wedge from 0 to $\pi/4$:

```
pi = 3.141592
CIRCLE (279,110), 150, , -0.00001, -pi/4
```

The result of this CIRCLE statement appears in Figure 5-7. Notice that in order to draw a radius at an angle of 0, we actually must supply a very small negative number. (You also need to include an appropriate screen mode statement before the CIRCLE statement is called. Figure 5-7 is the result of a SCREEN 2 graphics mode orientation and a Color Graphics Adapter.)

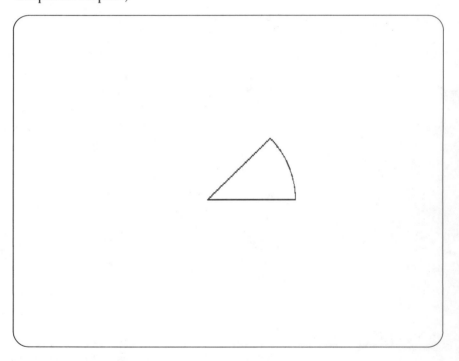

Figure 5-7.   *A wedge from 0 to* $-\pi/4$*, drawn with a CIRCLE statement.*

To draw a pie chart, then, the *QuickChart* program must loop through a list of numeric values and issue the CIRCLE statement once for each number, producing a proportional wedge to represent the value. You'll see exactly how this is done when you examine the program itself.

The VIEW and WINDOW statements

Although QuickBASIC's graphics statements are easy to use in themselves, figuring out where on the screen to display a graphic can get complicated when you must keep track of hundreds of pixel coordinates. QuickBASIC helps with two graphics statements: VIEW and WINDOW. Used together, these two statements alter the coordinate system for addresses on a graphics screen, yielding a new system that matches the requirements of a given task.

The VIEW statement identifies a rectangular portion of the graphics screen as a "viewport," or text and graphics work area. The statement's basic syntax is:

VIEW (x1,y1) — (x2,y2)

The two addresses in the statement provide opposite corners of the rectangle that becomes the work area: (x1,y1) represents the upper-left corner and (x2,y2) represents the lower-right corner. If no corners are specified, the entire screen becomes the viewport. Within this work area, the WINDOW statement assigns a new coordinate system:

WINDOW (x1,y1) — (x2,y2)

Inside the work area defined by VIEW, the WINDOW coordinate pair of (x1,y1) becomes the address of the lower-left corner, and (x2,y2) becomes the address of the upper-right corner.

For example, consider the following statements:

```
VIEW (80,20) - (480,180)
WINDOW (0,0) - (50,20)
```

The VIEW statement establishes a 400-pixel by 160-pixel rectangle as the work area. The WINDOW statement then assigns a new coordinate system to this rectangle. The corner coordinates of the work area, before and after the WINDOW statement, are shown in Figure 5-8.

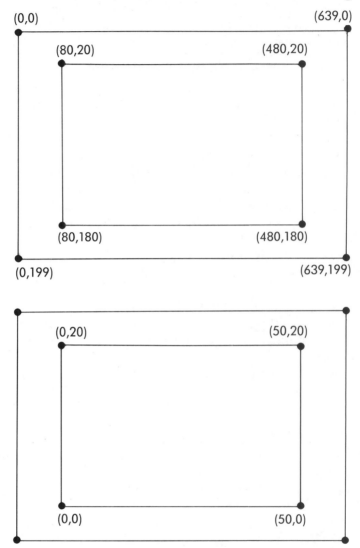

Figure 5-8. *A before-and-after WINDOW comparison.*

As you can see, the "origin" (0,0) of the new coordinate system is at the lower-left corner of the work area. Given this new system, the following

LINE statements produce, in effect, a vertical y-axis, a horizontal x-axis, and a diagonal line inside the quadrant represented by the work area:

```
LINE (0,0) - (0,20)
LINE (0,0) - (50,0)
LINE (10,4) - (40,15)
```

Figure 5-9 shows the result of this entire sequence of statements—the VIEW, WINDOW, and LINE statements together.

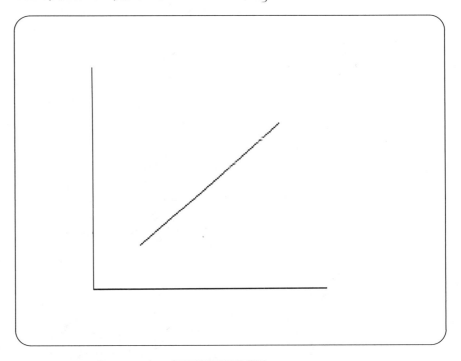

Figure 5-9. *A demonstration of VIEW, WINDOW, and LINE statements (see text).*

The significance of VIEW and WINDOW for creating line charts is clear: You use these two statements to avoid the messy arithmetic that would otherwise be necessary to convert the default SCREEN 2 coordinate system into appropriate addresses for the chart area. We will also be making our programs *device independent* with respect to screen displays. If we choose to run our programs in a screen mode that uses a different resolution, we can simply change the SCREEN statements—VIEW and WINDOW will do the rest.

A SAMPLE RUN OF THE *QUICKCHART* PROGRAM

QuickChart first presents the user with a menu of options and features. This menu, created by the *Menu* subprogram in Chapter 3, lets you press one letter to select an option, then the Enter key to confirm your selection, or the Esc key to cancel the selection.

Figure 5-10 shows the menu that appears. The first option, *Get data*, obtains a table of data for the program to work with. The program can read as many different data tables as you wish, but only one table at a time stays in memory. (When the program reads a new table, any previous data is lost.)

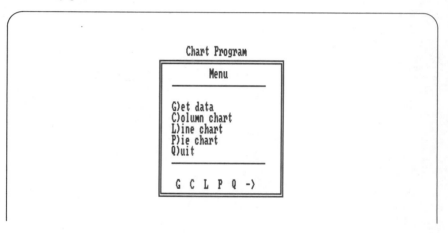

Figure 5-10. *The main menu for the* QuickChart *program.*

Choosing the *Get data* option displays the submenu shown in Figure 5-11. As you can see, *QuickChart* gives you three different ways to supply data: as new data input from the keyboard; as a *QuickChart* data file; or as a SYLK file (more on this later). If you select the *Keyboard input* option, *QuickChart* begins an input dialog to accept your data from the keyboard.

After you enter an entire table of data, the program lets you save the table on disk as a data file. Thanks to this feature, you never have to rekey data. You can specify any disk location and filename you wish for storing the data.

Figure 5-11. *The* Get data *submenu.*

After you create a data file and save it on disk, you can read it into the program by invoking the *Data file* option. When you select this option, the program asks for the filename (include any appropriate drive or pathnames), searches for the file, and then reads it into memory. The data file must conform to the format that *QuickChart* recognizes; in other words, it must be either a file that the program itself has created or one that has an identical format. The data file specifications are simple, as you will see later in this chapter.

The *SYLK* option in the *Get data* submenu lets you specify a SYLK file. SYLK, which stands for "Symbolic Link," is a Microsoft data-file format, designed for sharing data among different application programs. For example, you can create a table of data on a Microsoft Multiplan worksheet, instruct Multiplan to save the worksheet in the SYLK file format, and then run the *QuickChart* program to create charts from the data. *QuickChart* reads the SYLK file as long as you follow a few simple rules when you enter data onto your Multiplan worksheet. We'll look at an example later.

The fourth option in the *Get data* submenu, *Look at data,* lets you examine the data table that is currently in memory. No matter which method you use to read the data into the program, this option displays the data values on the screen (Figure 5-1 provides an example of this). If no data is currently in memory, you are returned to the main menu.

If the *Get data* submenu is currently displayed on the screen, you can return to the main menu by choosing *Cancel.*

When the program has a table of data to work with, you can invoke any of the three chart options from the main menu.

The *Column chart* and *Line chart* options immediately display the specified chart, derived from the data table currently in memory. As you will see, the *Pie chart* option requires one additional instruction before the program can display a pie chart on the screen.

The main menu comes back onto the screen after each activity you perform. (This is sometimes called a *recurring menu.*) After you look at one chart, you can produce the other chart types for the same data table. Or, you can choose *Get data* to read a new data table into the program.

Since the program cannot create charts until you give it a set of data, the *Get data* option is always your first activity. If you try to choose a chart option before the program has read any data, the main menu immediately reappears.

You can quit the program from the main menu by pressing *Q* and then Enter.

If your hardware system has a text-only monochrome adapter, *QuickChart* displays an abbreviated main menu that lets you choose *Get data, Column chart,* or *Quit.* Otherwise, the behavior of the program is identical. In particular, the *Get data* submenu offers all the same options for reading and displaying data tables. (You don't have to tell *QuickChart* anything about your hardware configuration; the program determines what kind of display device you have and presents the appropriate main menu.)

Besides the two controlling menus, the program presents very few other dialog screens. To examine these screens, we will work with the sample data table shown in Figure 5-12. This data belongs to a small (imaginary) insurance brokerage; the table records the number of policies that the agency has sold during a five-year period. Each column contains the sales figures for a given year. The rows divide the sales into four insurance-policy categories: life, home, auto, and other. The figure shows the tabular format that the program presents on the screen when you select the *Look at data* option from the *Get data* submenu.

```
Insurance Policies Sold
            1982          1983         1984         1985         1986
Life         34            58           52           75           41
Home         14            29           42           45           78
Auto         40            75           89           95           92
Other        49            62           75           89          117

Press <Enter> to continue.
```

Figure 5-12. *A sample data table.*

Suppose you just started the *QuickChart* program to enter this sales data and produce some charts. You select the *Get data* option from the main menu and then the *Keyboard input* option from the submenu. In response, the program initiates an input dialog designed to accept your data from the keyboard. Figure 5-13 shows part of the ensuing dialog. (Note that each prompt of the input dialog is presented one at a time.)

```
How many rows of data? (no more than 10) ==> 4
How many data values in each row? (no more than 10) ==> 5

Title of graph? Insurance Policies Sold

    Category names:
                column 1 ==> 1982
                column 2 ==> 1983
                column 3 ==> 1984
                column 4 ==> 1985
                column 5 ==> 1986

    Series name for row 1 ==> Life
      Numeric data values:
                1982 ==> 34
                1983 ==> 58
                1984 ==> 62
                1985 ==> 75
                1986 ==> 41

    Series name for row 2 ==> Home
      Numeric data values:
                1982 ==> 14
                1983 ==>
```

Figure 5-13. *Part of a sample input dialog, using values in Figure 5-12.*

The first information the program needs is the size of your data table—that is, the number of rows and columns of numeric data in the table, not counting any labels. To conserve memory and maintain chart readability, the maximum table size that the current version of the program allows is 10 rows by 10 columns, for a total of 100 data values. (You will see how to increase these maximum values later when we examine the program.) The insurance table has four rows and five columns of data, so you type these values in response to the first two questions.

Next, the program prompts you for a title for your table. This title will appear at the top of each chart produced from the table.

In the dialog that follows, the program unobtrusively introduces two terms that we will use for describing dimensions of a data table. The program refers to the columns of your table as *categories* and to the rows as *series*. The headings at the top of the columns are thus category names, and the row labels are series names. You will see in a moment how categories and series translate into the elements of a chart.

The program next asks you to enter a complete set of category names, one for each column of your table. In the case of the insurance table, the category names are the five years, from 1982 to 1986.

After you enter the category names, the next task is inputting the rows of numbers, or data series. The program handles this by first prompting you for the first name in the series, then for the values in its category. The program displays the corresponding category name (or column heading) as a prompt for each data value. If you are reading data from a two-dimensional table like the one in Figure 5-12 (on the previous page), this prompt helps you keep your place and thus avoid input errors. After you enter the last value for the first series, the program prompts you for the name of the next series, then its values, and so on until the values of all the series and categories you specified have been entered.

The current version of the program works only with data sets that consist exclusively of positive numbers. If you try to enter a negative number, the program displays an error message instructing you to enter positive numbers only and then waits for you to reenter a positive value.

After you enter the entire data table, the program gives you a chance to save the table on disk as a data file:

```
Enter a filename for storing this data.
This will be your only chance to do so.
(Or press Enter if you do not wish to save data.) ==>
```

When you enter a filename (and optionally a disk and/or path specification), the program saves your data on disk. If you press Enter, the program retains the table in memory but does not save it on disk. (In this case, the data is lost when the program reads a new data table or when you stop the program.)

Once a data table is stored in memory, the program's charting functions become active. The main menu reappears, and you can choose to see the data table in the form of one of the three charts. Figures 5-14, 5-15, and 5-16 (on the following pages) show a column chart, a line chart, and a pie chart (representing 1986 sales) derived from the insurance sales table (a pie chart actually requires an extra step, which we will discuss shortly). The following pages take a closer look at how each of these charts are put together from the table.

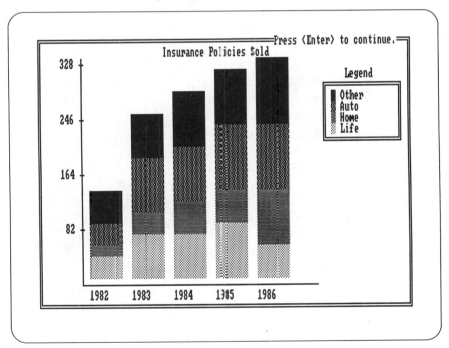

Figure 5-14. *A column chart based on the data table in Figure 5-12.*

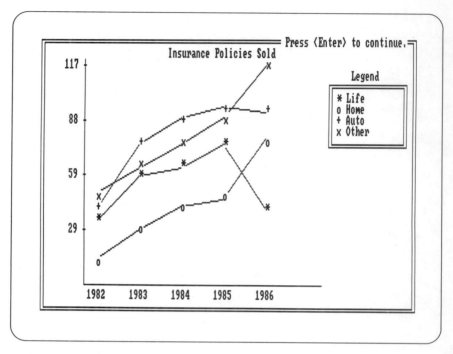

Figure 5-15. *A line chart based on the data table in Figure 5-12.*

In a column chart, the data values in a particular row (or series, to use the program's term) of your data table are represented by a given pattern in each column of the chart. The category names of your table (that is, the column headings) become labels along the horizontal axis of the chart. The series names (that is, the row labels) become the labels in the chart's legend. Since the program creates stacked column charts, the height of each chart column represents the total of all the numeric values in a given column of your data table.

In a line chart, each row of data becomes one line in the chart. Each point marker on a line represents the actual data value in a given row-column coordinate. Again, the category names of your table become labels along the chart's horizontal axis, and the series names become labels in the legend. The numbers along the vertical axis provide a scale for determining the value represented by each data point.

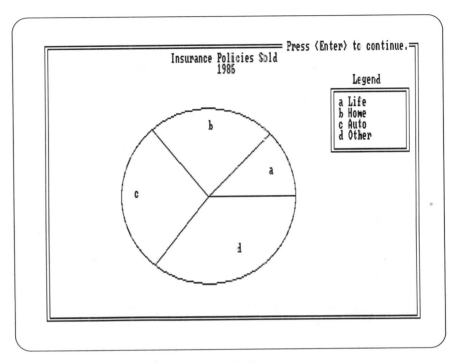

Figure 5-16. *A pie chart for the year 1986 based on the data table in Figure 5-12.*

Although a single column or line chart can display all the data categories in one chart, a pie chart can only model one category at a time. Before drawing a pie chart, the *QuickChart* program asks you which category of data you wish to use for the chart; the dialog for eliciting this information is shown in Figure 5-17 (on the next page). The program lists the category names of your data table. You simply enter a number corresponding to the category of data you want to chart. The category name becomes the subtitle on the pie chart, and the series names become labels in the chart's legend. Notice that the program identifies the wedges of the chart with lowercase letters, matching each wedge with a label displayed in the legend.

```
Select a column of data for the pie chart:
    1. 1982
    2. 1983
    3. 1984
    4. 1985
    5. 1986

      1 to  5 ==> 5
```

Figure 5-17.   *The dialog for selecting a year*
for a pie chart.

The *QuickChart* program never varies its method of translating
the series and categories of your data into the elements of a given
chart. However, you actually control the way the charts will appear
when you decide how to arrange your data. To produce a different set
of charts, you can always transpose the row-column orientation of the
data table itself.

For example, let's say we want to create a pie chart that represents
all the life insurance the agency sold during the five-year period. Each
wedge in the chart should represent one year of sales. To achieve this
effect, we have to reenter the data table into the program. The revised
table will contain five rows of data, representing the five years of sales;
and one column, representing life insurance sales. (The actual life insurance data is the same as before; only the row-column orientation is
new.) Figure 5-18 shows the data table after it has been stored in memory and Figure 5-19 shows the resulting pie chart.

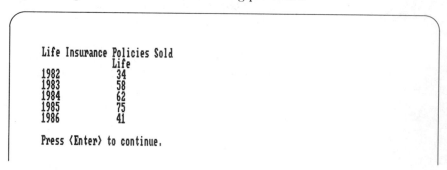

```
Life Insurance Policies Sold
                    Life
1982                 34
1983                 58
1984                 62
1985                 75
1986                 41

Press <Enter> to continue.
```

Figure 5-18.   *Transposing the life insurance*
information of Figure 5-12.

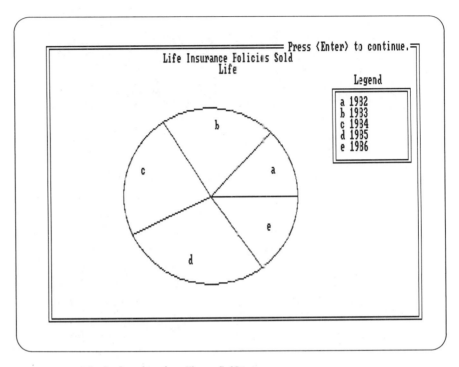

Figure 5-19. *A pie chart based on Figure 5-18.*

Reading data files

So far we've seen only the first of the three methods available for entering data into the program: manual data entry from the keyboard. The other two methods involve directing the program to read a data file. As we discussed, the program can read two different data-file formats: (1) files that the program has created itself, or (2) SYLK files.

When you choose the *Get data* option from the main menu and the *Data file* option from the *Get data* submenu, the program asks you to enter the name of the data file. The input dialog for this appears in Figure 5-20. You must specify a data file that *QuickChart* created during a previous session, or a file that matches its format exactly. When the file has been loaded you press the Enter key and the main menu reappears on the screen. Again, you can use any chart option to create charts from the data.

```
Enter the name of the file you want to read.
(Include the base name and the extension,
along with the drive designation if necessary.)
==) lifeins.dat


Reading data file...

Press <Enter> to continue.
```

Figure 5-20. *Reading a data file.*

QuickChart's data-file format

Figure 5-21 shows the data-file format that *QuickChart* uses. This example corresponds to the original insurance sales table in Figure 5-12. The format is simple. Here is a summary of its elements:

- The first line contains two integers separated by a comma. The first integer is the number of rows in the data table, and the second integer is the number of columns.

- The second line contains the title of the table, followed by the category names (that is, the column headings). Again, values are separated by commas.

- Subsequent lines represent rows of data. Each line begins with the series name (that is, the row label) and is followed by the numeric data values belonging to the row.

```
4,5
Insurance Policies Sold, 1982, 1983, 1984, 1985, 1986
Life,   34,  58,  62,  75,   41
Home,   14,  29,  42,  45,   78
Auto,   40,  75,  89,  95,   92
Other,  49,  62,  75,  89,   117
```

Figure 5-21. QuickChart's *data-file format.*

If you prefer, you can use a text editor or word processor to create a data file in this format. (The only stipulation is that you must

ORDER CARD

The Companion Disk to Microsoft® QuickBASIC contains all the programs found in Chapters 4–8. It makes a handy and valuable resource for anyone using this book. This disk is available only by ordering directly from Microsoft Press.

YES...please send me _____ copies of the Companion Disk to
Microsoft QuickBASIC at $15.95 each (U.S. funds only) .... $ _____

California residents add 6% sales tax ($.96) per disk; Washington State residents
add 8.1% sales tax ($1.29) per disk. .... $ _____

Postage and Handling Charges: $1.00 per disk (domestic orders) .... $ _____
$2.00 per disk (foreign orders). .... $ _____

TOTAL $ _____

Name _____

Address _____
(Please print)

City _____ State _____ Zip _____

Daytime Phone # : (____) _____

Payment: ☐ Check/Money Order   ☐ VISA   ☐ MasterCard   ☐ American Express
                                        (13 or 16 numbers)   (16 numbers)   (15 numbers)

Credit Card No. [ ]¹[ ]²[ ]³[ ]⁴[ ]⁵[ ]⁶[ ]⁷[ ]⁸[ ]⁹[ ]¹⁰[ ]¹¹[ ]¹²[ ]¹³[ ]¹⁴[ ]¹⁵[ ]¹⁶ Exp. Date _____

Signature _____

BUSINESS REPLY CARD

FIRST CLASS   PERMIT NO. 108   BELLEVUE, WA

POSTAGE WILL BE PAID BY ADDRESSEE

MICROSOFT PRESS
Attn: Microsoft QuickBASIC
       Companion Disk Offer
13221 SE 26th
Suite L
Bellevue, WA 98005

save your file as an ASCII text file, without any special word-processing control characters.) For example, you might use the QuickBASIC editor to enter (or edit) and save such a data file. As long as you follow the required format, the *QuickChart* program can read your data.

Alternatively, you can take advantage of the program's ability to read SYLK files. For example, Figure 5-22 shows a Microsoft Multiplan worksheet containing the insurance sales table. Saved as a SYLK file, this worksheet provides the same data table as in Figure 5-12.

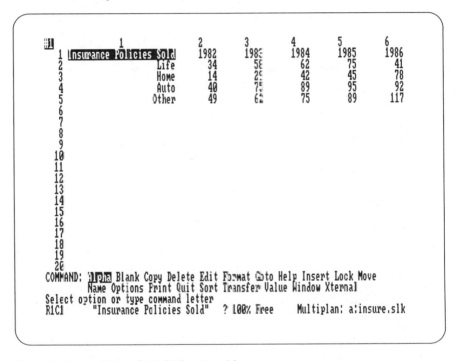

Figure 5-22. *A Microsoft Multiplan spreadsheet containing the same data table as Figure 5-12.*

QuickChart does impose some simple requirements on the format of the source worksheet:

- Cell R1C1 must contain the title of the table.
- Row 1 must contain the category names (column headings).
- Column 1 must contain the series names (row labels).
- The numeric data values must appear in the rectangular range of cells immediately below the category names and to the right of the series names.

After you prepare such a worksheet the steps for creating a SYLK file from Multiplan are:

1. Select the Transfer command and then choose the Options subcommand.

2. Select the Symbolic option so that the subsequent save operation results in a SYLK file.

3. Select the Transfer command again, and choose the Save subcommand.

Figure 5-23 displays the SYLK file that results from the insurance sales worksheet. We'll discuss the details of this format when we examine the subprogram responsible for reading it.

```
ID;PMP
F;DG0R10
F;W1 1 23
B;Y5;X6
C;Y1;X1;K"Insurance Policies Sold"
C;X2;K1982
C;X3;K1983
C;X4;K1984
C;X5;K1985
C;X6;K1986
C;Y2;X1;K"Life"
C;X2;K34
C;X3;K58
C;X4;K62
C;X5;K75
C;X6;K41
C;Y3;X1;K"Home"
C;X2;K14
C;X3;K29
C;X4;K42
C;X5;K45
C;X6;K78
C;Y4;X1;K"Auto"
C;X2;K40
C;X3;K75
C;X4;K89
C;X5;K95
C;X6;K92
C;Y5;X1;K"Other"
C;X2;K49
C;X3;K62
C;X4;K75
C;X5;K89
C;X6;K117
W;N1;A1 1;C7 0 7
E
```

Figure 5-23. *The SYLK file of the Multiplan spreadsheet in Figure 5-22.*

Back in the *QuickChart* program, you can simply choose the *Get data* option from the main menu and then the *SYLK file* option from the submenu to direct the program to read your SYLK file. The filename you enter at the prompt must have a *SLK* extension, for example:

```
POLICIES.SLK
```

Before attempting to read the numeric values stored in a data file or a SYLK file, *QuickChart* checks to be sure the file conforms to the expected format. If it does not, the program displays an appropriate message and then returns you to the main menu.

INSIDE THE *QUICKCHART* PROGRAM

Now that we have looked at the various options in *QuickChart,* we can begin studying the structure and algorithms of the program itself. The program is organized into some two dozen short subprograms, each of which is devoted to one small part of the action. We will examine the most significant subprograms in turn, concentrating on the repetition loops, arrays, and graphics statements in the program.

Figure 5-24 (on the next page) shows a structure chart of the *QuickChart* program. As we focus on the details of the subprograms, this tool will help us understand how the parts relate to the whole.

The *QuickChart* program uses both the ON ERROR GOTO and the RESUME NEXT commands, and these require some extra work from the compiler. To successfully compile the program, you must first switch on the *On Error* and *Resume Next* options in the dialog box of the Compile... command.

Before it can display the main menu, the program must first:

1. Declare a select group of arrays and variables as global.

2. Test the adapter card to see if it displays text-only images or graphics images.

3. Initialize several arrays and variables to their starting values.

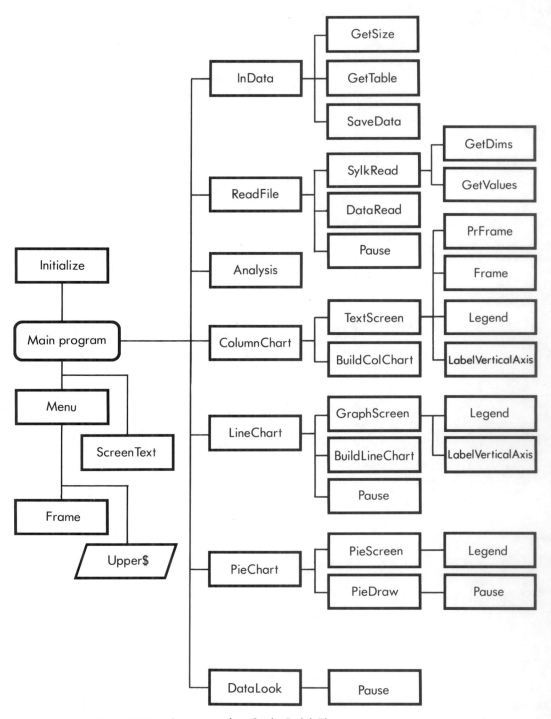

Figure 5-24. *A structure chart for the* QuickChart *program.*

The global variable declarations area

The *QuickChart* program (shown in Figure 5-25) begins with a series of global variable declarations. The program's primary variable is an array of strings, named *table$*. This array stores the current table of data from which charts will be created. Establishing the variable as an array of strings helps solve an otherwise inconvenient problem: A given array can hold only one type of data, but the program's data table consists of strings (series and category names) and numbers (the data values themselves). To store both strings and numeric values in a single array, the program temporarily converts the numbers in the data table to their string equivalents and stores them in *table$*. When the program needs the actual values, it converts them back to numbers. (The STR$ and VAL functions perform these conversion tasks.)

```
'   QCHART.BAS
'   Draws charts from input data or from data stored in disk files.

'   QuickChart uses several global variables:  table$ is a two-
'       dimensional array of string data values; dataExists% is a Boolean
'       value that indicates the presence of a valid table of data
'       in memory; rows% and columns% indicate the dimensions of table$;
'       largestValue, lineFactor, largestColTotal, and columnFactor are used
'       in the analysis of the data itself; columnChart$, prColumnChart$,
'       lineChart$, and pieChart$ are string arrays for use in the charts;
'       maxVals% is the maximum number of row and column values (set at 10
'       in this version of the program); menuChoices% is the number of
'       menu choices in the main menu; and noFile% is a Boolean value that
'       is true if the user requests a file that cannot be found.


'--------------------| Global Variable Declarations |--------------------

    COMMON SHARED table$(2), dataExists%, rows%, columns%, _
        largestValue, lineFactor, largestColTotal _
        columnFactor, columnChart$(1), prColumnChart$(1), _
        lineChart$(1), pieChart$(1), maxVals%, _
        menuChoices%, noFile%, file$

'   ---- Declare Boolean variables true% and false%
    COMMON SHARED true%, false%
    true% = -1
    false% = 0

'   ---- Initialize dataExists% to false (no data exists).
    dataExists% = false%

'   ---- Set the upper row and column limit to 10.
    maxVals% = 10
```

Figure 5-25. *The* QuickChart *program.*   *(more...)*

The *table$* array is used throughout the program, as are a few other variables that store miscellaneous items of information that the program requires. For convenience, the program declares this carefully selected group of arrays and variables as global. This means that the information they contain is available to any *QuickChart* subprogram. The declaration is in the form of a COMMON SHARED statement:

```
COMMON SHARED table$(2), dataExists%, rows%, columns%, _
    largestValue, lineFactor, largestColTotal, _
    columnFactor, columnChart$(1), prColumnChart$(1), _
    lineChart$(1), pieChart$(1), maxVals%, _
    menuChoices%, noFile%, file$
```

The following table explains how *QuickChart* uses these arrays and variables:

table$	The current array of data values, arranged in the format table$(rows, columns)
dataExists%	A Boolean variable that tells whether or not the program currently has a valid data table to work with.
rows%, columns%	The number of rows and columns (of numeric values only) contained in the current data table.
largestValue, lineFactor, largestColTotal, columnFactor	A set of statistical values and scaling factors, calculated from the current data table, used by later subprograms to determine x- and y-axes for line and column charts. (These values are all established by the *Analysis* subprogram.)
columnChart$, prColumnChart$, lineChart$, pieChart$	Arrays of characters that are used to represent the charting information currently in memory.
maxVals%	The maximum number of rows and columns allowed in the data table. (This value is set at 10 in the current version of the program.)
menuChoices%	The number of menu choices in the main menu (depends on the display adapter in your machine).
noFile%	A Boolean value that is true if a requested data file cannot be located on disk.
file$	The name of the current data file.

```
'    ---- Dimension the four dynamic arrays that will eventually contain
'         the current charting information.
     DIM columnChart$(maxVals%), prColumnChart$(maxVals%), _
         lineChart$(maxVals%), pieChart$(maxVals%)


'-------------------------| Function Area |-------------------------

'    ---- Read in and compile BASIC user-defined function.
     REM  $INCLUDE : 'UPPER.BAS'


'-------------------------| Main Program Area |-------------------------

     CALL ScreenTest

'    ---- Dimension the dynamic array mainMenu$ with the results of the
'         ScreenTest subprogram and the static array dataMenu$ with a fixed
'         value of five.
     DIM mainMenu$(menuChoices%), dataMenu$(5)

     CALL Initialize

'    ---- Read the two sets of menu choices from DATA lines.  The number
'         of choices in the main menu depends upon the value of menuChoices%
'         --that is, whether this is a text screen or a graphics screen.

     IF (menuChoices% = 3) THEN
         READ mainMenu$(1)
         READ mainMenu$(2)
         READ garbage$
         READ garbage$
         READ mainMenu$(3)
     ELSE
         FOR i% = 1 TO menuChoices%
             READ mainMenu$(i%)
         NEXT i%
     END IF

     FOR i% = 1 TO 5
         READ dataMenu$(i%)
     NEXT i%

'    ---- Display the menus, read the user's response, and act appropriately.
     WHILE choice% <> menuChoices%
         LOCATE 2,33: PRINT "Chart Program"
         CALL Menu(mainMenu$(), choice%)

'    ---- The Get Data submenu offers options for reading data.
         IF (choice% = 1) THEN
             LOCATE 2,27: PRINT "Get Data for Chart Program"
             CALL Menu(dataMenu$(), dataChoice%)
             IF (dataChoice% = 1) THEN
                 CALL InData
             ELSEIF (dataChoice% = 2) OR (dataChoice% = 3) THEN
                 CALL ReadFile(dataChoice%)
             ELSEIF (dataChoice% = 4) AND (dataExists%) THEN
                 CALL DataLook
             END IF
```

Figure 5-25. *The QuickChart program (continued).* *(more...)*

Notice that the five arrays in the global declaration are all dynamic arrays. Their names are followed in parentheses by the number of dimensions they will ultimately contain. They are defined by DIM or REDIM statements later in the program. The *table$* array is dynamic because its size may change each time a new data table is entered.

The one-dimensional arrays store a variety of ASCII characters used for building and identifying chart elements. The sizes of these arrays are all set at the value of *maxVals%*:

```
maxVals% = 10
DIM columnChart$(maxVals%), prColumnChart$(maxVals%), _
    lineChart$(maxVals%), pieChart$(maxVals%)
```

Thanks to this technique, you can change the size of all these arrays simply by revising the assignment statement that initializes *maxVals%*.

The global variable declaration area also declares the global Boolean variables *true%* and *false%*. These will be used throughout the program in logical operations. After this declaration, the Boolean variable *dataExists%* is initialized with a value of *false%* meaning that no charting information is resident in memory.

The main program area

The main program area of the *QuickChart* program begins by calling the *ScreenTest* subprogram.

The *ScreenTest* subprogram

The purpose of *ScreenTest* is to assign one of two values to the global variable *menuChoices%*—5 for a graphics display adapter or 3 for a monochrome (text-only) display adapter. The subprogram begins by assigning the variable a value of 5:

```
menuChoices% = 5
```

ScreenTest then issues a SCREEN 2 statement to switch the display into the high-resolution graphics mode. If the display hardware supports text characters only, this statement has no effect. The key to testing the status of the hardware comes next. The subprogram issues a graphics command that can only be performed on a graphics screen:

```
PSET(0,0)
```

```
'    ---- Once a valid set of data is available (dataExists% is true),
'         the charting options are available from the main menu.
        ELSEIF (choice% <> menuChoices%) AND (dataExists%) THEN
            CALL Analysis
            IF (choice% = 2) THEN
                CALL ColumnChart
            ELSEIF (choice% = 3) THEN
                CALL LineChart
            ELSE
                CALL PieChart
            END IF
        END IF
    WEND

    END

'---------------------------| Data Area |---------------------------

'    ---- This section contains all the DATA statements used by the
'         QuickChart program in the order in which they are called.

'    ---- ASCII codes for the column chart characters (called by Initialize).
    DATA 176, 177, 178, 219, 240, 19, 35, 88, 79, 72
'    ---- The line chart characters (called by Initialize).
    DATA *, o, +, x, v, @, #, z, -, =

'    ---- The menu choices (called by the Main Program).
    DATA get data, column chart, line chart, pie chart, quit
    DATA keyboard input, data file, SYLK file, look at data, cancel


'---------------------------| Subprogram Area |---------------------------

'    ---- Read in and compile BASIC subprograms.
    REM  $INCLUDE : 'FRAME.BAS'
    REM  $INCLUDE : 'PRFRAME.BAS'
    REM  $INCLUDE : 'MENU.BAS'


'    The Initialize subprogram reads text characters for the various
'        chart types from DATA statements located in the data area directly
'        below the main program area.

SUB Initialize STATIC
'    ---- Read the column chart characters.
    FOR i% = 1 TO maxVals%
        READ temp%
        columnChart$(i%) = CHR$(temp%)
    NEXT i%

'    ---- Read the line chart characters.
    FOR i% = 1 TO maxVals%
        READ lineChart$(i%)
    NEXT i%
```

Initialize

Figure 5-25. *The QuickChart program (continued).* *(more...)*

If the display hardware displays only text characters, QuickBASIC would normally respond to this graphics command by terminating the program and supplying an error message. Anticipating this event, *ScreenTest* cushions the PSET command inside an error trap found directly below the *ScreenTest* subprogram:

```
ON ERROR GOTO IfMono
PSET(0,0)
ON ERROR GOTO 0
```

An ON ERROR GOTO command tells QuickBASIC that if some subsequent statement results in an error that would terminate the program, QuickBASIC should instead branch to the error trap—that is, to the program line identified in the ON ERROR GOTO statement. In this case, the error trap is at the alphanumeric label *IfMono:*

```
IfMono:
    menuChoices% = 3
RESUME NEXT
```

The *IfMono* error trap assigns *menuChoices%* a new value of 3 (indicating that this is a text-only display device). Then the RESUME NEXT statement returns control of the program to the line following the command that caused the error. In the *ScreenTest* subprogram, this line is an ON ERROR GOTO 0 statement, which simply restores QuickBASIC's normal error checking. (From this point on any runtime error stops the program.) Finally, *ScreenTest* issues a SCREEN 0 command to return the display to text mode because the general design of the *QuickChart* program is to keep the SCREEN mode set to 0 (text-only) unless pie charting or line charting operations are being performed.

In summary, *ScreenTest* first sets *menuChoices%* = 5. It uses a SCREEN 2 statement to set up a graphics screen, and then uses a PSET graphics statement to test the display adapter. If the monitor can produce graphics images, the statement is correct, and *ScreenTest* leaves *menuChoices%* = 5; if it's a text-only display adapter, an error results. Since we don't want an error to stop the program, we include an ON ERROR GOTO error trap that sends QuickBASIC to an error-handling routine that sets *menuChoices%* = 3. After that, QuickBASIC returns to the *ScreenTest* subprogram, where error trapping is re-initialized and control is passed back to the main program.

```
'    ---- Create the arrays prColumnChart$ and pieChart$, for the
'         printable column chart and the pie chart, respectively.
     FOR i% = 1 TO maxVals%
         prColumnChart$(i%) = CHR$(64 + i%)
         pieChart$(i%) = CHR$(96 + i%)
     NEXT i%

END SUB


'    The ScreenTest subprogram determines whether we are working with
'         a graphics or text-only display adapter.  The variable menuChoices%
'         is the number of choices there will be in the main menu--3 if
'         this is a text screen; 5 if this is a graphics screen.

SUB ScreenTest STATIC
     menuChoices% = 5

'    ---- Try performing a graphics command in SCREEN 2.  If an error
'         results, the machine is using a text-only display adapter; if not,
'         a graphics display resides.  The error routine, IfMono, sets
'         menuChoices% to 3 if the routine is performed.

     SCREEN 2
     ON ERROR GOTO IfMono
     PSET(0,0)


     ON ERROR GOTO 0
     SCREEN 0
END SUB

'    ---- The error routine sets menuChoices% to 3 if this is a
'         text-only screen.
IfMono:
     menuChoices% = 3
RESUME NEXT


'    The ReadFile subprogram elicits the name of a sequential
'         data file or a SYLK file, checks to make sure the file
'         actually exists, opens the file, and calls either
'         DataRead or SylkRead to read the file.

SUB ReadFile(format%) STATIC
     PRINT: PRINT: PRINT
     PRINT "     Enter the name of the file you want to read."
     PRINT "     (Include the base name and the extension,"
     PRINT "     along with the drive designation if necessary.)"
     INPUT "     ==> ", file$
     PRINT: PRINT
     noFile% = false%

'    ---- Check to make sure the requested file actually exists.
     ON ERROR GOTO IfNoFile
         OPEN file$ FOR INPUT AS #1
     ON ERROR GOTO 0
```

ScreenTest

ReadFile

Figure 5-25. *The* QuickChart *program (continued).*   *(more...)*

After *ScreenTest* determines the display hardware, the main program section can establish the correct sizes of the global string arrays *mainMenu$* and *dataMenu$*. The following DIM statement does this:

```
DIM mainMenu$(menuChoices%), dataMenu$(5)
```

The *Initialize* subprogram

Next, the main program calls the *Initialize* subprogram to assign values to the four arrays associated with charting. *Initialize* consists of three FOR...NEXT loops, each of which works with one or two of the arrays. For example, the *columnChart$* array receives the ten ASCII graphics characters that the program uses to build column charts:

```
FOR i% = 1 TO maxVals%
    READ temp%
    columnChart$(i%) = CHR$(temp%)
NEXT i%
```

For each iteration of the loop, a READ statement reads one of the ASCII codes (stored in the DATA line in the DATA area) into the integer variable *temp%*. A subsequent assignment statement uses the CHR$ function to convert *temp%* to an ASCII character.

A similar process reads characters into the array *lineChart$*, which is used for identifying the data points of a line chart. Finally, a single FOR...NEXT loop stores the uppercase letters *A* to *J* in *prColumnChart$* (used for creating the printable column chart), and the lowercase letters *a* to *j* in *pieChart$* (used for identifying the wedges of a pie chart):

```
FOR i% = 1 TO maxVals%
    prColumnChart$(i%) = CHR$(64 + i%)
    pieChart$(i%) = CHR$(96 + i%)
NEXT i%
```

The formulas in this loop make use of the fact that the letters of the uppercase alphabet have ASCII codes that start at 65, and the lowercase alphabet begins at ASCII code 97.

The main program next assigns values to two string arrays, *mainMenu$* and *dataMenu$*. As their names suggest, these arrays store the two sets of menu choices that the program offers. Although the data menu always offers five choices, the main menu will have either three or five, depending on the capabilities of your display hardware. The main program uses the *menuChoices%* variable to determine how

```
'    ---- If it does exist, call the appropriate subroutine--to read
'         either a data file or a SYLK file.
    IF NOT noFile% THEN
        IF (format% = 2) THEN CALL DataRead ELSE Call SylkRead
        PRINT
        PRINT "    ";
        CALL Pause
        CLOSE
    END IF
END SUB


'    ---- The error routine displays an error message if a requested file
'         cannot be found.
IfNoFile:
    PRINT "    " FN Upper$(file$) " does not exist."
    PRINT
    PRINT "    ";
    CALL Pause
    noFile% = true%
RESUME NEXT


'    The Pause subprogram simply creates a pause in the action of the
'         program until the user presses the Enter key.  Although any key will
'         work, Enter is used because of its familiarity.

SUB Pause STATIC
    PRINT "Press <Enter> to continue.";
    character$ = ""
    WHILE character$ = ""
        character$ = INKEY$
    WEND
    CLS
END SUB


'    The InData subprogram accepts a set of data from the keyboard,
'         and optionally saves the data in a disk file.

SUB InData STATIC
'    ---- Find out the size of the data table.
    CALL GetSize

'    ---- The table$ array will hold the data.
    REDIM table$(rows%, columns%)

'    ---- Get the data.
    CALL GetTable

'    ---- Store the data in a disk file if the user so requests.
    PRINT "Enter a filename for storing this data "
    PRINT "This will be your only chance to do so "
    PRINT "(Or press Enter if you do not wish to save data.)";
    INPUT " ==> ", file$

    IF (LEN(file$) <> 0) THEN CALL SaveData
    CLS
    dataExists% = true%
END SUB
```

Pause

InData

Figure 5-25. *The* QuickChart *program (continued).*   *(more...)*

many options the main menu should have. Recall that the *ScreenTest* subprogram has already tested the display hardware connected to your machine to see if it can display graphic images on the screen or not. If graphic images can be displayed (meaning the attached display adapter and monitor support SCREEN 2), *menuChoices%* now holds a value of 5; if they cannot (meaning the attached hardware only supports SCREEN 0), *menuChoices%* now holds a value of 3. The significance of these numbers is apparent if you recall that the main menu contains five options for a graphics display, but only three options for a text-only display.

A sequence of READ statements assigns values to the *mainMenu$* array based on the value of *menuChoices*. Either a FOR...NEXT loop reads all five main menu options into the elements of *mainMenu$* or a sequence of READ statements assigns the first two DATA strings (*get data* and *column chart*) and the last one (*quit*) to the elements of *mainMenu$*. Since DATA values can only be read sequentially, the program simply reads (and then abandons) the third and fourth strings, employing a variable named *garbage$*.

The statements that work through this complicated task are:

```
IF (menuChoices% = 3) THEN
    READ mainMenu$(1)
    READ mainMenu$(2)
    READ garbage$
    READ garbage$
    READ mainMenu$(3)
ELSE
    FOR i% = 1 TO menuChoices%
        READ mainMenu$(i%)
    NEXT i%
END IF
    [other program lines]
DATA get data, column chart, line chart, pie chart, quit
```

The *dataMenu$* array always contains five elements, regardless of the display device:

```
FOR i% = 1 TO 5
    READ dataMenu$(i%)
NEXT i%
    [other program lines]
DATA keyboard input, data file, SYLK file, look at data, cancel
```

```
'    The GetSize subprogram finds out how many rows and columns of
'        numerical data the user wants to enter.

SUB GetSize STATIC
'    ---- Set Boolean variable ok% to false (-1)
    ok% = false%

    WHILE NOT ok%
        PRINT "How many rows of data? ";
        PRINT "(no more than" STR$(maxVals%);
        INPUT ") ==> ", rows%
        PRINT "How many data values in each row? ";
        PRINT "(no more than" STR$(maxVals%);
        INPUT ") ==> ", columns%
        PRINT
        ok% = (rows% > 0) AND (rows% <= maxVals%) _
            AND (columns% > 0) AND (columns% <= maxVals%)
    WEND
END SUB
```

GetSize

```
'    The GetTable subprogram accepts the user's data from the keyboard.
'        It stores series names in row 0, and category names in column 0.

SUB GetTable STATIC
    INPUT "Title of graph"; table$(0,0)
    PRINT
    PRINT "     Category names:"
    FOR i% = 1 to columns%
        PRINT TAB(20) "column" i%;
        INPUT "==> ", table$(0,i%)
    NEXT i%

    PRINT
    FOR i% = 1 to rows%
        PRINT "     Series name for row" i%;
        INPUT "==> ", table$(i%,0)
        PRINT "       Numeric data values:"
        FOR j% = 1 to columns%
            PRINT TAB(27) table$(0,j%);
            temp = -1
            WHILE (temp < 0)
                INPUT " ==> ", temp
                IF temp < 0 THEN
                    PRINT "          Redo. ";
                    PRINT "(Positive numbers only.) ";
                END IF
            WEND
            table$(i%,j%) = STR$(temp)
        NEXT j%
        PRINT
    NEXT i%
END SUB
```

GetTable

```
'    The SaveData subprogram saves a data set that has been entered from
'        the keyboard.
```

Figure 5-25. *The* QuickChart *program (continued).*   *(more...)*

181

Recall that the *Menu* subprogram makes a couple of changes in these strings before displaying them as menu options. Specifically, the routine converts the first character of each string to an uppercase letter and inserts a closing parenthesis to set off the first character from the rest of the string.

With all these initial tasks complete, the main program is ready to display the main menu on the screen. The main menu reappears after each charting activity. To produce this recurring menu, the program uses a WHILE...WEND loop:

```
WHILE choice% <> menuChoices%
    LOCATE 2,33: PRINT "Chart Program"
    CALL Menu(mainMenu$(), choice%)
        [carry out the user's charting request]
WEND
```

The *Menu* subprogram displays the main menu on the screen and passes back an integer—here stored in the variable *choice$*—representing the user's selection. Thus the WHILE...WEND loop repeatedly displays the main menu on the screen until the user selects the *Quit* option. (The number of this option is the same as the value of *menuChoices%*: 3 for a text-only screen or 5 for a graphics screen.)

The *Get data* menu options

For each iteration of the WHILE...WEND loop, the program's specific action depends on the value of *choice$*. If *choice$* equals 1, the user has selected the *Get data* option; in response, the program displays the corresponding submenu:

```
IF (choice% = 1) THEN
    LOCATE 2,27: PRINT "Get Data for Chart Program"
    CALL Menu(dataMenu$(), dataChoice%)
```

Again, the *Menu* subprogram passes back an integer representing the menu choice; this time the value is stored in the variable *dataChoice%*. If the value is 1, the user chose *Keyboard input,* and the *InData* subprogram is called; if the *dataChoice%* value is 2 or 3, the user chose the *Data file* option or the *SYLK file* option, and the *ReadFile* subprogram is called to read either a data file in *QuickChart's* own format or a data file in SYLK format; if the value of *dataChoice%* is 4, the user chose *Look at data,* and *DataLook* is called to display the data itself on the screen in table form.

```
SUB SaveData STATIC
    OPEN file$ FOR OUTPUT AS #1
    WRITE #1, rows%, columns%
    FOR i% = 0 to rows%
        FOR j% = 0 to columns%
            PRINT#1, table$(i%,j%);
            IF (j% < columns%) THEN PRINT #1, ", ";
        NEXT j%
        PRINT #1,
    NEXT i%
    CLOSE #1
END SUB


'   The DataRead subprogram reads a data file.  The routine expects the
'       file to match the format of files created by the InData routine.

SUB DataRead STATIC
        PRINT "    Reading data file..."
        INPUT #1, rows%, columns%
'   ---- The first two values must be integers in the range 1 to
'       maxVals%.  If not, the program cannot use the file.  (Note
'       that INPUT# assigns values of 0 to rows% and columns% if the
'       first two values in the file are nonnumeric.  This might
'       happen if the user inadvertently requested the reading of
'       a SYLK file by this routine.)

    ok% = (rows% > 0) AND (rows% <= maxVals%) _
        AND (columns% > 0) AND (columns% <= maxVals%)
    IF ok% THEN

'   ---- If rows% and columns% contain valid values, read the rest of
'       the data set into the table$ array.
        REDIM table$(rows%,columns%)

        FOR i% = 0 to rows%
            FOR j% = 0 to columns%
                INPUT #1, table$(i%,j%)
            NEXT j%
        NEXT i%

        dataExists% = true%

'    ---- Otherwise, display an error message, and set the global
'        Boolean variable dataExists% to false (C).
    ELSE
        PRINT
        PRINT "    Cannot use this data file."
        dataExists% = false%
    END IF
END SUB


'   The SylkRead subroutine reads a SYLK file.  The routine first checks
'       to make sure that the file contains a usable data set, and then
'       reads only the "K" fields in the "C" records.  Other records
'       and fields are ignored.

SUB SylkRead STATIC
    dataExists% = false%
    PRINT "    Reading SYLK file..."
    PRINT
```

SaveData

DataRead

SylkRead

Figure 5-25. *The QuickChart program (continued).*   *(more...)*

The chart options

If the user chooses one of the chart options on the main menu, *choice%* takes on a value of 2, 3, or 4. In this case, the program must check the value of the global Boolean variable *dataExists%* before processing the menu choice:

```
ELSEIF (choice% <> menuChoices%) AND (dataExists%) THEN
```

The subprograms that read a data table (either from the keyboard or from a disk file) assign a value of true to *dataExists%* if the input process is successful and a data set is actually available in memory. Only then does the program go ahead with the charting procedure: first calling *Analysis* (to compute scaling factors from the data) and then one of the actual charting subprograms, *ColumnChart*, *LineChart*, or *PieChart*.

Let's now review the highlights of *QuickChart's* major subprograms, starting with the data input routines.

Reading a data table: The *InData* and *ReadFile* subprograms

Whether the data table is to be read into memory from the keyboard or a previous data file, the program must first determine the size of the table and redimension the *table$* array to store the data. Although each data input subprogram has its own approach to this task, the *table$* array is always organized in the same way:

- The element *table$(0,0)* stores the title of the data table.

- The elements represented by *table$(i%,0)*—where *i%* ranges from 1 to the number of rows in the data table—contain the series names (that is, the row labels) of the table.

- The elements represented by *table$(0,j%)*—where *j%* ranges from 1 to the number of columns in the data table—contain the category names (that is, the column headings) of the table.

- The elements represented by *table$(i%,j%)*—where *i%* and *j%* range from 1 to the number of rows and columns, respectively—contain the numeric data values.

Notice that the program makes use of the "zeroth" elements of this two-dimensional array (since OPTION BASE 0 is the default, no statement is needed to signify this).

```
'    ---- The first record should be the ID record.  If not, the program
'         must assume that this is not a SYLK file.
     INPUT #1, sylkString$

     IF (LEFT$(sylkString$,4) = "ID;P") THEN
         CALL GetDims
         IF (rows% <= maxVals%) AND (rows% > 0) AND _
         (columns% <= maxVals%) THEN
             REDIM table$(rows%,columns%)
             CALL GetValues(ok%)
         ELSE
             ok% = false%
         END IF

         IF NOT ok% THEN
             PRINT "    This SYLK file does not match"
             PRINT "    the requirements of the program."
         ELSE
             dataExists% = true%
         END IF
     ELSE
         PRINT "    This is not a SYLK file."
     END IF
END SUB

'    The GetDims subprogram reads the "B" record of a SYLK file, which
'         indicates the row and column dimensions of the data set.

SUB GetDims STATIC
'    ---- Ignore all records until the "B" record is read.
     sylkString$ = ""
     WHILE (LEFT$(sylkString$,1) <> "B") AND (NOT EOF(1))
         INPUT #1, sylkString$
     WEND

'    ---- In the event that the file does not contain a "B" record
'         (i.e., EOF is true at this point), the program must reject the
'         data set as unusable.  Otherwise, the routine finds values for
'         rows% and columns% in the "Y" and "X" fields, respectively.

     IF NOT EOF(1) THEN
         yPosition% = INSTR(sylkString$,"Y") + 1
         xPosition% = INSTR(sylkString$,"X") + 1
         lengthY% = xPosition% - yPosition% - 2
         rows% = VAL(MID$(sylkString$,yPosition%,lengthY%)) - 1
         columns% = VAL(MID$(sylkString$,xPosition%)) - 1
     ELSE
         rows% = 0
     END IF
END SUB


'    The GetValues subprogram reads the data set from a SYLK file.
'         The routine stores the data in the global array variable
'         table$.  In the event that the SYLK file does not contain
'         all the necessary data to fill table$, the routine returns
'         a Boolean value of false in the parameter goodFile%.
```

`GetDims`

Figure 5-25. *The* QuickChart *program (continued).*   *(more...)*

The *InData* subprogram conducts the interactive dialog that elicits the entry of a data table from the keyboard. As shown in the *QuickChart* structure chart (Figure 5-24), *InData* calls three more subprograms: *GetSize,* to elicit the size of the table; *GetTable,* to elicit the data values themselves; and *SaveData,* to store the table in a data file if the user chooses that option.

The *GetSize* subprogram

GetSize uses a pair of INPUT statements to retrieve values for the global variables *rows%* and *columns%,* representing the dimensions of the data table. To ensure that both these variables contain valid values (from 1 to *maxVals%*), *GetSize* employs a WHILE...WEND loop that repeats the dialog, if necessary, until the dimensions are within the specified size:

```
ok% = false%
WHILE NOT ok%
    [prompt user for rows% and columns%]
    ok% = (rows% > 0) AND (rows% <= maxVals%) _
        AND (columns% > 0) AND (columns% <= maxVals%)
WEND
```

Notice how the Boolean variable *ok%* is used in this passage. It is initialized to a value of *false%* (0) to be sure the statements inside the WHILE...WEND loop are performed at least once. Then, at the bottom of the loop, an assignment statement evaluates a compound logical expression and assigns the result to *ok%.* If the entered values for *row%* and *column%* are within the valid range, a value of true is assigned to *ok%.* If the values are outside this range, a value of false is assigned to *ok%.* This logical expression ensures that *rows%* and *columns%* contain valid numeric values.

When control returns to the *InData* subprogram, a REDIM statement establishes the current size of the dynamic array, *table$*:

```
REDIM table$(rows%, columns%)
```

```
SUB GetValues (goodFile%) STATIC
'    ---- Set the Boolean variable goodFile% to true (-1).
     goodfile% = true%

     sylkString$ = ""
     count% = 0
     y% = 0
     x% = 0
     WHILE sylkString$ <> "E"
         INPUT #1, sylkString$

'    ---- Read only the "C" records; all others are irrelevant.
         IF (LEFT$(sylkString$,1) = "C") THEN
             count% = count% + 1
             kPosition% = INSTR(sylkString$,"K")
             sylkString$ = MID$(sylkString$,kPosition% + 1)
             stringLength% = LEN(sylkString$)

'    ---- The "K" field (always the last field in the "C" record)
'         may contain a string value enclosed in double quotes, or
'         a numeric value.  For rows% > 0 and columns% > 0, all values
'         should be numeric for the data set to be accepted as valid.
             IF (LEFT$(sylkString$,1) = CHR$(34)) THEN
                 table$(y%,x%) = MID$(sylkString$,2,stringLength% - 2)
                 IF (y% > 0) AND (x% > 0) THEN goodFile% = false%
             ELSE table$(y%,x%) = sylkString$
             END IF
             x% = x% + 1
             IF (x% > columns%) THEN
                 x% = 0
                 y% = y% + 1
             END IF
         END IF
     WEND

'    ---- If any of the "C" records did not contain "K" fields
'         (indicating that one or more worksheet cells were blank)
'         then some required data is missing; the data set must
'         therefore be rejected.

     IF (count% <> (rows% + 1) * (columns% + 1)) THEN goodFile% = false%
END SUB


'    The Analysis subprogram examines the data set, and computes
'         a set of statistical values required by the charting routines:
'             -- largestValue is the largest numeric value.
'             -- largestColTotal is the largest column total.
'             -- lineFactor is a scaling factor used for line charts.
'             -- columnFactor is a scaling factor used for column charts.
'         All four of these variables are global.

SUB Analysis STATIC
     linesInChartingArea% = 20
     largestValue = 0
     largestColTotal = 0
```

Figure 5-25.   *The* QuickChart *program (continued).*   *(more...)*

187

The *GetTable* subprogram

Next, the *GetTable* subprogram fills the *table$* array with data. *GetTable's* job is organized into several different loops. First a single FOR...NEXT loop elicits the category names:

```
FOR i% = 1 to columns%
    PRINT TAB(20) "column" i%;
    INPUT "==> ", table$(0,i%)
NEXT i%
```

Then a pair of nested loops moves through the rows one by one, eliciting a series name and then a series of numbers. Here is a summary of these loops:

```
FOR i% = 1 to rows%
    INPUT "==> ", table$(i%,0)
    FOR j% = 1 to columns%
        INPUT " ==> ", temp
  [make sure temp is a positive number]
        table$(i%,j%) = STR$(temp)
    NEXT j%
    PRINT
NEXT i%
```

Notice that the loop counters *i%* and *j%* become subscripts of the *table$* array; they ensure that each input value is stored in the correct array element. This passage demonstrates why a carefully structured FOR...NEXT loop is such an economical tool for working with an array. (Note that a nested loop structure must use a different variable name for the counter in each individual loop.)

Next, the *InData* subprogram elicits a filename, *file$*, for storing the data table on disk:

```
PRINT "Enter a filename for storing this data."
PRINT "This will be your only chance to do so."
PRINT "(Or press Enter if you do not wish to save data.)";
INPUT " ==> ", file$
IF (LEN(file$) <> 0) THEN CALL SaveData
```

```
        FOR j% = 1 to columns%
            temp = 0
            FOR i% = 1 to rows%
                IF (VAL(table$(i%,j%)) > largestValue) THEN _
                    largestValue = VAL(table$(i%,j%))
                temp = temp + VAL(table$(i%,j%))
            NEXT i%
            IF (temp > largestColTotal) THEN largestColTotal = temp
        NEXT j%

        columnFactor = linesInChartingArea% / largestColTotal
        lineFactor = linesInChartingArea% / largestValue
    END SUB


    '   The ColumnChart subprogram draws a column chart in two different
    '       versions.  The first version uses "text graphics" characters
    '       from the extended character set to produce an attractive
    '       chart on both text-only and graphics screens.  The second version
    '       uses characters from the standard character set (uppercase
    '       letters and punctuation characters) to produce a chart that
    '       can be sent to any printer with the Shift-PrtSc key combination.

    SUB ColumnChart STATIC
    '   ---- TextScreen and BuildColChart create the elements of the
    '       chart display.  The call to each routine requires a Boolean
    '       argument:  false% (or 0) results in the first version of the
    '       graph; true% (or -1) results in the printable version.

        CALL TextScreen(false%)
        CALL BuildColChart(false%)
        LOCATE 1,52: CALL Pause
        PRINT: PRINT: PRINT
        INPUT "    Do you want a printable version of this column chart"; yesno$
        CLS

        IF (LEFT$(FN Upper$(yesno$), 1) = "Y") THEN
            CALL TextScreen(true%)
            CALL BuildColChart(true%)
            ch$ = ""
            WHILE ch$ = "": ch$ = INKEY$: WEND
            CLS
        END IF
    END SUB


    '   The BuildColChart subprogram creates the "stacked" columns of the
    '       chart itself, and displays a category name below each column.

    SUB BuildColChart (printableChart%) STATIC
        columnWidth% = (48 \ columns%) - 2
        currentX% = 12
```

ColumnChart

BuildColChart

Figure 5-25. *The QuickChart program (continued).*   *(more . . .)*

If the user presses Enter without giving a filename, no file will be created on disk. If one is supplied, the *SaveData* subprogram then saves the data in a sequential data file under the name given. (A *sequential file* is designed to be read from beginning to end. In contrast, data in a *random-access file* can be accessed in any order. We will discuss both kinds of files further in Chapters 6 and 7.)

The *SaveData* subprogram

SaveData begins by opening the file specified in the *InData* subprogram for a write operation:

```
OPEN file$ FOR OUTPUT AS #1
```

If no pathname is specified when the user enters a name in response to the file prompt, a file is opened in the current working directory.

A WRITE# statement sends the values of *rows%* and *columns%* to the file. A pair of nested FOR ... NEXT loops then sends the data corresponding to the chart's rows and columns to *file$* via the PRINT# statement:

```
WRITE #1, rows%, columns%
FOR i% = 0 to rows%
    FOR j% = 0 to columns%
        PRINT#1, table$(i%,j%);
```

As in BASICA, the WRITE# statement puts a comma between each argument sent to an external file. It also surrounds strings with double quotation marks. The PRINT# statement does not include these delimiters in its transmissions to files, leaving that task to the program itself. If you examine *SaveData,* you will see how the routine delimits the data. (You might also want to review the resulting data-file format, an example of which appears in Figure 5-21.)

The *ReadFile* subprogram

The *ReadFile* subprogram reads an existing data file from disk—either a *QuickChart* file or a SYLK file. *ReadFile* first prompts the user for the name of the file and stores the filename in the global string variable *file$*. The following command opens the file for reading:

```
OPEN file$ FOR INPUT AS #1
```

```
      FOR j% = 1 to columns%
         LOCATE 24,currentX%
         PRINT LEFT$(table$(0,j%), columnWidth%);
         currentY% = 22
         FOR i% = 1 to rows%
            height% = CINT(columnFactor * VAL(table$(i%,j%)))
            FOR h% = 1 to height%
               LOCATE currentY%,currentX%
               IF (NOT printableChart%) THEN
                  PRINT STRING$(columnWidth%, columnChart$(i%));
               ELSE
                  PRINT STRING$(columnWidth%, prColumnChart$(i%));
               END IF
               currentY% = currentY% - 1
               IF (currentY% < 3) THEN currentY% = 3
            NEXT h%
         NEXT i%
         currentX% = currentX% + columnWidth% + 2
      NEXT j%
END SUB


'   The TextScreen subprogram prepares the screen for the column chart:
'      it displays the legend, creates the axes, displays numeric
'      values along the value axis, and draws a frame around the
'      perimeter of the screen.

SUB TextScreen (printableChart%) STATIC
      LOCATE 4,67: PRINT "Legend"
      IF (NOT printableChart%) THEN
         CALL Frame(1, 80, 1, 25)
         CALL Frame(62, 78, 5, rows% + 6)
         CALL Legend(columnChart$(), -1)
         verticalCh$ = CHR$(179)
         crossMark$ = CHR$(197)
         horizontalLine$ = STRING$(50, 196)
         origin$ = CHR$(192)
      ELSE
         CALL PrFrame(1, 80, 1, 25)
         CALL PrFrame(62, 78, 5, rows% + 6)
         CALL Legend(prColumnChart$(), -1)
         verticalCh$ = "|"
         crossMark$ = "+"
         horizontalLine$ = STRING$(50, "-")
         origin$ = "+"
      END IF

'   ---- Draw the axes.
      LOCATE 23,10: PRINT origin$
      LOCATE 23,11: PRINT horizontalLine$

      FOR i% = 22 to 3 STEP -1
         LOCATE i%,10
         IF ((i% + 2) MOD 5 = 0) THEN PRINT crossMark$ ELSE PRINT verticalCh$
      NEXT i%

      CALL LabelVerticalAxis(largestColTotal)
END SUB
```

Figure 5-25. *The* QuickChart *program (continued).*   (*more . . .*)

However, if the user enters a nonexistent filename and QuickBASIC can't find *file$* on the disk, this statement produces an error and terminates the program. To handle this possibility, *ReadFile* sets up the program's second error trap: If *file$* can't be found, control is sent to an error-handling routine directly below the *ReadFile* subprogram labeled *IfNoFile*:

```
ON ERROR GOTO IfNoFile
    OPEN file$ FOR INPUT AS #1
ON ERROR GOTO 0
```

The routine at IfNoFile displays an error message on the screen:

```
IfNoFile:
PRINT "    " FN Upper$(file$) " does not exist."
```

After the message is displayed, the *Pause* subprogram is called to give the user a chance to read it. The *Pause* routine simply displays the *Press <Enter> to continue* message on the screen and waits for the user to press Enter (or any other key) before allowing the program to continue. Then, just before sending control back to the *ReadFile* subprogram, the routine assigns a value of *true%* (−1) to the Boolean variable *noFile%*:

```
    noFile% = true%
RESUME NEXT
```

If *noFile%* is true, the *ReadFile* subprogram takes no further action. However, if the variable is false (the user-input file *does* exist), *ReadFile* calls either *DataRead,* to read a data file, or *SylkRead,* to read a SYLK file. The decision of which subprogram call to make is determined by the *format%* parameter, a value sent to *ReadFile* by the main program. If *format%* equals 2, the *DataRead* subprogram is called; if *format%* does not equal 2, the *SylkRead* subprogram is called.

After the file is read into the *table$* array, *ReadFile* calls the *Pause* subprogram again and issues a CLOSE command to close the file.

The *DataRead* subprogram

The *DataRead* subprogram, called by *ReadFile* if the user-entered data-file name is on disk and is in the *QuickChart* data-file format, reads the data file into the *table$* array. It begins by reading the first two values stored in the file, which specify the size of the table:

```
INPUT #1, rows%, columns%
```

```
'    The Legend subprogram creates the legend for all three chart types.
'        Legend has two parameters:  symbols$ is an array of graphics
'        characters that represent the elements in the graph; and
'        backward% is a Boolean value that indicates whether the legend
'        strings should be displayed from bottom to top (true%) or from
'        top to bottom (false%).

SUB Legend (symbols$(1),backward%) STATIC
    FOR i% = 1 to rows%
        IF (backward%) THEN LOCATE rows% + 6 - i%, 64 ELSE LOCATE 5 + i%, 64
        PRINT symbols$(i%) " " LEFT$(table$(i%,0),11)
    NEXT i%

    titleLength% = LEN(table$(0,0))
    LOCATE 2,(80 - titleLength%) \ 2: PRINT table$(0,0);
END SUB
```

```
'    The LabelVerticalAxis subprogram displays an array of numbers along
'        the vertical value axis for column charts and line charts.
'        LabelVerticalAxis has one parameter, axisMax, which contains the
'        largest numeric value represented on the chart.

SUB LabelVerticalAxis (axisMax) STATIC
    FOR i% = 1 to 4
        LOCATE (23 - (i% * 5)), 2
        IF (axisMax > 9999999) THEN
            PRINT USING "##.#^^^^"; axisMax * (0.25 * i%);
        ELSE
            PRINT USING "#######"; axisMax * (0.25 * i%);
        END IF
    NEXT i%
END SUB
```

```
'    The LineChart subprogram draws a line chart on a graphics screen
'        defined by the QuickBASIC statement SCREEN 2.

SUB LineChart STATIC
    SCREEN 2
    CALL GraphScreen
    CALL BuildLineChart
    LOCATE 1,52: PRINT " ";
    CALL Pause
    SCREEN 0
END SUB
```

```
'    The BuildLineChart subprogram draws the lines of a line chart and
'        marks the actual data points with character symbols.  The
'        key commands here are VIEW and WINDOW which establish a new
'        coordinate system and simplify use of the LINE command.

SUB BuildLineChart STATIC
'    ---- Establish view window.
    VIEW (80,20)-(479,180)
    WINDOW (0,0)-(50,INT(largestValue))
```

Legend

LabelVerticalAxis

LineChart

BuildLineChart

Figure 5-25. *The* QuickChart *program (continued).*   *(more...)*

193

After validating these dimensions, *DataRead* issues a REDIM command to establish the new size of the *table$* array. Each value is then read into *table$* by a pair of nested FOR ... NEXT loops:

```
FOR i% = 0 to rows%
    FOR j% = 0 to columns%
        INPUT #1, table$(i%, j%)
    NEXT j%
NEXT i%
```

If the file is not in the proper format, an error message is printed and the global Boolean variable *dataExists%* is set to *false%* (meaning that the *table$* array does not contain a valid set of charting data).

The *SylkRead* subprogram

If the user specifies a SYLK file, program control branches to the *SylkRead* subprogram. A SYLK file created by Multiplan contains extensive information about a worksheet's format, structure, data, and formulas. Since many programs that read such a file are not always interested in all this information, the SYLK file-format is structured to let a program pick and choose the information it requires and ignore the rest.

If you look back at Figure 5-23, you will see that a SYLK file consists of many one-line records. Each record begins with a letter that identifies the kind of information it stores. The *QuickChart* program needs only four kinds of SYLK records:

- The ID record, which is always the first record in a SYLK file. (If *QuickChart* does not find this record, the program assumes that the current file is not really a SYLK file.)

- The B record, which contains the number of rows and columns in the source worksheet (each SYLK file has only one B record).

- The C records, which supply the actual data values from the cells of the source worksheet (a SYLK file typically has many C records).

- The E record, which always marks the end of a SYLK file.

These records are in turn divided into fields; the various field types are also identified by letters. Inside the one-line records, each field is separated from the next by a semicolon.

```
'    ---- Draw the line chart.
     between% = 48 \ columns%
     FOR i% = 1 to rows%
         PSET(2, VAL(table$(i%,1)))
         FOR j% = 2 to columns%
             LINE -(between% * (j%-1) + 2, VAL(table$(i%,j%)))
         NEXT j%
     NEXT i%

'    ---- Once the lines have been drawn, the symbols in the lineChart$
'         array are displayed to represent the actual data points.
'         Since these are text symbols, LOCATE and PRINT are used to
'         display them, rather than any of the graphics commands.

     FOR j% = 1 to columns%
         LOCATE 24, (11 + (between%*(j%-1)))
         PRINT LEFT$(table$(0,j%), between%-2);
         FOR i% = 1 to rows%
             yPosition% = 23 - CINT(lineFactor * VAL(table$(i%,j%)))
             LOCATE yPosition%, 13 + between% * (j%-1)
             PRINT LineChart$(i%)
         NEXT i%
     NEXT j%
END SUB


'   The GraphScreen subprogram prepares the screen for the line chart,
'        displaying the legend, drawing the axes, and placing a frame
'        around the perimeter of the screen.

SUB GraphScreen STATIC
'    ---- Produce frame.
     LINE (0,2)-(639,199),,B
     LINE (5,4)-(634,197),,B

     LOCATE 4,67: PRINT "Legend"
     LINE (490,34)-STEP(133,rows% * 8 + 13),,B
     LINE (495,36)-STEP(123,rows% * 8 + 9),,B
     CALL Legend(LineChart$(), 0)

     LINE (74,16)-(74,180)
     LINE -(479,180)

     FOR y% = 20 TO 140 STEP 40
         LINE (72,y%)-(76,y%)
     NEXT y%
     CALL LabelVerticalAxis(largestValue)
END SUB


'   The PieChart subprogram draws a pie chart from the selected column
'        of data.

SUB PieChart STATIC
'    ---- If the current data set (in the table$ array) contains
'         more than one column, allow the user to select a column
'         for the pie chart.
```

GraphScreen

PieChart

Figure 5-25. *The* QuickChart *program (continued).* (*more . . .*)

The B record contains a Y field, which supplies the number of rows in the worksheet, and an X field, which gives the number of columns. For example:

```
B;Y5;X6
```

Each C record includes a K field, which stores the data value from the corresponding worksheet cell. String values are enclosed in quotes in the K field, and numeric values follow after the K. For example:

```
C;Y1;X1;K"Insurance Policies Sold"
C;X2;K1982
```

These are really all the SYLK characteristics that the *SylkRead* subprogram needs to know. The routine begins by reading the first record of the file into the *sylkString$* variable:

```
INPUT #1, sylkString$
```

The reading continues only if this first string contains the appropriate SYLK file identification header, "ID;P":

```
IF (LEFT$(sylkString$,4) = "ID;P") THEN
    [continue reading and checking the SYLK file]
ELSE
    PRINT "    This is not a SYLK file."
END IF
```

The *GetDims* and *GetValues* subprograms

If the file identification is correct (*ID;P*), *SylkRead* calls two subprograms to continue the read process: *GetDims* looks for the B record and reads the dimensions of the table from it; and *GetValues* reads data values from all the subsequent C records.

Each routine uses a WHILE...WEND loop to read one record after another, while ignoring any records that do not contain relevant information. For example, *GetDims* uses the following loop to read the file, line by line, until it encounters the B record.

```
WHILE (LEFT$(sylkString$,1) <> "B") AND (NOT EOF(1))
    INPUT #1, sylkString$
WEND
```

Both subprograms read items of information from particular fields of the record. Since the one-line records are always read as string values, this task requires the help of a variety of QuickBASIC's string-handling functions, including INSTR, MID$, LEN, VAL, and CHR$.

```
        IF (columns% > 1) THEN
            PRINT: PRINT: PRINT
            PRINT "    Select a column of data for the pie chart:"
            PRINT
            FOR i% = 1 TO columns%
                PRINT TAB(8) STR$(i%) ". " table$(0,i%)
            NEXT i%
            PRINT
            columnToBePie% = 0
            WHILE (columnToBePie% < 1) OR (columnToBePie% > columns%)
                PRINT TAB(12) "1 to " columns%;
                INPUT "==> ", columnToBePie%
            WEND
        ELSE
            columnToBePie% = 1
        END IF

        CLS
        CALL PieScreen(columnToBePie%)
        CALL PieDraw(columnToBePie%)
    END SUB


    '   The PieScreen subprogram prepares the pie chart screen by drawing a
    '       frame, displaying the legend, and creating the title and subtitle
    '       portions of the chart.

    SUB PieScreen(columnToBePie%) STATIC
        SCREEN 2
        LINE (0,2)-(639,199),,B
        LINE (5,4)-(634,197),,B

        LOCATE 4,67: PRINT "Legend"
        LINE (490, 34)-STEP(133, rows% * 8 + 13),,B
        LINE (495, 36)-STEP(123, rows% * 8 + 9),,B
        CALL Legend(pieChart$(), 0)

        subTitleLength% = LEN(table$(0, columnToBePie%))
        LOCATE 3, ((80 - subTitleLength%)\ 2)
        PRINT table$(0, columnToBePie%);
    END SUB


    '   The PieDraw subprogram draws the pie chart itself.

    SUB PieDraw(targetColumn%) STATIC
    '   ---- Calculate columnTotal, the total of the column of numeric values.
        columnTotal = 0
        FOR i% = 1 to rows%
            columnTotal = columnTotal + _
                VAL(table$(i%,targetColumn%))
        NEXT i%

    '   ---- Assign constant values for the center coordinates, the
    '        radius, the starting point, and the value of 2 * pi.
    '        (Note that the variables start and neg2Pie receive negative
    '        values so that CIRCLE will draw the sides of each wedge.)
```

PieScreen

PieDraw

Figure 5-25. *The* QuickChart *program (continued).*   *(more...)*

As you have seen, the data input routines (*InData*, *DataRead*, and *SylkRead*) all assign a value of *true%* to the global variable *dataExists%* when a valid table of data has been stored in the *table$* array. As soon as *dataExists%* is true, you can begin using the charting subprograms to draw charts from the available data.

When you select one of the valid charting options from the main menu, the main program first calls the *Analysis* subprogram which computes some essential values based on the data table.

The *Analysis* subprogram

To draw charts to scale in the space available on the screen, *QuickChart* needs to calculate a small set of statistical values from the data table; this is handled by the *Analysis* subprogram.

For column charts and line charts, the program allocates 20 lines on the screen in which to display the elements of the charts. Given the current data table, the program has to then determine the range of numeric values that those 20 lines will represent. Furthermore, the program needs a scaling factor that will successfully translate each individual data value into the height (for a column chart) or position (for a line chart) that will accurately represent the value within the chart area of 20 screen lines.

In a line chart, this scaling factor is based on the largest numeric value in the data set. The 20 screen lines then are proportioned to represent values from 0 to this largest number.

In a column chart, the scaling factor is based on the largest column total in the data set. Determining this value requires adding each column of data and identifying the largest total. The 20 screen lines are proportioned to represent values from 0 to this total.

To meet these requirements, *Analysis* first calculates the values of four global variables:

- *largestValue* is the largest numeric value in the data table.

- *largestColTotal* is the largest column total in the data table.

- *lineFactor* is the scaling factor for line charts, calculated from *largestValue*.

- *columnFactor* is the scaling factor for column charts, calculated from *largestColTotal*.

```
        xCenter% = 279
        yCenter% = 110
        radius% = 150
        start = -0.00001
        neg2Pie = -3.141592 * 2

'       ---- Use the CIRCLE command to draw the wedges of the pie
'           chart, each wedge representing one of the values in
'           the selected column.

        FOR i% = 1 to rows%
            portion = (VAL(table$(i%, targetColumn%)) _
               / columnTotal) * neg2Pie
            IF (i% < rows%) THEN wedge = start + portion _
               ELSE wedge = neg2Pie
            CIRCLE (xCenter%, yCenter%), radius%,, start, wedge

'       ---- Calculate the coordinates for positioning an identifying
'           symbol inside each wedge; display the symbol.
            angle = -1 * (start + (portion / 2))
            rowLocation% = INT(-6 * SIN(angle) + 14.5)
            columnLocation% = INT(15 * COS(angle) + 35.5)
            LOCATE rowLocation%, columnLocation%: PRINT pieChart$(i%);
            start = wedge
        NEXT i%

        LOCATE 1, 52: PRINT " ";
        CALL Pause
        SCREEN 0
    END SUB


'       The DataLook subprogram displays the current data set (in the table$
'           array) on the screen.  This is the fourth option in the
'           Get Data submenu.

    SUB DataLook STATIC
        PRINT
        FOR i% = 0 to rows%
            FOR j% = 0 to columns%
                PRINT TAB((j% * 15) + 1) table$(i%, j%);
            NEXT j%
            PRINT
        NEXT i%
        PRINT
        CALL Pause
    END SUB
```

DataLook

Figure 5-25. *The* QuickChart *program (continued).*

LargestValue and *largestColTotal* are determined within a pair of nested
FOR...NEXT loops. First, the routine initializes *linesInChartingArea%*
to 20 and both *largestValue* and *largestColTotal* to 0. Then the
FOR...NEXT loops move column by column through the data table
and row by row through each column, searching for the largest individual value and column sum in the table.

The IF statement inside the inner loop compares each new data value with the current value of *largestValue.* Whenever a number is found that is greater than *largestValue,* that number becomes the new value of *largestValue.*

An assignment statement, also inside the inner loop, accumulates the total of a given column in the variable *temp.* Each time the inner loop counts through an entire column, an IF statement (located just outside the inner loop) compares *temp* with the current value of *largestColTotal.* A column total that is larger than *largestColTotal* becomes the new value of *largestColTotal.*

Finally, when the looping is complete, the following statements compute the two required scaling factors:

```
columnFactor = linesInChartingArea% / largestColTotal
lineFactor = linesInChartingArea% / largestValue
```

Since the charting area is to be 20 lines long, the program can multiply any individual data value by *lineFactor* to find the screen position that corresponds to the value in the line chart. Likewise, multiplying a given value by *columnFactor* yields the correct height that corresponds to that value in the column chart.

The *ColumnChart* subprogram

The *ColumnChart* subprogram facilitates the drawing of the two different versions of the column chart. The first is made up of graphics characters from the IBM extended character set, and the second— produced only at the user's request—consists of printable characters from the standard character set that can be sent to any printer.

To build both versions, *ColumnChart* simply makes calls to two subsidiary subprograms named *TextScreen* and *BuildColChart.* Both take a single Boolean argument. A value of *false%* produces the extended character set version:

```
CALL TextScreen(false%)
CALL BuildColChart(false%)
```

A value of *true%* results in the printable version:

```
CALL TextScreen(true%)
CALL BuildColChart(true%)
```

The *TextScreen* subprogram

The *TextScreen* subprogram supplies all the screen elements except those for the chart itself: It draws the axes, prints the numeric values along the vertical axis, prepares the legend, and draws a frame around the entire screen.

To perform all these tasks, the routine calls on several small subprograms. The *Legend* subprogram places the chart's legend and title on the screen. The *LabelVerticalAxis* subprogram computes and displays the numbers along the value axis. (Both of these subprograms will be used again to prepare screen elements for the other chart types.)

TextScreen calls either the *Frame* or the *PrFrame* subprogram to draw a frame around the chart. These routines, which we discussed in Chapter 2, are both read into the program as $INCLUDE files at the beginning of the subprogram section.

The *BuildColChart* subprogram

The *BuildColChart* routine uses three nested FOR...NEXT loops to draw the stacked columns on the screen. During the course of the looping, the program uses two variables, *currentX%* and *currentY%*, to keep track of the constantly changing text-screen addresses where individual graphics characters are displayed. (The program uses these addresses as the arguments of the LOCATE command.) The variable *currentX%* is the current horizontal screen address, which starts at 12 for the position of the left-most column of the chart:

```
currentX% = 12
```

The current vertical screen address, *currentY%*, locates the base of each new chart column at the bottom of the chart area, row 22:

```
currentY% = 22
```

After each element of a given column is displayed on the screen, the program decrements the vertical address by 1, to move upward by one character position on the screen:

```
currentY% = currentY% - 1
```

Another important value that the subprogram calculates is *columnWidth%*, the number of characters in the width of each chart column. This value depends on the number of columns to be drawn. Given that the designated chart area is 48 characters wide, the formula for determining the width of each column is:

```
columnWidth% = (48 \ columns%) - 2
```

So, for example, if the data table has four columns of values, each column in the chart is 10 characters wide. After each column is drawn, the program calculates the horizontal screen address of the next column with the formula:

```
currentX% = currentX% + columnWidth% + 2
```

Notice that this formula leaves two spaces between each column.

Let's look at the action of the three nested loops in *BuildColChart*. The outer loop produces each chart column, from left to right. It begins by displaying a category name as a label at the bottom of each chart column. The loop reads each category name from the first row of the table$ array:

```
FOR j% = 1 to columns%
    LOCATE 24,currentX%
    PRINT LEFT$(table(0,j%), columnWidth%);
```

If any category name is too long to be displayed in its entirety, the LEFT$ function displays only the first *columnWidth%* characters.

For each chart column, the middle loop draws the stacked sections, from bottom to top. The height in characters of each section is calculated from the actual *table$* array value that the section is designed to represent; here is where the scaling factor *columnFactor* (computed by the *Analysis* subprogram) comes into play:

```
FOR i% = 1 to rows%
    height% = CINT(columnFactor * VAL(table$(i%,j%)))
```

Notice that the CINT function rounds the product of *columnFactor* and the selected *table$* array value to the nearest integer.

Finally, the inner loop moves row by row up the calculated column height and prints an appropriate width of chart characters—either IBM extended character set graphic characters from the *columnChart$* array or standard character set printable characters from the *prColumnChart$* array—at each vertical position:

```
FOR h% = 1 to height%
    LOCATE currentY%,currentX%
    IF (NOT printableChart%) THEN
        PRINT STRING$(columnWidth%, columnChart$(i%));
    ELSE
        PRINT STRING$(columnWidth%, prColumnChart$(i%));
    END IF
```

The Boolean variable *printableChart%* determines which characters make up the chart; it contains the value that was originally passed as an argument to *BuildColChart*.

BuildColChart represents yet another demonstration of the power and economy of nested FOR…NEXT loops. In fewer than two dozen lines of code, this routine arranges hundreds of screen characters to create an attractive and accurately scaled column chart.

Next we will see how the program creates line charts.

The *LineChart* subprogram

The *LineChart* routine begins by switching into the SCREEN 2 (graphics) display mode, and then calls two subprograms that actually do the charting: *GraphScreen* and *BuildLineChart*.

The *GraphScreen* and *BuildLineChart* subprograms

The *GraphScreen* subprogram prepares the display screen for the line chart. It creates the legend (with a call to the *Legend* subprogram), draws the axes, and displays the numeric values along the vertical axis (with a call to *LabelVerticalAxis*).

GraphScreen produces the frame around the chart area using pairs of LINE statements rather than the *Frame* subprogram. For example, the routine produces the double-line frame around the entire perimeter of the screen with the statements:

```
LINE (0,2)-(639,199),,B
LINE (5,4)-(634,197),,B
```

The *BuildLineChart* subprogram draws the lines. The routine begins by issuing VIEW and WINDOW statements, to reorient the system of pixel addresses into an arrangement that is better suited to the task of drawing the lines. First, the VIEW command establishes the designated chart area:

```
VIEW (80,20)-(479,180)
```

Then, within this area, the WINDOW command sets a new system of pixel addresses, starting with (0,0) at the lower-left corner of the chart area designated by the VIEW statement:

```
WINDOW (0,0)-(50,INT(largestValue))
```

Notice that the vertical coordinate of the upper-right corner pixel is taken as *largestValue*. This, you will recall, is the largest numeric value in the data table, as determined by the *Analysis* subprogram. Given this new coordinate system, the program then can plot the numeric values in the *table$* array directly as vertical addresses in the chart area; no further scale calculations are required.

The routine performs one more preliminary task before starting the chart. An assignment statement computes the number of spaces between each plotted point on the chart; the variable *between%* receives the value:

```
between% = 48 \ columns%
```

Finally, a pair of nested FOR...NEXT loops draws the lines of the chart. The outer loop moves row by row through the data table and draws a line for each series of data. The initial task inside this loop is to plot the first data value of each row, using the PSET statement:

```
FOR i% = 1 to rows%
    PSET (2, VAL(table$(i%,1)))
```

The inner loop then draws a line segment from that first point to the point that represents each subsequent value in a given row of data:

```
FOR j% = 2 to columns%
    LINE -(between% * (j%-1) + 2, VAL(table$(i%,j%)))
```

Recall from the beginning of this chapter that this particular LINE syntax draws a line from the last plotted point to the designated address. Here, the horizontal address coordinate is calculated from *between%*; the vertical address coordinate is simply the data value itself.

BuildLineChart's last task is to supply text characters (from the array *lineChart$*) to mark the actual data points. A pair of nested loops use the LOCATE and PRINT commands to display the characters and the scaling factor *lineFactor* to compute the vertical screen positions.

The final charting routine is the *PieChart* subprogram.

The *PieChart* subprogram

PieChart begins by asking the user to select the data column from which it will create the pie chart. The routine elicits a number from 1 to the number of columns in the data table and stores the input value in the variable *columnToBePie%*. *PieChart* then sends this value as an argument to each of two subsidiary subprograms—*PieScreen*, which prepares the chart screen; and *PieDraw*, which draws the chart.

The *PieScreen* subprogram

The *PieScreen* subprogram performs the usual preliminaries: switching the display into the SCREEN 2 graphics mode; drawing a frame around the perimeter of the screen with LINE statements; producing the legend with a call to the *Legend* subprogram; and displaying the title of the chart.

The *PieDraw* subprogram

The *PieDraw* subprogram receives the data table column number in the *targetColumn%* parameter:

```
SUB PieDraw(targetColumn%) STATIC
```

At the beginning of the routine a FOR...NEXT loop totals the values stored in *targetColumn%* column; the total is accumulated in the *columnTotal* variable:

```
columnTotal = 0
FOR i% = 1 to rows%
    columnTotal = columnTotal + _
        VAL(table$(i%, targetColumn%))
NEXT i%
```

Next, *PieDraw* initializes a set of variables to use for drawing the pie chart. The center coordinates and the radius of the circle are assigned to the *xCenter%*, *yCenter%*, and *radius%* variables:

```
xCenter% = 279
yCenter% = 110
radius% = 150
```

The variable *start* receives the starting angle of the pie's first wedge. In principle, this value should be 0 radians; but since angles must be expressed as negative radian values in order for CIRCLE to draw the sides of the wedges, *start* actually uses a small negative number as its initial value:

```
start = -0.00001
```

Finally, the variable *neg2Pie* receives the value of -2π, the angle that represents the entire circle:

```
neg2Pie = -3.141592 * 2
```

A single FOR...NEXT loop moves one by one through the row data values in the target column and draws a wedge of the pie that corresponds to each value. At the top of the loop the program calculates the absolute angle of the current wedge; this angle is assigned to the *portion* variable:

```
FOR i% = 1 to rows%
    portion = (VAL(table$(i%, targetColumn%)) _
        / columnTotal) * neg2Pie
```

This calculation divides the current data value by the total of all the values and multiplies the result by *neg2Pie*.

Inside the circle, the relative ending angle of the current wedge is normally the sum of *start* and *portion*; however, the final wedge should end at precisely *neg2pie*:

```
IF (i% < rows%) THEN wedge = start + portion _
    ELSE wedge = neg2Pie
```

Given the relative starting and ending angles, *start* and *wedge,* the program is ready to draw the current wedge:

```
CIRCLE (xCenter%, yCenter%), radius%,, start, wedge
```

The next task is to position a text character (from the *PieChart$* array) in the center of the wedge. This character will match one of the characters in the legend and thus identify the value that the wedge represents. Oddly enough, calculating the proper screen position for this character is probably the most difficult conceptual task in the entire program.

In effect, the program must define a second circumference around which to display the identification characters. The addresses for these text characters will appear as vertical and horizontal text screen coordinates in a LOCATE statement. In this context the program cannot use the CIRCLE command; instead the text address coordinates, *rowLocation%* and *columnLocation%,* are calculated with the SIN and COS functions, respectively:

```
angle = -1 * (start + (portion / 2))
rowLocation% = INT(-6 * SIN(angle) + 14.5)
columnLocation% = INT(15 * COS(angle) + 35.5)
LOCATE rowLocation%, columnLocation%: PRINT pieChart$(i%);
```

You can see what a powerful statement CIRCLE is, since it condenses all these equations into one line.

Finally, before attempting to draw the next wedge (in the subsequent loop iteration), the program must assign a new value to the *start* variable:

```
start = wedge
```

In other words, the starting angle of the next wedge is the same as the ending angle of the previous wedge.

CONCLUSION

In this chapter we have seen many variations of FOR...NEXT loops and WHILE...WEND loops, most of which were devoted to working with the data values stored in one two-dimensional array named *table$*. The *QuickChart* program clearly demonstrates the important programming relationship between loops and arrays.

If you would like to work further with the *QuickChart* program, here are a few suggestions for additions, revisions, and improvements:

1. Write a subprogram that transposes the shape of the current data table, substituting rows for columns and columns for rows. (As a result, *QuickChart* changes the series and category orientation of the charts.) Include a *Transpose* option in the *Get data* submenu.

2. Rework the *ColumnChart* and *LineChart* routines so that the program can handle negative numbers in the data table. The position of the horizontal category axis will have to be calculated in a manner that results in an appropriate scale for displaying both negative and positive numbers.

3. Add routines to offer additional chart types; for example, a bar chart, producing horizontal bars to represent data values; and an x-y (or "scatter") chart, in which ordered pairs of Cartesian coordinates are plotted against an x-axis and a y-axis.

4. Add more error information and help screens to aid the user.

5. Allow revisions of the data currently in the *table$* array (such as adding a data column).

6. Enhance the quality of the output by including colors in the charts. If you have an IBM Enhanced Graphics Adapter and an IBM Enhanced Color Monitor, modify the SCREEN statements and display dimensions to support the higher resolution available.

Sequential Data Files: *A Business Survey Program*

Many QuickBASIC applications need a way of storing data on disk for future use. In this context, a data file is a medium of communication between one program and another, or between one performance and the next of a given program. QuickBASIC provides commands for working with two different types of data files.

The two types of data files are *sequential* and *random access.* In a sequential data file, discrete units of information, or *data elements,* are streamed onto the disk in the order they are created. Later, when the program needs to access a particular file element, it must start at the beginning of the file and look at every data element until it comes to the one it needs. In a random-access file, on the other hand, the file elements are stored with special electronic markers that enable the program to jump over file elements and go directly to the element needed. A sequential file, then, is designed for processing an entire collection of data as a unit. For an application that does not require direct access to individual records, sequential files are generally easier to use than random-access files.

Random-access files are discussed in the next chapter. In this chapter, we concentrate on the QuickBASIC language elements that work with sequential files. Specifically, we review the commands and functions that perform these tasks:

- Opening a sequential file for reading (OPEN . . . FOR INPUT)

- Reading items of information from the open file (INPUT#)

- Determining when the reading process has reached the end of the file (EOF)

- Opening a new sequential file for writing (OPEN . . . FOR OUTPUT) or opening an existing file for appending information to the end of the file (OPEN . . . FOR APPEND)

- Writing information to the open file (PRINT# or WRITE#)

- Closing a sequential file when the current operation is complete (CLOSE)

The principles of sequential file-handling are modeled in this chapter in the *Survey* program. The program is designed to generate all kinds of questionnaires—such as customer-satisfaction surveys, consumer-attitude surveys, and opinion polls—and to analyze the responses. In general, the *Survey* program aids in gathering and analyzing information about large groups of people who have some trait or activity in common—for example, customers, employees, voters, TV viewers, newspaper readers, students, consumers, churchgoers, computer owners, cat lovers, club members, sports fans, and so on.

Survey does not keep data for individuals in a group, such as names, addresses, and phone numbers, but rather aims to generalize the opinions, attitudes, and characteristics of the group as a whole. So, because *Survey* works with entire categories of data rather than discrete entries, it's an ideal application for sequential files.

Using *Survey*, you can:

- Generate and save surveys that contain any number of multiple-choice questions.

- Print forms to distribute to survey participants.

- Record the responses.

- Determine the percentage of participants who answered a given question in a particular way and print a report that displays this information.

Before we look at this program, however, let's review QuickBASIC's vocabulary of commands and functions that are devoted to sequential file-handling.

SEQUENTIAL FILE-HANDLING IN QUICKBASIC

A program opens a sequential file for one of three individual operations: *reading* a file into memory so a program can use its information, *writing* information to a new file, or *appending* information to the end of an existing file. A sequential file may only be used for one of these operations at a time. For example, imagine a program that creates a file and subsequently needs to read information from the same file. The program would follow these steps:

1. Open the file for writing.
2. Write items of information to the file.
3. Close the file.
4. Open the file for reading.
5. Read items of information from the file.
6. Close the file.

The OPEN command opens a sequential file for one of the three possible operations. The syntax for the three statements that open sequential files for reading, writing, and appending is:

```
OPEN "fileName" FOR INPUT AS #fileNumber
OPEN "fileName" FOR OUTPUT AS #fileNumber
OPEN "fileName" FOR APPEND AS #fileNumber
```

In all three statements, the FOR clause specifies the operation that the program performs with the open file. The filename that identifies the file on the disk must be a legal DOS name of a maximum of eight characters, plus an optional three-character extension. The filename may also include path and drive specifications.

The AS clause supplies a file number for each open file. This number is an integer in the range 1 to 255, the maximum number of files that may be open at one time. After a file is open, you identify it in subsequent commands by its file number. For example, the INPUT#, PRINT#, and WRITE# commands all refer to a specific file by number.

Reading a sequential file

The following statement opens an existing file named *SAMPLE.NUM*, located on a disk in drive B, and prepares to read information from the file:

```
OPEN "B:SAMPLE.NUM" FOR INPUT AS #1
```

Notice that the statement gives *SAMPLE.NUM* a file number of 1. As long as the file is open, any commands that deal with the file refer to it by this number. Although you can use any positive integer in the range 1 to 255 for the file number, a particular number can be assigned to only one currently open file. Most programmers assign 1 to the first file they open, 2 to the second file, and so on.

The INPUT# command reads items of information from the file. Its general syntax is:

```
INPUT #fileNumber, variableList
```

For example, assume that data is stored in file #1 as a series of paired strings and integers; the following INPUT# command reads a string and an integer value from file #1:

```
INPUT #1, title$, number%
```

Notice the punctuation of the statement: A comma follows the file number, and the variables in the subsequent list are also separated by commas. If this example is the first INPUT# command issued after the corresponding OPEN statement, the command reads the first and second data values stored in the file and assigns the values to the variables *title$* and *number%*, respectively. Alternatively, these same values could have been read by two individual INPUT# commands:

```
INPUT #1, title$
INPUT #1, number%
```

The next INPUT# command after these reads the third value in the file, and then the fourth, and so on until reaching the end of the file.

Typically, the INPUT# statements that read a sequential file are located within a FOR...NEXT or WHILE...WEND loop. Each iteration of the loop reads one or more values from the file. A common error occurs when a program attempts to read more data values than the file actually contains. When a sequential file is created or when data is appended to a sequential file, an electronic end-of-file "marker" is set after the last data element. When an INPUT# command reads the last value in a file, QuickBASIC records the end-of-file condition for that file. If a subsequent INPUT# statement tries to read another value from the file, the resulting runtime error *Input past end* terminates the program.

Fortunately, the built-in EOF function avoids this problem. EOF takes a file number as its argument. While data values are available to be read from the specified file, EOF returns a value of false. But when QuickBASIC records the file's end-of-file marker, EOF returns a value of true. Using this function as the condition of a WHILE...WEND structure, you can loop through the file, reading each element until the last element is retrieved.

Consider the following example:

```
WHILE (NOT EOF(1))
    INPUT #1, phoneNumber$
    CALL AddToList(phoneNumber$)
WEND
```

As long as the expression (NOT EOF(1)) is true, this WHILE...WEND loop continues reading individual values from file #1 into the variable *phoneNumber$*. A call to a subprogram named *AddToList* performs some operation on each value before the loop reads the next value in the file. The looping stops after the last value is read and processed.

An alternative to the EOF method of avoiding the *Input past end* error is to record the number of data elements in a file in a counter variable. Then your program can employ a FOR...NEXT loop to read the correct number of data values from the file. The *Survey* program uses both approaches: a conditional WHILE...WEND loop that relies on the EOF function, and a FOR...NEXT loop that relies on specific information about the length of the file.

When you design a program to read a sequential file, you must know what types of values are stored in the file. The variable types in the INPUT# statement should correspond correctly to the values read from the file. If they do not correspond, QuickBASIC makes data-type conversions where possible, but unexpected results may occur. For example, if an INPUT# statement reads a string value from a sequential file and assigns the value to a numeric variable, the numeric variable receives a value of 0.

An additional problem arises when QuickBASIC cannot find the disk file referred to in the OPEN statement. This problem is particularly common in programs designed to elicit a filename from the user at the keyboard and then to open the file for reading. The following sequence illustrates these steps:

```
INPUT "What file do you want to read"; fileName$
OPEN fileName$ FOR INPUT AS #1
```

In this example, the name of the file is stored in the string variable *fileName$,* and the OPEN statement looks on the disk for the filename stored in the variable. (If no path is specified, the current drive and directory are searched.) The danger is that the user will enter a filename that does not actually exist on disk. If this happens, a *File not found* runtime error results, and the program terminates.

There are two ways to guard against this problem. The first is to show the user a list of the files that are actually available on disk. The FILES command shows such a directory on the screen. The format for the FILES command is:

FILES *fileSpec*

where *fileSpec* is a filename, a pathname, a drive letter, or a combination of these elements.

For example, the following command from the *Survey* program uses the "*" wildcard character to display files that have extension names of *SUR* in the current drive and directory:

```
FILES "*.SUR"
```

If drive B is the current drive, the resulting display looks like this:

```
B:\
CUSTOMER.SUR     SAMPLE.SUR      EMPLOYEE.SUR
 288768 Bytes free
```

This display lets the user request a file that actually exists on the current disk and in the current directory/path.

But even with this directory display, errors often occur during the file-opening process. The user might simply mistype the filename, for example. For this reason, the ultimate safeguard against a bad filename in an OPEN statement is to create an error trap, using the ON ERROR GOTO statement. One example of this technique appears in the charting program in Chapter 5. Another example is in the *Survey* program in this chapter.

After the necessary reading and writing is complete, a program should close a file, using the CLOSE statement. The format for the CLOSE statement is:

CLOSE *#fileNumber(s)*

where *#fileNumber(s)* is a list of file numbers under which the files were opened, separated by commas. If no file number is specified, all files currently open are closed.

You close a sequential file when you finish working with it or when you plan to manipulate the file from the *beginning* the next time you open it.

For example, the following statement closes file #1:

```
CLOSE #1
```

If two or more files are open, they can be closed explicitly in a single CLOSE statement; for example, this statement closes files #1 and #3:

```
CLOSE #1, #3
```

After you close a file, the file number is available again for opening some other file. A specific number is only associated with a file while the file is open.

If you want a program to read the same sequential file more than once, close the file after the first reading and reopen it for a subsequent reading. Each time you open a file for reading, QuickBASIC prepares to start reading values from the beginning of the file.

Next, let's look at the various ways to write information to a sequential file.

Writing data to a sequential file

QuickBASIC has two commands for writing to sequential files: PRINT# and WRITE#. These are equivalent to the familiar BASIC commands PRINT and WRITE, except that they transfer information to a file rather than to the display screen. These commands are only available after you open a sequential file on disk for output. They write information in two ways: to sequential files open for output, or to sequential files open for appending.

Creating new sequential files: Opening for OUTPUT

The format for opening a new file is:

OPEN *"fileName"* FOR OUTPUT AS *#fileNumber*

where *fileName* is a string expression consisting of an optional drive letter, an optional pathname, and a required filename, respectively.

The following statement creates the new file *SAMPLE.NUM* on a disk in drive B, assigns it a file number of 1, and prepares to write data values to it:

```
OPEN "B:SAMPLE.NUM" FOR OUTPUT AS #1
```

After this statement appears in a program, you can subsequently use the WRITE# statement or the PRINT# statement to send data values to the sequential file.

If you open for OUTPUT a file that already exists on disk, the file's current contents are overwritten and lost. Any subsequent information sent to the file begins accumulating in an empty file. Use the OPEN command in this way when you want to replace an existing file with a new, updated one.

Adding to existing sequential files: Opening for APPEND

We have just seen that QuickBASIC's OPEN statement opens a new file and prepares it to receive data, or opens and empties an existing file and prepares it to receive data. You can also open files for APPEND to add data to the end of an existing file. Its syntax is similar to opening a file for OUTPUT:

OPEN *"fileName"* **FOR APPEND AS** #*fileNumber*

where *fileName* is a string expression consisting of an optional drive letter, an optional pathname, and a required filename, respectively.

The following statement opens an existing disk file on drive B named *SAMPLE.NUM* and prepares to append data values after the current end of the file:

```
OPEN "B:SAMPLE.NUM" FOR APPEND AS #1
```

If *SAMPLE.NUM* does not exist, QuickBASIC creates a new file and prepares to write data to it. In this one special case, opening a file for APPEND behaves the same as opening a file for OUTPUT.

The distinction between these two output methods is very important. To summarize:

- The OPEN FOR OUTPUT method creates a new file and prepares to write data to it. If the file already exists, its contents are overwritten and lost.

- The OPEN FOR APPEND method opens an existing file and prepares to append data to the end of the file. If the named file does not exist, APPEND creates it.

After you open a new file or an existing file, you store data in it by using QuickBASIC's WRITE# and PRINT# statements.

The WRITE# statement

A WRITE# command sends one or more values to the file. The general form of WRITE# is:

WRITE #*fileNumber, expressionList*

where *expressionList* can be constants, expressions, or variables. For example, the following command sends a string constant and an integer variable to file #1:

```
WRITE #1, "India", population%
```

WRITE# formats the data values sent to a file: It encloses string values in quotation marks when it writes them to the file, and it supplies commas as "delimiters" between values sent to the file.

A delimiter is an ASCII character that separates one data value from the next in a sequential file. The delimiters that QuickBASIC recognizes for separating any two values are:

- The comma character

- The carriage return/line feed combination

- One or more consecutive space characters (valid as a delimiter between numeric values)

One advantage of the WRITE# statement is that it supplies delimiters where they are needed. For example, consider this sequence:

```
string1$ = "first line": variable1% = 1
string2$ = "second line": variable2% = 2
OPEN "B:SAMPLE.NUM" FOR OUTPUT AS #1
WRITE #1, string1$, variable1
WRITE #1, string2$, variable2
CLOSE #1
```

The two WRITE# statements send two lines of values to the file, each line consisting of a string value and an integer. This is what the file looks like:

```
"first line",1
"second line",2
```

As you can see, the string values are enclosed in quotes and a comma separates the two values in each line. Each WRITE# statement sends a carriage return/line feed sequence after the final data value in a line.

The quotation marks around string values can prove particularly important when a program writes lines of text to a file. For example, the *Survey* program stores the questions and multiple-choice answers of a given survey in a sequential file. Sometimes one of these lines of text will itself contain a comma. However, in this case the comma is simply one of the characters in a string data value; the comma should not be considered a delimiter *between* data values. To prevent

QuickBASIC from reading the comma as a delimiter, the entire string must be enclosed in quotes. As we'll see when we examine the *Survey* program, the easiest way to accomplish this is via the WRITE# statement.

The PRINT# statement

The PRINT# statement also sends values to a data file, but does not include either the comma delimiter between values or the quotation marks around strings (it still uses the carriage return/line feed sequence to delimit lines, however). If a file requires either of these elements, you must supply them in a PRINT# statement. For example, consider the following statements:

```
string1$ = "A": string2$ = "B": string3$ = "C"
PRINT #1, string1$ "," string2$ "," string3$
```

This PRINT# statement sends three string values to a file and also sends two commas as delimiters between the values. The strings are not enclosed in quotes. Here is the resulting line of data in the file:

```
A,B,C
```

Examples in the *Survey* program will give us the opportunity to compare and contrast both of these statements.

Other sequential file commands and features

You can also use an abbreviated form of the OPEN command. For example, the following three statements open files for reading, writing, and appending, respectively:

```
OPEN "I", 1, "SAMPLE.NUM"
OPEN "O", 2, "OUTFILE.TXT"
OPEN "A", 3, "DATA.NUM"
```

You might encounter this cryptic form of OPEN in programs written in an older version of BASIC, so you should learn to recognize it. However, the longer form is easier to understand and therefore preferable.

The OPEN statement also includes an optional LEN clause, which specifies the size of the buffer that QuickBASIC establishes for each open data file. A buffer is an area in QuickBASIC's memory set aside for storing data that is on its way to or from a file. If you omit the LEN clause in the OPEN statement, the default size of this buffer is 128 bytes. Increasing the size results in faster reading and writing processes for sequential files because more data is stored in memory at a time, where it can be processed electronically, and the program doesn't have to go to the disk as much, which involves a slower mechanical process. For example, the following statement, taken from the *Survey* program, establishes a buffer size of one kilobyte (1024 bytes):

```
OPEN surFile$ FOR INPUT AS #1 LEN = 1024
```

If too much memory is taken from QuickBASIC's operating area, however, QuickBASIC can run out of room and slow up substantially because it then has to access the disk for instructions it normally keeps in memory but that have been displaced by program information. The LEN clause is actually more important for opening random-access files, in which case the clause specifies the record length of the file. Chapter 7 presents more information about the LEN function.

In addition, the QuickBASIC OPEN statement has *shared* and *lock* clauses for controlling file operations that take place in a multiuser networked environment. Chapter 7 briefly discusses this subject; for more information, consult the QuickBASIC documentation.

QuickBASIC has two less commonly used input commands that are designed for reading sequential files: The LINE INPUT# command and the INPUT$ function. The LINE INPUT# command reads an entire *line* of a file, up to and including a carriage return/line feed sequence, regardless of other delimiter characters or quotation marks that may be within the line, and puts the result in a string variable. The command takes the following format:

LINE INPUT *#fileNumber, stringVariable$*

For example, the following command reads the next line from file #1 and stores the contents of the line in the string variable *first$*:

```
LINE INPUT #1, first$
```

In contrast, the INPUT$ function reads a specified number of *characters* from a sequential file. The function has the following form:

INPUT$ *(numberOfCharacters, #fileNumber)*

The first argument, *numberOfCharacters,* is an integer value specifying the number of characters the function will read from the file. For example, the following statement reads one character from file #1 and displays the character's ASCII code number.

```
PRINT ASC(INPUT$(1, #1))
```

Figure 6-1 shows a simple QuickBASIC program illustrating some of the sequential file commands we have just discussed. The output of the program appears in Figure 6-2 (on the next page).

```
'    INTEST.BAS
'    An exercise with LINE INPUT# and INPUT$.

     string1$ = "A"
     string2$ = "B"
     variable1% = 1
     variable2% = 2

'    ---- Send newly declared variables to the file "TEST.DAT".  Use WRITE
'         statements so a delimiter (,) is included between each value.
     OPEN "TEST.DAT" FOR OUTPUT AS #1
     WRITE #1, string1$, variable1%
     WRITE #1, string2$, variable2%
     CLOSE #1

     PRINT "Here is the file TEST.DAT:"
     PRINT STRING$(26, "-")
     PRINT

'    ---- Read and print the elements of the newly created file "TEST.DAT".
     OPEN "TEST.DAT" FOR INPUT AS #1
     LINE INPUT#1, first$
     LINE INPUT#1, second$
     PRINT first$
     PRINT second$
     CLOSE #1

     PRINT: PRINT: PRINT
     PRINT "Here are the ASCII characters that the file contains:"
     PRINT STRING$(53, "-")
     PRINT

'    ---- Print an ASCII numeral for each character in "TEST.DAT".
     OPEN "TEST.DAT" FOR INPUT AS #1
     WHILE NOT EOF(1)
         PRINT ASC(INPUT$(1, #1));
     WEND
     CLOSE #1

     PRINT: PRINT
     PRINT "(Notice in particular the carriage return/line feed"
     PRINT " sequences:  ASCII 13 and ASCII 10.)

     END
```

Figure 6-1. *A sample sequential file program*

```
Here is the file TEST.DAT:
-----------------------------

"A",1
"B",2


Here are the ASCII characters that the file contains:
------------------------------------------------------

 34  65  34  44  49  13  10  34  66  34  44  50  13  10

(Notice in particular the carriage return/line feed
 sequences:  ASCII 13 and ASCII 10.)
```

Figure 6-2. *A screen display of the program listed in
Figure 6-1.*

SAMPLE RUN OF THE *SURVEY* PROGRAM

Figure 6-3 shows the recurring menu for the *Survey* program, which
offers four main options:

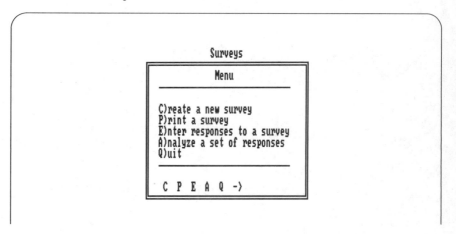

```
                        Surveys
                  ┌──────────────────────┐
                  │         Menu         │
                  │ ──────────────────── │
                  │                      │
                  │ C)reate a new survey │
                  │ P)rint a survey      │
                  │ E)nter responses to a survey │
                  │ A)nalyze a set of responses  │
                  │ Q)uit                │
                  │                      │
                  │ ──────────────────── │
                  │                      │
                  │  C  P  E  A  Q  -)   │
                  └──────────────────────┘
```

Figure 6-3. *The* Survey *program's main menu.*

● *Create a new survey.* This option presents a series of input screens
  from which you enter the questions and multiple-choice answers
  for a new survey. The program saves the survey on disk in a sequential data file. You can create as many surveys as you want and
  store each under its own name on disk.

- *Print a survey.* This option begins by eliciting the filename of a survey that you want to print. The program then opens the file and prints the survey in a questionnaire form that you can distribute to participants.

- *Enter responses to a survey.* This option presents input screens for recording the responses you receive from participants. You can enter answers from as many questionnaires as you receive. The program saves these responses in a data file.

- *Analyze a set of responses.* This option examines the responses you entered in the preceding option. For each question, the program computes the percentage of survey participants who checked it. The *Analyze responses* option produces a printed report incorporating these percentages with a copy of the questionnaire.

As we examine each of these options, we will develop and analyze a sample questionnaire: a customer-satisfaction survey for an imaginary small business named Sam's Friendly Auto Repair.

The *Create* option and the survey files

The *Create* option starts out by displaying a screen of instructions, explaining the input process for generating a new survey. These instructions are shown in Figure 6-4. In brief, each question in the survey can

```
Create a new survey.
------ - --- -------

Each question may be from one to four
lines long, and you may supply from two
to ten responses per question.

To complete a question or a group
of responses, press the (Enter) key
when you see the new input prompt.

Enter the filename for this survey:
(The extension .SUR will automatically
be added to the filename.)

     -) CARSHOP
```

Figure 6-4. *Instructions for the* Create *option.*

comprise from one to four lines of text, followed by as many as ten multiple-choice answers.

At the bottom of the instruction screen, the *Survey* program elicits a filename for storing the new survey. As shown in Figure 6-4, we will use the descriptive filename *CARSHOP*.

Next, the program requests a title for the survey with the prompt:

```
Enter a title for this survey:
```

We will use the survey title *Sam's Friendly Auto Repair,* and this title will then appear at the top of each printed questionnaire.

After supplying a filename and a title, you are ready to enter the survey questions. The program first displays a prompt for each line of the question. You type each line (up to 80 characters) and then press Enter. For example:

```
        Question # 1


Line # 1: How did you first hear about Sam's Friendly
Line # 2: Auto Repair Shop?
```

Although the program allows a maximum of four lines of text for the question, you can stop after one, two, or three lines. To do so, press Enter when you see the next line prompt.

To prompt you for the multiple-choice answers, the program supplies uppercase letters, potentially from A to J, to represent each of the possible 10 responses:

```
        Responses to Question # 1


A:
```

The responses should be less than 67 characters.

After you enter a response, the program displays a prompt for the next one. The program requires at least two responses for each question, and you can stop anytime between two and ten responses by pressing Enter at a new response prompt. The response-input dialog also stops after you enter the tenth response.

Files created by the *Survey* program

When you create a new survey, the *Survey* program immediately generates three different disk files. The three files have extension names of

SUR (for *survey*), *ALT* (for *alternate*), and *NUM* (for *number*). For example, the *CARSHOP* questionnaire creates the following files:

```
CARSHOP.SUR
CARSHOP.ALT
CARSHOP.NUM
```

The primary file in this example, containing the complete text of the questionnaire, is *CARSHOP.SUR*. This file stores each question line and each response in sequential order. The lines of text are enclosed in quotation marks in the file. Figure 6-5 shows the complete file; it contains six questions which were entered into an input screen.

```
"How did you first hear about Sam's Friendly"
"Auto Repair Shop?"
"From a friend."
"In our newspaper advertisement."
"From our radio commercial."
"In the phone book."
"By passing the shop on the street."
"Other."
"Including the latest visit, how many times"
"have you brought your current car to be serviced"
"at Sam's Auto Repair?"
"Once"
"Twice"
"Three to five times"
"Six times or more"
"Every service up to now"
"What impressed you most favorably about your most "
"recent car service at Sam's?"
"The fast service and prompt delivery."
"The thorough explanation of what needed to be done."
"The courteous attendants."
"The reasonable price for the service."
"All of the above."
"Was there anything you were not happy about in"
"your recent car service at Sam's?"
"The time taken for the repair."
"The attitude of the attendants."
"The explanation of the service."
"The price."
"None of the above."
"What was the reason you brought your car in "
"for your most recent service at Sam's Friendly"
"Auto Repair Shop?"
"Routine service."
"A problem that you couldn't identify yourself."
"A specific repair that you knew had to be done."
"A follow-up on an inadequate previous service."
"Would you recommend Sam's Friendly Auto Repair"
"Shop to a friend?"
"Yes"
"No"
```

Figure 6-5. *The CARSHOP.SUR main survey sequential file.*

To read this file correctly, the program needs to find out the number of lines in each question and the number of corresponding multiple-choice answers. As we have seen, both these numbers can vary from question to question: The question itself can be from one to four lines long, and there can be from two to ten responses.

The *ALT* file supplies the dimensions of the survey. Figure 6-6 shows *CARSHOP.ALT*. You can see that the file gives three items of information describing each question in the survey:

```
"How did you fir"
2
6
"Including the l"
3
5
"What impressed "
2
5
"Was there anyth"
2
5
"What was the re"
3
4
"Would you recom"
2
2
```

Figure 6-6. *The* CARSHOP.ALT *file, supplying the dimensions of the survey.*

1. The first 15 characters of the question itself

2. The number of lines in the question (from 1 to 4)

3. The number of multiple-choice answers (from 2 to 10)

For example, the description of the first question in the *CARSHOP* survey appears as follows:

```
"How did you fir"
2
6
```

The two numerical values in this description instruct the program to read the first survey question as follows: The first two lines in *CARSHOP.SUR* are the lines of the question itself, and the next six lines are the responses for the question. We will see exactly how *Survey* uses this information as we progress through the program. We will also find out why the *ALT* file includes a short excerpt from the beginning of the question text.

The *Survey* program creates a third short file, *NUM*, to describe the questionnaire. The *NUM* file contains only two items of information:

1.   The title of the survey

2.   The total number of questions in the survey

For example, here is the entire *CARSHOP.NUM* file, which describes a survey entitled "Sam's Friendly Auto Repair" containing six questions:

```
"Sam's Friendly Auto Repair"
6
```

The program does not create this little file until you complete the input process for the new survey. Since you may not know in advance the number of questions, the program counts them as you go along and records the number in the *NUM* file when you finish.

Each subsequent program option uses all or some of the three files produced during the *Create* option. Let's turn now to the *Print* option.

The *Print* option

To print a working copy of a survey stored on disk, you use the *Print* option. *Print* shows you a directory of all the *SUR* files on the current disk and asks which one you want to print. You can see this directory and input prompt in Figure 6-7 (on the next page). To open a survey file, enter the base name of the file, without the extension.

If you mistype the filename—producing a name that does not exist on the disk—the program displays an error message and returns you to the main menu.

Although only the filenames with the *SUR* extension are displayed, the program actually tries to open all three of the survey files: *SUR*, *ALT*, and *NUM*. If any one of the files is missing from your disk, the program won't be able to work with the survey and will therefore display a file-error message.

```
Print a Survey
----- - ------


Here are the survey files in the current directory:

----------------------------------------------------------------
A:\
CARSHOP .SUR      SERVICE .SUR      MIKE    .SUR      COMPUTE .SUR
DAVE    .SUR      DOCTOR  .SUR      FOOD    .SUR
 316416 Bytes free
----------------------------------------------------------------

Do you want to print one of these surveys (Y or N)?
```

Figure 6-7. *The filename display and input prompt for
the* Print *option.*

However, if the files are opened successfully, the program is
ready to read them and produce a printed survey form. To give you a
chance to prepare your printer for the operation, the program pauses
and displays the following message on the screen:

```
Press the space bar
when your printer is
ready to operate.
```

When you press the space bar, the program begins reading the survey
files and then sends each question to the printer. Figure 6-8 shows the
customer-satisfaction survey for Sam's Friendly Auto Repair. Notice
that the program prints a pair of square brackets at the left of each response for participants to indicate their answers.

```
        Survey: Sam's Friendly Auto Repair


1 - How did you first hear about Sam's Friendly
        Auto Repair Shop?

        [ ]   A: From a friend.
        [ ]   B: In our newspaper advertisement.
        [ ]   C: From our radio commercial.
        [ ]   D: In the phone book.
        [ ]   E: By passing the shop on the street.
        [ ]   F: Other.
```

Figure 6-8. *The printed* CARSHOP *survey.*   *(more...)*

```
2 - Including the latest visit, how many times
        have you brought your current car to be serviced
        at Sam's Auto Repair?

        [  ]  A: Once
        [  ]  B: Twice
        [  ]  C: Three to five times
        [  ]  D: Six times or more
        [  ]  E: Every service up to now


3 - What impressed you most favorably about your most
        recent car service at Sam's?

        [  ]  A: The fast service and prompt delivery.
        [  ]  B: The thorough explanation of what needed to be done.
        [  ]  C: The courteous attendants.
        [  ]  D: The reasonable price for the service.
        [  ]  E: All of the above.


4 - Was there anything you were not happy about in
        your recent car service at Sam's?

        [  ]  A: The time taken for the repair.
        [  ]  B: The attitude of the attendants.
        [  ]  C: The explanation of the service.
        [  ]  D: The price.
        [  ]  E: None of the above.


5 - What was the reason you brought your car in
        for your most recent service at Sam's Friendly
        Auto Repair Shop?

        [  ]  A: Routine service.
        [  ]  B: A problem that you couldn't identify yourself.
        [  ]  C: A specific repair that you knew had to be done.
        [  ]  D: A follow-up on an inadequate previous service.


6 - Would you recommend Sam's Friendly Auto Repair
        Shop to a friend?

        [  ]  A: Yes
        [  ]  B: No
```

Figure 6-8. *The printed* CARSHOP *survey (continued).*

Now imagine that you have produced a survey like the one for Sam's auto shop and that you have begun receiving completed questionnaires from your customers. No matter how many responses you receive for a given survey—dozens, hundreds, or even thousands— you will want an efficient way to record all the answers in one place and to tally the results. The *Enter responses* and *Analyze responses* options of the *Survey* program provide these operations.

The *Enter responses* option

A programmer must think carefully about designing an input process that might involve large amounts of data. For example, the process for entering survey responses should be simple and efficient, allowing a good typist to store a large amount of data as quickly as possible. The screen prompts for this process should display just enough information to identify a question and elicit an appropriate single-letter response. Furthermore, the program should require only one keystroke for each answer and should ignore alphabetic case. Finally, the program should recognize and reject inappropriate responses and alert the typist with an audible signal.

All these features are built into the *Enter responses* option's input dialog. When you select this option, the program first shows you a directory of survey files and prompts you to choose one. Then, to make sure you have chosen the correct file, the program displays the survey title on the screen before beginning the input process. For example:

```
Survey title: Sam's Friendly Auto Repair
Is this the correct survey? (Y or N) ->
```

If you answer affirmatively, the input begins. Figure 6-9 shows a sample, using the survey for Sam's auto shop. For each question, the

```
        1 - How did you fir...
              A B C D E F -> C

        2 - Including the l...
              A B C D E -> E

        3 - What impressed ...
              A B C D E -> D

        4 - Was there anyth...
              A B C D E -> E

        5 - What was the re...
              A B C D -> A

        6 - Would you recom...
              A B -> A


  Another? (Y or N) ->
```

Figure 6-9. *The input dialog for survey responses.*

230

program displays the question number, along with a short "teaser" quotation from the text of the question itself. (The program reads this excerpt from the *ALT* file.) Then, below the text, the program shows the appropriate responses. For example, here is the first question from Sam's survey:

```
1 - How did you fir...
    A B C D E F ->
```

To answer this question, press a letter key. The program records the response and moves to the next question.

Notice in Figure 6-9 that the prompt shows the exact sequence of appropriate letters for each question: Question 1 has six possible responses (A through F), and Question 2 has five (A through E). If you enter a letter that is not in this set, the program sounds a beep from the computer's speaker.

After going through all the questions for a single questionnaire form, the program asks if there is to be another round:

```
Another? (Y or N) ->
```

Again, only a single keystroke response is necessary: *Y* or *N*. Depending on your answer, input dialog begins for the next questionnaire or you are returned to the main menu.

As you enter questionnaire responses, the *Enter responses* option creates an additional fourth data file for the survey. This file has an extension name of *RES* (for *responses*). For example, Figure 6-10 shows a selection of responses for Sam's customer-satisfaction survey, stored in

```
B, C, A, D, B, A
D, E, A, B, C, A
A, B, C, D, A, A
A, D, A, B, C, A
D, E, E, A, C, B
D, D, A, C, D, A
D, A, B, C, D, A
B, C, D, A, C, A
D, D, A, B, B, A
C, C, B, D, A, B
A, C, D, E, A, A
F, D, B, C, A, A
D, D, A, B, C, A
A, C, C, B, A, A
D, C, C, B, B, A
```

Figure 6-10. *The CARSHOP.RES questionnaire-response file.*

the file *CARSHOP.RES*. For each completed questionnaire received for a given survey, the *RES* file contains one line of responses. You can see that in this case each line of the file contains six one-letter entries, separated by commas. These entries are one participant's responses to the six questions of the survey.

The *RES* file can grow to be the largest sequential data file of the four files that the program produces. Each time you select the *Enter responses* option, the program prepares to append new lines of data to the bottom of the file. This lets you enter questionnaire responses during different input sessions over a period of time, as you receive them.

Finally, the *Analyze responses* option goes through the *RES* file and tallies the responses for a given question.

The *Analyze responses* option

When you select the *Analyze responses* option, the *Survey* program again displays the files with *SUR* extensions in the current directory and asks if you would like to print one. If you respond affirmatively you are then asked to supply the filename.

The output of the *Analyze responses* option is a printed report, supplying the tallied responses. Accordingly, the program pauses while you prepare your printer and begins the report when you press the space bar (you may also press the Esc key at this time to return to the main menu).

Figure 6-11 shows a sample report for Sam's auto shop. You can see that the output is similar to the original questionnaire form, except for two new details. Beneath the title line, the report shows the number of questionnaires analyzed in the report. Then, beneath each

```
        Survey: Sam's Friendly Auto Repair
               242 Survey Responses Received

1 - How did you first hear about Sam's Friendly
       Auto Repair Shop?

       30%    A: From a friend.
       15%    B: In our newspaper advertisement.
       6%     C: From our radio commercial.
       45%    D: In the phone book.
       0%     E: By passing the shop on the street.
       5%     F: Other.
```

Figure 6-11. *The results of the* Analyze responses *option for the* CARSHOP *survey.* *(more...)*

```
2 - Including the latest visit, how many times
        have you brought your current car to be serviced
        at Sam's Auto Repair?

    10%    A: Once
    5%     B: Twice
    50%    C: Three to five times
    25%    D: Six times or more
    11%    E: Every service up to now


3 - What impressed you most favorably about your most
        recent car service at Sam's?

    35%    A: The fast service and prompt delivery.
    20%    B: The thorough explanation of what needed to be done.
    25%    C: The courteous attendants.
    11%    D: The reasonable price for the service.
    10%    E: All of the above.


4 - Was there anything you were not happy about in
        your recent car service at Sam's?

    15%    A: The time taken for the repair.
    30%    B: The attitude of the attendants.
    15%    C: The explanation of the service.
    25%    D: The price.
    16%    E: None of the above.


5 - What was the reason you brought your car in
        for your most recent service at Sam's Friendly
        Auto Repair Shop?

    38%    A: Routine service.
    22%    B: A problem that you couldn't identify yourself.
    30%    C: A specific repair that you knew had to be done.
    10%    D: A follow-up on an inadequate previous service.


6 - Would you recommend Sam's Friendly Auto Repair
        Shop to a friend?

    61%    A: Yes
    39%    B: No
```

Figure 6-11. *The* CARSHOP *Analyze responses option (continued).*

question, the program supplies the percentage of participants who chose a given response. For a given question, these percentages will add up to 100% (or approximately so, since the program rounds them to the nearest integer).

Of course, you might want to expand the scope of the *Survey* program to generate more sophisticated statistical analyses of the response data. We will discuss some possibilities at the end of this

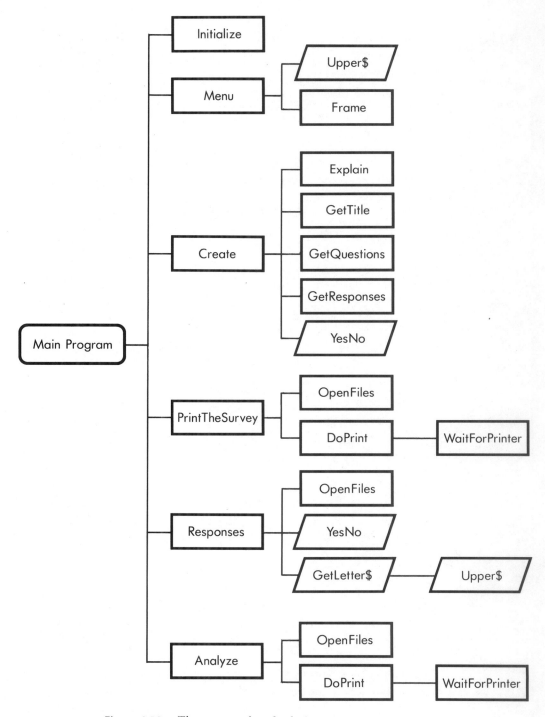

Figure 6-12. *The structure chart for the* Survey *program.*

chapter. For now, keep in mind that all the raw data from question-naire responses is available in the *RES* file, and you can write routines to manipulate this data any way you wish.

In summary, *Survey* creates four different sequential-access data files for each survey that you generate. These files are identified by their extension names:

- *SUR* is the file that stores the text of the questionnaire itself.

- *ALT* specifies the length of each question (in lines) and the number of responses; it also supplies a "teaser" quotation from the question, for use in the *Enter responses* option.

- *NUM* gives the title of the survey and the number of questions in the survey.

- *RES* stores the responses from the survey. Each time you choose the *Enter responses* option, the program adds data to *RES*.

As we turn now to the listing of the *Survey* program, we'll concentrate on the creation and handling of these four files. Figure 6-12 shows the structure chart of the *Survey* program.

INSIDE THE *SURVEY* PROGRAM

Figure 6-13 shows the complete listing of the *Survey* program. Turn to it often as you read the following descriptions.

```
'   SURVEY.BAS
'   The Survey program supplies a number of operations that are useful
'       for a company or organization that conducts surveys or opinion
'       polls.  Using the program, you can create a survey consisting of
'       multiple-choice questions.  The program will print the survey,
'       conduct an input dialog for recording responses from the survey,
'       and then analyze the resulting file of responses.

'--------------------| Global Variable Declarations |--------------------


DIM mainMenu$(5)
COMMON SHARED mainMenu$(), indent%, okFile%, altFile$, resFile$, _
    response%(2), true%, false%, currentDirEmpty%, choice%

'   ---- Initialize Boolean variables true% and false%.
    true% = -1
    false% = 0


'   ---- Initialize indent% for later output formatting use.
    indent% = 15
```

Figure 6-13. *The* Survey *program.*

(*more...*)

There is an important procedure to remember when running the program: Since one routine in the program contains an error trap—implemented by the ON ERROR GOTO and RESUME NEXT statements—you must select the following two compiler options in the *Compile...* window before attempting a compilation:

- On Error
- Resume Next

In addition, *Survey* assumes that the following subroutines and functions are in the current directory: *YesNo.Bas, Upper.Bas, Frame.Bas,* and *Menu.Bas.* As always, if these subroutines are in another directory, you must reference them by including a path in the related $INCLUDE statements or by adding them to a user library (see Chapter 3 for more information on user libraries).

The global variable declarations area

This area declares the *Survey* program's global variables and initializes the Boolean variables *true%* and *false%* and the integer variable *indent%.* The following table describes how each global variable is used throughout the program.

mainMenu$	A static array holding the five main-menu strings.
indent%	An integer variable used for formatting screen output.
okFile%	A Boolean variable set to true when all files are in the proper format.
altFile$	A string variable containing the current filename and an *ALT* extension.
resFile$	A string variable containing the current filename and a *RES* extension.
response%	A two-dimensional dynamic array holding survey responses.
true%	An integer variable that maintains the Boolean value of true (-1) throughout program execution.
false%	An integer variable that maintains the Boolean value of false (0) throughout program execution.
currentDirEmpty%	A Boolean variable set to true if no *SUR* files exist in the current directory.
choice%	An integer variable representing the main-menu item chosen.

```
'------------------------------| Function Area |------------------------------


'    ---- Read in and compile BASIC user-defined functions.
     REM $INCLUDE : 'YESNO.BAS'
     REM $INCLUDE : 'UPPER.BAS'


'    The GetLetter$ function elicits a single letter (from A to J) for each
'        response of a given question.  This function is called by the
'        Responses subprogram, which conducts the input dialog for the
'        "Enter responses" option.

DEF FN GetLetter$(upTo%)
'    ---- For clarity, declare all of GetLetter$'s variables as local.
     STATIC i%, prompt$, legal$, answer$

'    ---- Create the prompt string, and the string of legal characters for
'        a given question.
     prompt$ = "": legal$ = ""
     FOR i% = 1 TO upTo%
         prompt$ = prompt$ + CHR$(64 + i%) + ' "
         legal$ = legal$  + CHR$(64 + i%)
     NEXT i%
     PRINT prompt$ "-> ";

'    ---- Elicit the response.  If the response is not a letter in the
'        proper range, sound a beep from the speaker.
     answer$ = ""
     WHILE (answer$ = "") OR (INSTR(legal$, answer$) = 0)
         answer$ = INKEY$
         answer$ = FN Upper$(answer$)
         IF (INSTR(legal$, answer$) = 0) THEN BEEP
     WEND

     PRINT answer$
     FN GetLetter$ = answer$
END DEF
'------------------------------| Main Program Area |------------------------------


     CALL Initialize

'    ---- Display the recurring menu and accept the user's menu choice.
'        Call the appropriate subprogram in response.
     WHILE choice% <> 5
         LOCATE 2,37: PRINT "Surveys"
         CALL Menu(mainMenu$(), choice%)

         IF (choice% = 1) THEN
             CALL Create
         ELSEIF choice% = 2 THEN
             CALL PrintTheSurvey
         ELSEIF choice% = 3 THEN
             CALL Responses
         ELSEIF choice% = 4 THEN
             CALL Analyze
         END IF
     WEND

     END
```

GetLetter

Figure 6-13. *The* Survey *program (continued).*   *(more...)*

The main program area

Survey's main program area performs the following three steps:

1.   Displays the menu on the screen

2.   Accepts the user's menu choice

3.   Calls one of four major subprograms to carry out the menu choice

The program repeats these steps continually until the user chooses the fifth menu choice, *Quit.*

To prepare the main menu, the program calls the *Initialize* routine. This subprogram stores the menu's five option strings in a string array named *mainMenu$*. Then, within a WHILE...WEND loop that creates the recurring menu, the main program sends this array as an argument to the *Menu* routine:

```
WHILE choice% <> 5
    LOCATE 2,37: PRINT "Surveys"
    CALL Menu(mainMenu$(), choice%)
```

The user's menu choice comes back from the *Menu* routine as an integer in the range 1 to 5. Given a *choice%* value of 1, 2, 3, or 4, a block of IF...THEN...ELSEIF statements calls one of the four main subprograms: *Create,* to generate a new survey; *PrintTheSurvey,* to print a working copy of a questionnaire; *Responses,* to record answers received from the survey; or *Analyze,* to prepare and print a report from the survey responses.

The *Create* subprogram

When the user selects the first menu option, *Create a new survey,* the *Create* subprogram produces the three disk files that the program uses to describe a new survey. *Create* also conducts the input dialog that elicits the file's name, and data and text values to store in these files.

The subprogram begins by calling the *Explain* routine, which displays instructions for the input procedure. Then *Create* elicits a filename for the new survey:

```
PRINT TAB(indent% + 5);: INPUT " -> ", fileName$
```

Create first ensures that the filename entered begins with an upper- or lowercase letter. If the user enters a filename that includes

```
'-------------------------| Subprogram Area |---------------------------


'    ---- Read in and compile BASIC subprograms.
     REM $INCLUDE : 'MENU.BAS'
     REM $INCLUDE : 'FRAME.BAS'


'    Initialize assigns option strings to the mainMenu$ array.

SUB Initialize STATIC
     FOR i% = 1 TO 5
          READ mainMenu$(i%)
     NEXT i%

     DATA create a new survey
     DATA print a survey
     DATA enter responses to a survey
     DATA analyze a set of responses
     DATA quit
END SUB


'    The Create subprogram conducts the input dialog for a new set of
'        survey questions.  The subprogram creates three different files:

'        name.SUR    contains the questions
'        name.ALT    describes the dimensions of the survey
'        name.NUM    contains the survey name and the number of questions

SUB Create STATIC
'    ---- Explain the input rules, and elicit a filename.
     CALL Explain
     PRINT TAB(indent% + 5);: INPUT " -> ", fileName$
'    ---- Make sure that fileName$ begins with a letter by checking its first
'        character against the appropriate ASCII boundaries.  The outOfRange$
'        variable is used to prevent null errors within the ASC function.
'        It has been assigned a value of nine, but any value out of range
'        will do.

     outOfRange$ = "9"
     IF (fileName$ = "") THEN fileName$ = outOfRange$
     WHILE (ASC(fileName$) < 65) OR (ASC(fileName$) > 122) _
          OR ((ASC(fileName$) < 97) AND (ASC(fileName$) > 90))
          INPUT "(Survey files must begin with a letter) -> ", fileName$
          IF (fileName$ = "") THEN fileName$ = outOfRange$
     WEND

'    ---- Isolate the base of the filename.
     IF (INSTR(fileName$, ".") <> 0) THEN _
          fileName$ = LEFT$(fileName$, INSTR(fileName$, ".") - 1)

     surFile$ = fileName$ + ".SUR"
     altFile$ = fileName$ + ".ALT"
     numFile$ = fileName$ + ".NUM"

'    ---- Open files for output, allocating buffers of 1024 bytes for files
'        ending with .SUR and .ALT and 128 bytes for files ending in .NUM.
     OPEN surFile$ FOR OUTPUT AS #1 LEN = 1024
     OPEN altFile$ FOR OUTPUT AS #2 LEN = 1024
     OPEN numFile$ FOR OUTPUT AS #3
```

Initialize

Create

Figure 6-13.   *The* Survey *program (continued).*   (*more...*)

an extension (despite instructions to the contrary), *Create* must eliminate the extension name:

```
IF (INSTR(fileName$, ".") <> 0) THEN _
    fileName$ = LEFT$(fileName$, INSTR(fileName$, ".") - 1)
```

This IF statement looks for a period (.) in the filename. If one exists,
the LEFT$ function isolates the base of the filename (that is, all the
characters located before the period) and stores them in the original
string variable, *fileName$*.

Next, the subprogram creates filenames (with identifyng extensions) for the three sequential data files:

```
surFile$ = fileName$ + ".SUR"
altFile$ = fileName$ + ".ALT"
numFile$ = fileName$ + ".NUM"
```

Given these three names, the following statements create the new files
and open them for writing:

```
OPEN surFile$ FOR OUTPUT AS #1 LEN = 1024
OPEN altFile$ FOR OUTPUT AS #2 LEN = 1024
OPEN numFile$ FOR OUTPUT AS #3
```

To improve handling efficiency, the program uses the LEN option to
allocate larger file buffers for the *SUR* and *ALT* files. (Since the *NUM* file
is so small, the default buffer size is adequate.)

With the files open, the *Create* subprogram clears the screen and
calls three input routines to receive the data for these newly opened
files: *GetTitle*, to elicit the survey title; *GetQuestions*, to accept a maximum of four lines of text for a survey question; and *GetResponses*, to
accept a maximum of ten responses for a given question. These routines actually write the data to the open files.

All three of the routines use the LINE INPUT statement to accept
lines of text from the keyboard. For example, here is how the *GetTitle*
subprogram receives the title of the survey:

```
LINE INPUT " -> "; title$
```

If the user enters a line of text that contains a comma, the INPUT
statement would read the comma as a delimiter between two different
input values. In contrast, the LINE INPUT statement considers the
comma part of the input text value. Thanks to LINE INPUT, then, the
user can punctuate lines of text properly.

```
      CLS
      CALL GetTitle
      query% = 1
      continue% = true%

'     ---- Get the questions and answers.
      WHILE continue%
          PRINT TAB(indent%) "Question #" query%
          PRINT
          CALL GetQuestions

          PRINT: PRINT
          PRINT TAB(indent%) "Responses to Question #" query%
          PRINT
          CALL GetResponses

          PRINT
          PRINT TAB(indent%);
          continue% = FN YesNo("Another question?")
          IF continue% THEN query% = query% + 1
          CLS
      WEND

      CLOSE #1, #2
      WRITE #3, query%
      CLOSE #3
END SUB


'   The Explain subprogram displays messages on the screen describing
'       the input process for a new survey.

SUB Explain STATIC
      PRINT: PRINT: PRINT
      PRINT TAB(indent%) "Create a new survey."
      PRINT TAB(indent%) "------ - --- -------"
      PRINT
      PRINT TAB(indent%) "Each question may be from one to four
      PRINT TAB(indent%) "lines long, and you may supply from two"
      PRINT TAB(indent%) "to ten responses per question."
      PRINT

      PRINT TAB(indent%) "To complete a question or a group
      PRINT TAB(indent%) "of responses, press the <Enter> key
      PRINT TAB(indent%) "when you see the new input prompt."
      PRINT

      PRINT TAB(indent%) "Enter the filename for this survey:"
      PRINT TAB(indent%) "(The extension .SUR will automatically"
      PRINT TAB(indent%) "be added to the filename.)"
      PRINT
END SUB


'   The GetTitle subprogram elicits a title for the survey.

SUB GetTitle STATIC
      PRINT: PRINT: PRINT
      PRINT TAB(indent%) "Enter a title for this survey:"
```

Explain

GetTitle

Figure 6-13. *The* Survey *program (continued).*   (*more...*)

After accepting the title string from the keyboard, the *GetTitle* routine writes the value to file #3, the *NUM* file:

```
WRITE #3, title$
```

Recall that the WRITE# statement encloses a text value in quotation marks in the file. Once again the program is allowing for punctuation within the line of text.

To elicit the text of the questions and the user's responses, *Create* calls the *GetQuestions* and *GetResponses* subprograms from within a WHILE...WEND loop. This loop continues the input dialog as long as the user wants to continue entering survey questions.

If you refer to the *Create* subprogram, you'll notice the use of the *YesNo* function to control the action of the loop. Given an affirmative response to the prompt *Another question?,* the *YesNo* function returns a value of true, and the looping continues.

The statement at the bottom of this loop:

```
IF continue% THEN query% = query% + 1
```

counts the number of questions that the user enters, and stores the count in the integer variable *query%*. The final action in the *Create* subprogram is to write the value of *query%* to the *NUM* file and then close the file:

```
WRITE #3, query%
CLOSE #3
```

The *GetQuestions* subprogram

Each time that the user enters a question, the *GetQuestions* and *GetResponses* subprograms write values to both the *SUR* and the *ALT* files. Within a WHILE...WEND loop, *GetQuestions* accepts each line of the question and stores it in the *SUR* file (currently open as file #1):

```
LINE INPUT ": "; surveyQuestion$
    [other program lines]
WRITE #1, surveyQuestion$
```

GetQuestions uses the counter variable *lineNumber%* to keep track of the number of lines that the user has entered for a given question (a maximum of four is allowed). After receiving the first line, the routine

```
'    ---- Do not accept an empty string for the title.
     title$ = ""
     WHILE title$ = ""
         PRINT TAB(indent%);
         LINE INPUT " -> "; title$
     WEND

'    ---- Store the title string in the name.NUM file, which is currently
'         open as file #3.
     WRITE #3, title$
     CLS
END SUB


'    The GetQuestions subprogram elicits a survey question, which may
'         be from one to four lines long.

SUB GetQuestions STATIC
     surveyQuestion$ = " ": lineNumber% = 1
     WHILE (surveyQuestion$ <> "") AND (lineNumber% <= 4)
         PRINT "Line #" STR$(lineNumber%);

'    ---- The LINE INPUT command allows the user to include commas in text.
         LINE INPUT ": "; surveyQuestion$

'    ---- Store each line of the question in the name.SUR file.  This is
'         currently open as file #1.  Store the first 15 characters of
'         each question in the name.ALT file, currently open as file #2.

         IF (surveyQuestion$ <> "") THEN
             WRITE #1, surveyQuestion$
             IF (lineNumber% = 1) THEN
                 sample$ = LEFT$(surveyQuestion$, 15)
                 WRITE #2, sample$
             END IF
             lineNumber% = lineNumber% + 1

'    ---- Require the user to enter at least one nonblank line for
'         the question.
         ELSEIF (lineNumber% = 1) THEN
             surveyQuestion$ = " "
         END IF
     WEND

'    ---- Record the number of lines in the question in the name.ALT file.
     lineNumber% = lineNumber% - 1
     WRITE #2, lineNumber%
END SUB


'    The GetResponses subprogram elicits a set of possible responses for a
'         given multiple-choice question.  Each question may include up
'         to 10 responses.

SUB GetResponses STATIC
     surveyResponse$ = " ": responseNumber% = 1
     WHILE (surveyResponse$ <> "") AND (responseNumber% <= 10)
         PRINT TAB(10) CHR$(64 + responseNumber%);
         LINE INPUT ": "; surveyResponse$
```

GetQuestions

GetResponses

Figure 6-13.   *The* Survey *program (continued).*   *(more...)*

stores the first 15 characters (the "teaser" text) in the *ALT* file (currently open as file #2):

```
IF (lineNumber% = 1) THEN
    sample$ = LEFT$(surveyQuestion$, 15)
    WRITE #2, sample$
END IF
```

Then, when the user has entered all the lines of text that make up the question, *GetQuestions* stores the number of lines in the *ALT* file:

```
WRITE #2, lineNumber%
```

The *GetResponses* subprogram

While the *GetQuestions* subprogram elicits and stores the survey questions, the *GetResponses* subprogram uses a similar procedure to elicit each response line, store the line in the *SUR* file (currently open as file #1), and keep track of the number of responses:

```
LINE INPUT ": "; surveyResponse$
    [other program lines]
WRITE #1, surveyResponse$
responseNumber% = responseNumber% + 1
```

When all the responses have been entered, the routine stores the value of *responseNumber%* in the *ALT* file (currently open as file #2):

```
WRITE #2, responseNumber%
```

Back in the *Create* subprogram, the following CLOSE statement closes the *SUR* and *ALT* files after the input dialog:

```
CLOSE #1, #2
```

This ends the process of generating a survey. The original three survey files—*SUR, ALT,* and *NUM*—are now stored safely on disk, their data ready to be used by other routines in the program.

The *PrintTheSurvey* subprogram

PrintTheSurvey prints a copy of a questionnaire form when you choose the second main-menu option, *Print a survey.* This routine in turn calls two other important subprograms: *OpenFiles,* to open the files describing a given survey, and *DoPrint,* to perform the actual printing process. Both of these subprograms are used elsewhere in the *Survey* program and are therefore designed to adjust their respective tasks appropriately to the situation at hand.

```
'    ---- Save the responses in name.SUR, currently open as file #1.
        IF (surveyResponse$ <> "") THEN
            WRITE #1, surveyResponse$
            responseNumber% = responseNumber% + 1

'    ---- Each question must have at least two responses.
        ELSEIF (responseNumber% = 1) OR (responseNumber% = 2) THEN
            surveyResponse$ = " "
        END IF
    WEND

'    ---- Save the number of responses in name.ALT, currently open as file #2.
    responseNumber% = responseNumber% - 1
    WRITE #2, responseNumber%
END SUB


'    The WaitForPrinter subprogram creates a pause in the action while the
'        user prepares the printer.  If the space bar is pressed, a value of
'        true is returned in the Boolean variable readyToGo% and the printing
'        process starts.  If the Esc key is pressed, a value of false is
'        returned to the calling program and the print operation is aborted.

SUB WaitForPrinter (readyToGo%) STATIC
    PRINT: PRINT: PRINT
    PRINT TAB(indent%) "Press the space bar when your printer is ready"
    PRINT TAB(indent%) "to operate or Esc to return to the main menu."
    character$ = ""
'    ---- Continue reading characters from the keyboard until one is either
'        the space character (" ") or the Esc character (ASCII 27).
    WHILE (character$ <> " ") AND (character$ <> CHR$(27))
        character$ = INKEY$
    WEND
    IF (character$ = CHR$(27)) THEN readyToGo% = false% _
        ELSE readyToGo% = true%
END SUB


'    The PrintTheSurvey subprogram controls the process of printing a survey.

SUB PrintTheSurvey STATIC
    PRINT: PRINT: PRINT
    PRINT "Print a Survey"
    PRINT "----- - ------"
    PRINT: PRINT

'    ---- OpenFiles gets the target filename and opens all necessary files.
'        When an argument of false% is sent to OpenFiles, no survey analysis
'        is done.
    CALL OpenFiles(false%)

    IF okFile% THEN

'    ---- Get the title of the survey and the number of questions in the
'        survey from the name.NUM file, currently open as file #3.
        INPUT #3, title$, numOfQuestions%
        CLOSE #3

'    ---- DoPrint actually prints the survey.  When an argument of 0 is sent,
'        DoPrint refrains from printing any analysis information.
        CALL DoPrint(title$, numOfQuestions%, 0)
```

WaitForPrinter

PrintTheSurvey

Figure 6-13. *The* Survey *program (continued).*   *(more ...)*

The *OpenFiles* subprogram

A call to *OpenFiles* takes an argument of *true%* or *false%*. Given an argument of *false%*, *OpenFiles* opens the original three survey files, *SUR*, *ALT*, and *NUM*, for reading. With an argument of *true%*, *OpenFiles* also opens the response file, *RES*. Below is the call from the *PrintTheSurvey* subprogram:

```
CALL OpenFiles(false%)
```

OpenFiles stores the incoming argument in the Boolean variable *all%*. The subprogram begins by using the FILES command to display a directory of *SUR* files on the screen.

If no files with *SUR* extensions exist in the current directory, the FILES statement generates a runtime error. This is averted by the *NoSurveyFiles* error trap, which displays a message on the screen and then sets the global Boolean variable *currentDirEmpty%* to *true%*.

If the *OpenFiles* subprogram was called by *PrintTheSurvey* or *Analyze* and the value of *currentDirEmpty%* is still false, the user then sees the following query:

```
Do you want to print one of these surveys (Y or N)?
```

If the *OpenFiles* subprogram was called by the *GetResponses* subprogram, the user sees this query:

```
Do you want to enter responses for one of these surveys (Y or N)?
```

These messages are printed by an IF...THEN...ELSEIF block that uses the global variable with the most recent main-menu selection, *choice%*.

If you respond positively, you are then prompted for a filename.

```
INPUT "Filename >", fileName$
```

OpenFiles combines the base filename with each of the four extension names, creating four different names (again, any extensions added by the user are stripped off). Then the routine makes an attempt to open the corresponding files:

```
ON ERROR GOTO MissingFile
    OPEN surFile$ FOR INPUT AS #1 LEN = 1024
    OPEN altFile$ FOR INPUT AS #2 LEN = 1024
    OPEN numFile$ FOR INPUT AS #3
    IF all% THEN OPEN resFile$ FOR INPUT AS #4 LEN = 1024
ON ERROR GOTO 0
```

```
      END IF
      CLOSE #1, #2
      CLS
END SUB


'     The DoPrint subprogram prints the survey in two different formats:
'         a blank survey sheet for a customer to fill in, or a survey
'         sheet that contains the calculated percentages from a group of
'         completed surveys.  A call to DoPrint takes three arguments:
'         surveyTitle$ is the title of the survey; numOfQuestions% is the
'         number of questions; and surveysReturned% is the number of survey
'         responses returned.  If surveysReturned% is 0, DoPrint prints a
'         blank survey sheet.

SUB DoPrint (surveyTitle$, numOfQuestions%, surveysReturned%) STATIC
      CALL WaitForPrinter(readyToGo%)
      IF readyToGo% THEN
'     ---- Print the survey title center aligned.
          surveyTitle$ = "Survey:  " + surveyTitle$
          space% = (80 - LEN(surveyTitle$)) / 2
          LPRINT TAB(space%) surveyTitle$

          IF surveysReturned% THEN
              LPRINT TAB(26) surveysReturned% "Survey Responses Received"
          ELSE
              LPRINT
          END IF
          LPRINT
          FOR i% = 1 TO numOfQuestions%

'     ---- Print the lines of the question.
              INPUT #2, garbage$
              INPUT #2, linesInQuestion%

              LPRINT i% "- ";
              FOR j% = 1 TO linesInQuestion%
                  INPUT #1, questionLine$
                  IF (j% > 1) THEN LPRINT SPACE$(10);
                  LPRINT questionLine$
              NEXT j%
              LPRINT

'     ---- Print the responses.
              INPUT #2, numOfResponses%
              FOR j% = 1 TO numOfResponses%
                  IF surveysReturned% THEN
                      percent% = CINT((response%(i%, j%) / surveysReturned%)*100)
                      LPRINT TAB(8) STR$(percent%) '%";
                  ELSE
                      LPRINT TAB(10) "[ ]";
                  END IF

                  INPUT #1, responseLine$

'     ---- Print a capital letter (starting with A) for each legal choice.
                  LPRINT TAB(15) CHR$(64 + j%);
                  LPRINT ": " responseLine$
              NEXT j%
              LPRINT: LPRINT
          NEXT i%
      END IF
END SUB
```

DoPrint

Figure 6-13. *The* Survey *program (continued).*   *(more...)*

Depending on the value of *all%*, this passage opens either three or four files for reading.

The ON ERROR GOTO statement sets up an error trap that will be activated if any of the files are missing. In this event, control of the program branches down to the error routine labeled *MissingFile*, shown directly below the *OpenFiles* subprogram:

```
MissingFile:
    okFile% = false%
RESUME NEXT
```

The Boolean variable *okFile%* is initialized to *true%* before the routine tries to open the files. If the value of *okFile%* has been switched to *false%* after the attempt, the condition indicates that the error routine has been performed and that there is not a complete set of files available. In this case, *OpenFiles* displays an error message, closes any files that may have been opened successfully, and returns control to the calling subprogram:

```
IF (NOT okFile%) THEN
    PRINT: PRINT
    PRINT "*** This file is not available. ***"
    CLOSE: PRINT
```

On the other hand, if *OpenFiles* locates and opens all the necessary files, *PrintTheSurvey* can begin the process of printing the questionnaire. Since the variable *okFile%* is declared global with the COMMON SHARED statement at the beginning of the program, *PrintTheSurvey* can use this Boolean value to decide if it should proceed. Assuming the survey files have been opened successfully, *PrintTheSurvey* reads two items of information from the *NUM* file: the title of the survey (*title$*) and the number of questions in the survey (*numOfQuestions%*). Then the routine closes the file:

```
IF okFile% THEN
    [intervening comments]
    INPUT #3, title$, numOfQuestions%
    CLOSE #3
```

These two values, *title$* and *numOfQuestions%*, are sent as arguments to the *DoPrint* subprogram:

```
CALL DoPrint(title$, numOfQuestions%, 0)
```

```
'   The OpenFiles subprogram performs several tasks.  It begins by
'       displaying the names of the survey files stored in the current
'       directory.  If none exist, an error message is displayed.  Then
'       it elicits the name of the target file, and attempts
'       to open that file.  If the attempt is unsuccessful, the routine
'       displays an error message.  A call to the routine takes one
'       Boolean argument, all%.  If true, the routine opens all four
'       associated files.  If false, the routine opens only the SUR,
'       ALT, and NUM files.

SUB OpenFiles (all%) STATIC
    PRINT  "Here are the survey files in the current directory:"
    PRINT
    PRINT STRING$(65, "-")

'   ---- Check for files with the SUR extension in the current directory.
'       Call the error-handling routine NoSurveyFiles if none are found.
    currentDirEmpty% = false%
    ON ERROR GOTO NoSurveyFiles
        FILES "*.SUR"
    ON ERROR GOTO 0

    PRINT STRING$(65, "-")
    PRINT

    IF (NOT currentDirEmpty%) THEN
'   ---- Print an appropriate header.
        IF (choice% = 2) OR (choice% = 4) THEN
            PRINT "Do you want to print one of these surveys";
            INPUT " (Y or N)"; reply$
        ELSEIF (choice% = 3) THEN
            PRINT "Do you want to enter responses for one of these surveys";
            INPUT " (Y or N)"; reply$
        END IF
        PRINT
'   ---- If the user would like to open a file, elicit a filename and open
'       all appropriate files.
        IF (LEFT$(reply$, 1) = "Y") OR (LEFT$(reply$, 1) = "y") THEN
            INPUT "Filename > ", fileName$
            PRINT
            IF (INSTR(fileName$,".") <> 0) THEN
                fileName$ = LEFT$(fileName$, INSTR(fileName$, ".") - 1)
            surFile$ = fileName$ + ".SUR"
            altFile$ = fileName$ + ".ALT"
            numFile$ = fileName$ + ".NUM"
            resFile$ = fileName$ + ".RES"
            okFile% = true%

'   ---- The error trap prevents termination if the files cannot be found.
            ON ERROR GOTO MissingFile
                OPEN surFile$ FOR INPUT AS #1 LEN = 1024
                OPEN altFile$ FOR INPUT AS #2 LEN = 1024
                OPEN numFile$ FOR INPUT AS #3
                IF all% THEN OPEN resFile$ FOR INPUT AS #4 LEN = 1024
            ON ERROR GOTO 0
```

Figure 6-13. *The* Survey *program (continued).*   *(more...)*

249

The call to *DoPrint* also takes a third argument: A value of 0 instructs the routine to print a questionnaire form; an integer value greater than 0 results in a survey analysis report.

The *DoPrint* subprogram

The *DoPrint* subprogram receives its three arguments in the parameter variables *surveyTitle$*, *numOfQuestions%*, and *surveysReturned%*.

The routine starts with a call to the *WaitForPrinter* subprogram. *WaitForPrinter* creates a pause, giving the user time to prepare the printer for the upcoming operation. At this time the user may either press the space bar to send the survey information to the printer, or press the Esc key to return to the main program. Notice that the Boolean variable *readyToGo%* is being sent by reference to the *WaitForPrinter* subprogram. If this variable returns with a value of true, the space bar was pressed and the survey is printed. If the user pressed the Esc key, *readyToGo%* carries a value of false, and the IF...THEN block of statements delimited by:

```
IF readyToGo% THEN
```

is skipped over, causing control to pass back to the main program.

If *readyToGo%* evaluates to true, *DoPrint* first prints the survey title at the center of the page with QuickBASIC's LPRINT statement:

```
LPRINT TAB(space%) surveyTitle$
```

If you are familiar with BASICA, you will recognize LPRINT as the statement that sends information to the printer connected to your machine's primary parallel port (LPT1). LPRINT functions the same as PRINT and PRINT USING, except that output goes to the printer rather than to the screen.

A FOR...NEXT loop controls the printing of each question in the survey:

```
FOR i% = TO numOfQuestions%
```

To print a question, *DoPrint* must read information from both the *ALT* file and the *SUR* file. Here is a summary of the necessary steps:

1.   From the *ALT* file (file #2), find out the number of lines in the current question (*linesInQuestion%*).

2.   Read *linesInQuestion%* lines from the *SUR* file (file #1) and send each line to the printer (indenting after the first line).

```
                IF (NOT okFile%) THEN
                    PRINT: PRINT
                    PRINT  "*** This file is not available. ***"
                    CLOSE: PRINT
                END IF
            ELSE
                okFile% = false%
            END IF
        END IF
        PRINT  "Press the space bar to continue."
        character$ = ""
        WHILE character$ <> " ": character$ = INKEY$: WEND
        CLS
END SUB

'    ---- The error handling routines for the OpenFiles subprogram:
NoSurveyFiles:
    PRINT
    PRINT "There are no .SUR files in the current directory."
    PRINT
    currentDirEmpty% = true%
RESUME NEXT

MissingFile:
    okFile% = false%
RESUME NEXT

'    The Responses subprogram conducts the input dialog for the
'        "Enter responses to a survey" option.

SUB Responses STATIC
    PRINT: PRINT: PRINT
    PRINT "Enter Responses to a Survey"
    PRINT "----- --------- -- - ------"
    PRINT: PRINT

'    ---- OpenFiles elicits a filename and opens the appropriate files.
    CALL OpenFiles(false%)
    IF okFile% THEN

'    ---- Get the title from the name.NUM file.
        INPUT #3, title$, numOfQuestions%
        CLOSE

'    ---- Make sure this is the file the user wants.
        PRINT: PRINT: PRINT
        PRINT TAB(indent%) "Survey title: " title$
        PRINT: PRINT TAB(indent%);

        IF FN YesNo("Is this the correct survey?") THEN
            CLS

'    ---- Store the responses in the name.RES file.
            OPEN resFile$ FOR APPEND AS #4
            continue% = true%
            WHILE continue%
                OPEN altFile$ FOR INPUT AS #2
                FOR i% = 1 to numOfQuestions%
```

Figure 6-13. *The* Survey *program (continued).* *(more...)*

Responses

3. From the *ALT* file again, find out the number of responses for the current question (*numOfResponses%*).

4. Read *numOfResponses%* lines from the *SUR* file and send each response to the printer.

Let's look briefly at the details of these steps. Recall that the *ALT* file contains three items of information for each question in the survey:

- A 15-character text excerpt from the first line of the question

- The number of lines in the question (*linesInQuestion%*)

- The number of multiple-choice responses for the question (*numOfResponses%*)

Although the *DoPrint* subprogram only requires the second and third items, the routine must read all three items in order. This is the nature of a sequential file. The following INPUT# statements read the text value and the value for *linesInQuestion%*:

```
INPUT #2, garbage$
INPUT #2, linesInQuestion%
```

As you can see, the text value is stored in a string variable named *garbage$*, to indicate that the value is of no particular use here.

Given *linesInQuestion%*, the number of lines in the current question, the following nested FOR . . . NEXT loop reads the correct number of lines from the *SUR* file and sends each line to the printer:

```
FOR j% = 1 TO linesInQuestion%
    INPUT #1, questionLine$
    IF (j% > 1) THEN LPRINT SPACE$(10);
    LPRINT questionLine$
NEXT j%
```

A similar process occurs for reading and printing the responses. The program reads the number of responses, *numOfResponses%*, from

```
'    ---- Get the dimensions of the file.
                INPUT #2, teaser$, garbage%, numOfResponses%
                PRINT TAB(indent%) i% "- " teaser$ "..."
                PRINT TAB(indent% + 7);
                answer$ = FN GetLetter$(numOfResponses%)
                PRINT #4, answer$;
                IF (i% <> numOfQuestions%) THEN PRINT #4, ", ";
                PRINT
            NEXT i%

            CLOSE #2
            PRINT #4,
            PRINT
            continue% = FN YesNo("Another?")
            CLS
         WEND
      ELSE
         CLS
      END IF
   END IF
   CLOSE
END SUB
'   The Analyze subprogram examines a set of survey responses and determines
'      the selection percentages for each individual answer.  Analyze
'      supplies a printed survey form that includes these percentages.

SUB Analyze STATIC
   PRINT: PRINT: PRINT
   PRINT "Analyze the Responses to a Survey"
   PRINT "------- --- --------- -- - ------"
   PRINT: PRINT

'   ---- OpenFiles opens the target files.  Sending an argument of true%
'      also opens the name.RES file, which contains the set of responses.
   CALL OpenFiles(true%)
   IF okFile% THEN
      INPUT #3, title$, numOfQuestions%
      CLOSE #3

'   ---- Confirm that the user has opened the right file.
      PRINT: PRINT: PRINT
      PRINT TAB(indent%) "Survey title: " title$
      PRINT
      PRINT TAB(indent%);

      IF (FN YesNo("Is this the correct survey?")) THEN
         PRINT
         range$ = "ABCDEFGHIJ"
         REDIM response%(numOfQuestions%, 10)
         total% = 0

'   ---- Analyze the response data. Go through the entire response file,
'      and tally the occurrences of each response. Store the tally in
'      the array response%.
```

Analyze

Figure 6-13. *The* Survey *program (continued).*   (*more . . .*)

the *ALT* file; then a second nested FOR ... NEXT loop reads each response from the *SUR* file and sends it to the printer:

```
INPUT #2, numOfResponses%
FOR j% = 1 TO numOfResponses%
    [print a percentage or an empty box]
    INPUT #1, responseLine$
    [print a capital letter for each survey choice]
    LPRINT ": " responseLine$
NEXT j%
```

When the entire survey has been printed, the *PrintTheSurvey* subprogram closes the *SUR* and *ALT* files:

```
CLOSE #1, #2
```

We will be looking again at the *DoPrint* routine later when we discuss the *Analyze* subprogram.

The *Responses* subprogram

The *Responses* subprogram conducts the input dialog for questionnaire responses and appends each group of responses to the end of the *RES* file. To elicit a filename, the routine starts by calling *OpenFiles* with an argument of *false%*. Assuming the program successfully opens the survey files (*okFile%* is true), *Responses* reads the survey title and the number of questions from the *NUM* file (currently open as file #3):

```
CALL OpenFiles(false%)
IF okFile% THEN
    INPUT #3, title$, numOfQuestions%
    CLOSE
```

Responses closes all the files again after this single read operation. As you will see, the subprogram issues its own OPEN statements to open the *ALT* and the *RES* files at appropriate moments during the input dialog. After the call to *OpenFiles,* the global string variables *altFile$* and *resFile$* supply the names of these two files.

Responses next displays the survey title on the screen and uses the *YesNo* user-defined function to ask the user to confirm that the correct files have been selected. If the answer is affirmative, the *Responses* subprogram opens the *RES* file in the APPEND mode, as file #4:

```
OPEN resFile$ FOR APPEND AS #4
```

```
            WHILE NOT EOF(4)
                FOR i% = 1 to numOfQuestions%
                    INPUT #4, answer$
                    answer% = INSTR(range$, answer$)
                    response%(i%, answer%) = response%(i%, answer%) + 1
                NEXT i%
                total% = total% + 1
            WEND

'    ---- DoPrint prints the survey form.
            CALL DoPrint(title$, numOfQuestions%, total%)
        END IF
    END IF
    CLS
    CLOSE
END SUB
```

Figure 6-13. *The* Survey *program (continued).*

If a *RES* file does not already exist, a new one is created. If a *RES* file does exist the OPEN statement prepares to write data values to the end of the response file.

Now the *Responses* subprogram is ready to start the input dialog. The routine uses the *ALT* file to guide the input process. For each complete set of questionnaire responses, the routine follows these steps:

1. Open the *ALT* file for reading, as file #2.

2. For each question in the survey:

    — Read the 15-character "teaser" string excerpt from the question text and the number of multiple-choice responses, both from the *ALT* file.
    — Display the teaser to identify the question, and display the correct sequence of single-letter responses as an input prompt.
    — Get the response from the keyboard.
    — Save the response in the *RES* file, currently open as file #4.

3. After eliciting an answer for all the survey questions, close the *ALT* file.

4. Ask the user if there is another survey to record.

For each round of the input dialog, the program has to read the entire *ALT* file from beginning to end. To accomplish this, the program opens the file at the beginning of a round:

```
OPEN altFile$ FOR INPUT AS #2
```

and closes it again at the end of a round:

```
CLOSE #2
```

To prepare the prompts that elicit a response to a given question, the program reads the corresponding description from the *ALT* file:

```
INPUT #2, teaser$, garbage%, numOfResponses%
```

The program displays the first of these variables, *teaser$*, to identify the question. The second of these three variables—indicating the number of lines in the question text—is irrelevant to this routine and is therefore read into the variable named *garbage%*.

The third value, *numOfResponses%*, is the number of possible responses to a given question. The *Responses* subprogram sends this value to a special input function named *GetLetter$*:

```
answer$ = FN GetLetter$(numOfResponses%)
```

The *GetLetter$* function

GetLetter$* elicits a valid single-letter response from the keyboard. The integer argument value tells *GetLetter$ how many letters of the alphabet are valid responses to a given question. For example, if the function receives an argument of 5, it displays the following input prompt on the screen:

```
A B C D E ->
```

If you press any one of these five letter keys, the function returns the character as the input answer. (The function rejects any invalid input characters and beeps to alert you of the error.)

The *Responses* subprogram stores the result of *GetLetter$* in the *answer$* variable. One by one, each value of *answer$* is stored in the *RES* file. The semicolon directly after the *answer$* variable causes each set of survey responses to be stored on the same line:

```
PRINT #4, answer$;
```

After each entry in the file (except for the final alphabetic character in a given line), the program stores a comma as a delimiter:

```
IF (i% <> numOfQuestions%) THEN PRINT #4, ", ";
```

A PRINT# statement sends a carriage return/line feed sequence after each line of the file:

```
PRINT #4,
```

As you can see by looking back at Figure 6-10, the PRINT# statement allows this routine to send data to the file in a table format.

Once a *RES* file exists for a given survey, the *Analyze* subprogram can produce its printed report, supplying a statistical description of the answers received.

The *Analyze* subprogram

Given a set of open survey files, the *Analyze* subprogram has two major tasks:

1. For each multiple-choice answer to each question in the survey, tally the total number of participants who selected the answer.

2. Print a survey report in which these tallies are converted to percentages.

This process requires information from all four of the survey files: *SUR* (the text of the questions and answers), *ALT* (the dimensions of the file), *NUM* (the survey title and the number of questions in the file), and *RES* (the recorded responses to the survey). To open all these files at once, the subprogram starts by calling the *OpenFiles* routine:

```
CALL OpenFiles(true%)
```

Recall that an argument of *true%* (−1) instructs *OpenFiles* to open all four survey files, including the *RES* file.

Like the *Responses* routine before it, *Analyze* displays the survey title on the screen and gives the user the opportunity to confirm the file selection. Once this is done, *Analyze* sets up a two-dimensional array of integers as a table for tallying the responses:

```
REDIM response%(numOfQuestions%, 10)
```

The first dimension of *response%* is the number of questions in the current survey. The second dimension is fixed at 10, the maximum number of responses for any question. You may have noticed that this dynamic array is declared global at the beginning of the *Survey* program.

In preparation for the tallying process, *Analyze* creates two other important variables. The integer variable *total%* will be used to count the total number of questionnaires that are recorded in the *RES* file. This variable is initialized to 0:

```
total% = 0
```

A string variable named *range$* receives the range of single-letter responses that the program can expect to find in the *RES* file:

```
range$ = "ABCDEFGHIJ"
```

The program will ultimately have to convert each letter response, *answer$*, into a number in the range 1 to 10. Using *range$* and the INSTR function, this is an easy task:

```
answer% = INSTR(range$, answer$)
```

For example, if *answer$* contains the letter *D*, this statement assigns a corresponding value of 4 to the integer variable *answer%*. Recall that the INSTR function returns the position—counting left to right—where the second string argument (*answer$* in this example) is found in the first string argument (*range$* in this example). Also note that QuickBASIC considers *answer$* and *answer%* two distinct variables, one a string and the other an integer.

A WHILE...WEND loop reads the *RES* file (currently opened as file #4) from beginning to end:

```
WHILE NOT EOF(4)
```

Inside this WHILE...WEND loop, a nested FOR...NEXT loop reads the answer to each question and performs the necessary letter-to-integer conversion:

```
FOR i% = 1 to numOfQuestions%
    INPUT #4, answer$
    answer% = INSTR(range$, answer$)
```

The integer *answer%* now represents the number of the answer that was selected on the current questionnaire. The following statement increments the corresponding element of the *response%* array to tally the answer:

```
response%(i%, answer%) = response%(i%, answer%) + 1
```

After reading an entire line of answers, the subprogram increments the value of *total%*, the total number of questionnaires received:

```
total% = total% + 1
```

Finally, to print the survey report, *Analyze* calls the *DoPrint* subprogram:

```
CALL DoPrint(title$, numOfQuestions%, total%)
```

The three arguments represent the title of the survey, the number of questions in the survey, and the total number of questionnaires returned and recorded.

As we have seen, the *DoPrint* subprogram receives the value of *total%* in the variable *surveysReturned%*. Since *surveysReturned%* does not equal 0, it maintains a value of true when used in the second IF...THEN statement of the *DoPrint* subprogram. As a result, *DoPrint* displays a message that reports the total number of questionnaires recorded:

```
IF surveysReturned% THEN
    LPRINT TAB(26) surveysReturned% "Survey Responses Received"
```

Then, before sending each line of answer text to the printer, *DoPrint* converts the corresponding element of *response%* to a percentage of the total number of questionnaires and prints the value:

```
IF surveysReturned% THEN
    percent% = CINT((response%(i%, j%) / surveysReturned%)*100)
    LPRINT TAB(8) STR$(percent%) "%";
```

This is the key to creating the statistical survey report.

CONCLUSION

We have seen that sequential files are designed to be used item by item, from the first value in the file to the last. QuickBASIC supplies a versatile set of commands and functions for performing sequential file input and output operations. In summary, these operations are:

- Opening a file for reading (OPEN ... FOR INPUT)
- Reading one or more data values from an open file (INPUT#)
- Reading an entire line from a file, regardless of delimiter characters within the line (LINE INPUT#)
- Reading a specified number of characters from the file (the INPUT$ function)
- Determining when the reading process has reached the end of the file (the EOF function)
- Creating a new file and preparing to write information to the file (OPEN ... FOR OUTPUT)

- Opening an existing file and preparing to append data to the end of the file (OPEN ... FOR APPEND)

- Writing data values to the file (WRITE# or PRINT#)

- Closing the file (CLOSE)

An application program that works with a particular set of data or text values might be designed to create more than one sequential file on disk to describe the data set. QuickBASIC allows a program to open multiple files at once. When the program is run, each open file is identified by a unique file number and is associated with a memory buffer that temporarily stores data going to and from the file.

The programmer's job is to devise a system of data files that conveniently stores and adequately describes the data set. For example, we have seen that the *Survey* program creates four different data files for each survey it generates. We can describe the purposes of these files in the following general terms:

- Storing the text of the survey

- Describing the length of each question

- Describing the length of the survey

- Storing data generated in response to the survey

Together, these four files give the *Survey* program all the information it needs to efficiently manage the various survey operations.

If you are inclined to attempt additional programming projects with the *Survey* application, a few suggestions follow:

1. Create a routine that expands the analysis of responses received from a survey. Specifically, write a subprogram that isolates all those respondents who answered a specified question in a given way; then, within this subgroup of participants, analyze the results of other questions. For example, in the customer-satisfaction survey for Sam's auto shop, we might like to look at the group of customers who came in for routine service (answer A of question 5) and find out how this group first heard about Sam's shop (question 1).

2. Go one step further with the analysis: Write a routine that looks for respondents who answered two or more questions in a certain way, and examine the characteristics of this subgroup. For example, imagine a survey aimed at characterizing consumers of a particular business software program. You might want to focus on all those respondents who are in a certain age group and income level.

3. Think of ways to improve the presentation of the statistical report produced by the *Analyze responses* option, both on the screen and on paper. One idea is to rearrange the response lines beneath each question in the order of the percentages, from the highest to the lowest. For example, the first question from Sam's survey shown in Figure 6-11 might be rearranged as:

```
1 - How did you first hear about Sam's Friendly
        Auto Repair Shop?
     45%    D: In the phone book.
     30%    A: From a friend.
     15%    B: In our newspaper advertisement.
     6%     C: From our radio commercial.
     5%     F: Other.
     0%     E: By passing the shop on the street.
```

To do this you need to include a sort routine in the *Survey* program; use a revision of either the *Sort* subprogram introduced in Chapter 3 or the simpler bubble sort described in Chapter 8.

CHAPTER 7

Random-access Files: A Database Management Program

*I*n the last chapter we explored QuickBASIC's ability to create and manipulate data stored in sequential files. Individual data elements are stored in a sequential file one after the other. Therefore, to find a particular data element in the middle of the file, QuickBASIC must read all the elements in sequence from the beginning of the file to the one it needs. Consequently, sequential files are best used for storing sets of information that will always be accessed from beginning to end.

To store and access individual data elements at selected locations within files, you can use a set of QuickBASIC statements for creating and manipulating *random-access files.* Unlike sequential files, random-access files permit programs to access individual data elements directly, without reading all the intervening elements.

Database management has evolved into one of the most important general applications for personal computers. Storing information on disk and accessing that information is an essential activity in business, in scientific and technological fields, and even in personal life. QuickBASIC is a good programming environment in which to develop customized database applications. The random-access file commands—combined with a few important tools like the *Sort* and *Search* subprograms presented in Chapter 3—enable QuickBASIC to perform a broad range of database management tasks.

A typical database management program has specific features that help the user build a database and access the information in it. For example, most databases provide easy steps for accomplishing the following:

- Entering records of information into the database

- Locating a specific record and displaying it on the screen

- Modifying the contents of a record

- Deleting records that are no longer relevant

- Printing tables of many records, arranged in a specified order

A *record* is the main organizational unit of a database. Records, in turn, are organized into *fields* of information. For example, the *Employee* program in this chapter manages a database of employee profiles. Each record in the database describes one employee. The program elicits several items of information about each new employee: name, social security number, date hired, job title, salary, and so on. These items become the fields of an employee record.

Using QuickBASIC, you can create a random-access file to store a database. Random-access files and the programs that manipulate them have three important characteristics:

1. The record length of the file is fixed (each record contains a specified number of characters).

2. To read records from—or write records to—the file, a program must first supply a specific structure for dividing the records into fields of information.

3. Records can be read from or written to the file in any order (thus the term *random-access file*).

We begin this chapter by reviewing the dozen or so commands and functions that create and handle random-access files. These language features enable a program to:

- Open a random-access file and define its field structure (OPEN and FIELD)

- Determine the current length of an open file (LOF)

- Read a record from any location in the file (GET#)

- Assign the data of a record to specified field variables (LSET and RSET) and subsequently store the entire record in the file (PUT#)

- Store numeric data in the file as strings in a space-saving format (MKI$, MKS$, and MKD$) and convert those strings into numeric values that the program can work with (CVI, CVS, CVD)

- Close a file when the program finishes working with it (CLOSE)

In addition to these commands and functions, several tools from our collection of subprograms play essential roles in the *Employee* program. The most significant are the *Sort* and *Search* subprograms from Chapter 3, which build and manage a special index in the employee database. This index lets the program directly locate any employee record, regardless of its position in the file.

RANDOM-ACCESS FILE HANDLING IN QUICKBASIC

Unlike sequential files, a random-access file can be opened for both reading and writing at once with the OPEN statement. We begin by looking at the syntax of this statement.

The OPEN statement

The virtue of a random-access file is that it lets QuickBASIC retrieve or send individual records by passing over all of the preceding records. QuickBASIC must know the size of all the records in a file so that it can

calculate how far it must jump to access a specific record. This means
that all the records in a particular file must be the same size; if they are
not, a jump might land in the middle of a record rather than at the beginning. Even though not every record necessarily uses all of its
allotted space, each record in a random-access file must be assigned
enough space to accommodate the largest record in the file.

The size of a random-access record is the total number of characters in the record. Because a record consists of a number of fields, the
total size of a record is the sum of all its field lengths, which are also
measured in characters. (Field lengths are defined with the FIELD
statement, which we examine shortly.)

The size of the records in a random-access file is established by
the OPEN statement, which uses the following format:

OPEN *"fileName"* **FOR RANDOM AS** *#fileNumber* **LEN** = *recordLength*

The filename can be any string of text that follows the DOS rules
for filenames: a base name of a maximum of eight characters followed
by an optional extension name of a maximum of three characters. You
can also include drive and path designations as part of the filename.

The OPEN statement also requires a file number. Since a
QuickBASIC program can open multiple files, a file number is necessary to identify each open file. (The maximum number of files that
may be open at any one time is 255.) When a file is open, subsequent
program statements refer to it by its number. For example, FIELD#1,
GET#1, and PUT#1 all work with a particular file identified as #1.

Finally, you can use the LEN clause of the OPEN statement to indicate the record length of the file you are opening. Specify the length in
characters (or bytes); the number should equal the sum of all field
widths listed in the FIELD statement. If you omit the LEN clause, the
default record length is 128 characters.

Here is an example of the OPEN statement, taken from the
Employee program:

```
OPEN "EMP.DAT" FOR RANDOM AS #1 LEN = 91
```

This statement opens a random-access file named *EMP.DAT*, assigns
it a file number of 1, and specifies a record length of 91 characters.
QuickBASIC sets aside 91 bytes in the computer's memory for storing

individual records that are written to or read from file number 1. This memory area is called a *buffer*. (If a program is given a record longer than the length specified in the LEN statement, only the number of characters corresponding to the LEN statement are written to the file.)

EMP.DAT may or may not already exist at the time this OPEN statement is performed. Opening a nonexistent random-access file does not result in a runtime error. If the file does not exist, it is created, although the file remains empty until you begin writing records into it. If the file does exist, QuickBASIC is ready to read from it or write to it.

The OPEN statement also has a more cryptic shorthand form. For example:

```
OPEN "R", #1, "EMP.DAT", 91
```

This statement opens *EMP.DAT* as a random-access file, with a file number of 1 and a record length of 91. The syntax is a carryover from older versions of BASIC. Although this shortened form may save you a few keystrokes, the first form is clearer and more readable.

Multiprocessing considerations for random-access files

One final note about the OPEN statement: QuickBASIC allows file sharing in multiprocessing environments, such as a network in which two or more computers share a storage device. If you write a database management program for such an environment, you must plan for more than one user attempting to access the same database simultaneously.

Unless a program takes this eventuality into account, a number of mishaps can occur. For example, one user might be reading a record while another is writing data to the same record. In this case, the first user is unaware that the data on the screen is no longer current. Another problem arises if two users try to write new data to a record simultaneously: the validity of the resulting record is suspect.

You can control the multiple use of QuickBASIC random-access files at the file level and at the record level. For control at the file level, the OPEN statement has optional ACCESS and LOCK clauses. The ACCESS clause specifies whether the current use of the file is for reading, writing, or both. The LOCK clause restricts any other use of the file while it is open. For example, the following statement opens the random-access file *EMP.DAT* for reading, but denies permission for anyone to write to the file:

```
OPEN "EMP.DAT" FOR RANDOM ACCESS READ LOCK WRITE AS #1
```

For control at the record level, QuickBASIC has the LOCK and UNLOCK statements. The LOCK statement restricts the use of specific records. The format for this statement is:

LOCK *#fileNumber, startingRecord* **TO** *endingRecord*

where *startingRecord* is the first record in a consecutive list of records to be locked, and *endingRecord* is the last. If you omit *endingRecord,* only *startingRecord* is locked.

For example, the following program segment prevents other processes from accessing record 12 in file #1 while the current program is using it; it makes the record available again with an UNLOCK statement:

```
LOCK #1, 12
    [other program lines]
UNLOCK #1, 12
```

These features are available only if QuickBASIC is running under MS-DOS versions 3.1 or later, which support networking. Consult the QuickBASIC documentation for further details.

The FIELD statement

The purpose of the FIELD statement is to divide up the record length of a random-access file into appropriate field widths. The sum of the widths of all the fields should equal the record length specified in the OPEN statement. Here is the syntax of the FIELD statement:

FIELD *#fileNumber, fieldWidth1* **AS** *fieldVariable1$* _
  fieldWidth2 **AS** *fieldVariable2$* _
  fieldWidth3 **AS** *fieldVariable3$* _
  [additional field definitions]

The FIELD statement specifies a width, *m* characters, for each field variable. As a result of the statement, the named field variables will refer to designated widths in the random-access file buffer. All fields must be represented as string variables and have names ending with the $ string suffix.

You can write FIELD statements that are easy to read by listing the field widths and variables on consecutive lines, using QuickBASIC's line-continuation symbol (_) to tie the statements together. For example, here is the FIELD statement in the *Employee* program:

```
FIELD #1, 15 AS lastName$, _          ' last name
        10 AS firstName$, _           ' first name
        11 AS socialSecurity$, _      ' social security number
        10 AS hireDate$, _            ' date hired
        15 AS dept$, _                ' department (or "departed")
        15 AS position$, _            ' position
        4  AS salary$, _              ' current salary
        1  AS salaryType$, _          ' salary type (hr, mo, yr)
        10 AS depDate$                ' date of departure from firm
```

As you can see, this statement creates nine field variables of varying widths. The sum of all these widths, 91, equals the record length specified in the file's OPEN statement.

Data is not put directly into a random-access file as it is with sequential files: It is first put in the record buffer and from there transferred to the file. Similarly, data is not read directly from the file; it is first placed in the record buffer, from which the program then retrieves it. After you establish the field variables, you can access a record from the file or send a record to the file with the GET# and PUT# statements. The PUT# statement writes a record from the record buffer to the file. The GET# statement reads a record from the file and stores it in the record buffer.

Reading a record from a random-access file: The GET# statement

The GET# statement takes the following syntax:

> **GET** *#fileNumber, recordNumber*

The file number must match the number you originally assigned to the file in the OPEN statement. The record number identifies the record that you want to read. When you use a GET# statement, the specified record is transferred to the file buffer; from there you use the field variables to access the data. For example, in the following statements:

```
GET #1, 12
PRINT lastName$, firstName$, socialSecurity$
```

the GET# statement reads record 12 into the buffer, and then the PRINT statement displays the first three fields of the record (which we previously defined with FIELD) on the screen.

The LOF function

If a GET# statement attempts to read a record number that is greater than the number of records actually stored in the file, results are unpredictable. For this reason, a program usually needs to determine the number of records currently stored in a random-access file. The built-in LOF (*length-of-file*)function returns the length, in bytes, of an open file. Dividing this value by the record length yields the number of records in the file.

LOF takes one numeric argument: a file number. The following expression determines the total number of records in file 1, in which the record length is 91 bytes. The statement assigns the result to the variable *numberOfRecords%*:

```
numberOfRecords% = LOF(1) / 91
```

The record number in a GET# statement is often expressed as a variable. Because the total number of records is also the number of the last record, the following statement reads the last record of the file into the file buffer:

```
GET #1, numberOfRecords%
```

In summary, the steps for reading records from a random-access file are:

1. Open the file and specify the record length (OPEN).

2. Use field variables to designate the length of each field within a record (FIELD).

3. (optional) Determine the current number of records in the file (LOF / record length).

4. Read a specific record from the file into the buffer (GET#).

5. Use the field variables to access particular field values from the buffer.

Retrieving specific fields with GET#

Significantly enough, you can supply more than one FIELD statement for dividing a file's record structure into field widths. Doing this allows a program to read record values in different ways.

For example, imagine a subprogram that only needs to read the first three fields of the employee database—*lastName$*, *firstName$*, and *socialSecurity$*—and print out a table of these three fields. The following FIELD statement meets the requirements of this subprogram.

```
FIELD #1, 36 AS nameNumber$, _   ' the employee's name and number
     55 AS garbage$              ' the remainder of the record
```

Notice that the field width of *nameNumber$* equals the sum of the first three field widths in the original FIELD statement and that the rest of the record is lumped together in the field variable *garbage$*. Thus, the *nameNumber$* string actually contains three items: the employee's last name, first name, and social security number. Given this second record structure, the program can read individual records from the file and print the *nameNumber$* field from each record. For example:

```
GET #1, 12
LPRINT nameNumber$
```

This second record structure can coexist with the first, and different parts of the program can establish different record structures, each of which is tailored to provide only the information required for the current operation.

To write records to a random-access file, you must understand some additional characteristics of field variables.

Understanding field variables

First, field variables that are established within a subprogram are, by default, local to that subprogram. In this respect, field variables are the same as regular program variables. However, in many programs field variables are more convenient to work with if you declare them global. For example, the following COMMON SHARED statement establishes all nine fields in the employee database as global:

```
COMMON SHARED lastName$, firstName$, socialSecurity$, _
    hireDate$, dept$, position$, salary$, salaryType$, deptDate$
```

Access to the record buffer itself is, in effect, global: Any subprogram can successfully issue a command that refers to a specific file by number (such as GET# or PUT#). Only the field variables that refer to portions of the buffer are local, unless you declare them otherwise.

Assigning string values to field variables

Assigning a value to a field variable requires special attention. You cannot use simple assignment statements or INPUT statements to store field values in the file buffer; doing so destroys the special status of the field variable. If the value is a string, QuickBASIC uses the LSET and RSET statements to assign it to field variables. LSET left-justifies the string within the field width and, if necessary, appends spaces to fill the width. RSET right-justifies the string within the field width, and, if necessary, appends spaces on the left to fill the width.

The following sequence prompts the user to enter a string value from the keyboard as an employee's last name, and then it stores the value in the appropriate field variable:

```
INPUT "Last name"; lastTemp$
LSET lastName$ = lastTemp$
```

Notice that the variable *lastTemp$* temporarily stores the input-string value. Placing the value directly into the field variable *lastName$* would be a mistake. For example, as a result of this statement:

```
INPUT "Employee's last name"; lastName$
```

QuickBASIC would subsequently treat *lastName$* as a standard string variable rather than as a field variable. Thereafter, *lastName$* would not be associated with the field buffer, and the input value itself would not be stored in the buffer.

Assigning numeric values to field variables

Another important programming issue is the storage format of numeric values in the random-access file. We have already noted that fields in random-access files are always represented as string variables with specified widths. How do you assign a numeric value to such a variable?

The functions MKI$, MKS$, and MKD$ convert numbers into fixed-length strings that can be assigned to string-type field variables. Briefly, these three functions work like this:

- MKI$ converts a specified integer value into a two-byte string equivalent.

- MKS$ converts a specified single-precision number into a four-byte string equivalent.

- MKD$ converts a specified double-precision number into an eight-byte string equivalent.

For example, the employee database includes a salary field for each employee's hourly rate. Normally, a program stores a salary as a single-precision number. However, the FIELD statement in the *OpenFile* subprogram designates the field variable *salary$* as a string field with a width of four characters:

```
FIELD #1, 15 AS lastName$, _              ' last name
    [intervening field declarations]
    4  AS salary$, _                       ' current salary
```

To assign a numeric value to this field variable, you use the MKS$ function to convert the value into a four-byte string format. For example, consider the following lines:

```
INPUT "Employee's salary"; salaryTemp
LSET salary$ = MKS$(salaryTemp)
```

The first statement elicits the employee's salary from the user at the keyboard and temporarily stores the input value in the numeric variable *salaryTemp*. In the second statement, the MKS$ function supplies a four-byte equivalent of the number, and the LSET statement assigns this converted value to the *salary$* field.

To use a converted numeric value that is stored in a random-access file, a program needs to change the value back into a number. To do this, QuickBASIC supplies three complementary functions: CVI (*convert integer*), CVS (*convert single-precision*), and CVD (*convert double-precision*). These functions convert strings to numbers; their purpose is the opposite of the MKI\$, MKS\$, and MKD\$ functions. For example, consider these two statements:

```
GET #1, 12
PRINT USING "Salary is $$#,###.##"; CVS(salary$)
```

The GET# statement reads employee record 12, and the PRINT USING statement displays the field associated with *salary\$* (the employee's salary) on the screen. CVS supplies the numeric single-precision equivalent of the four-byte string value stored in *salary\$*.

In summary, here are three essential characteristics of field variables in random-access files:

1. Unless a program declares them global, field variables are local to the subprogram in which they are defined.

2. A program must use either the LSET or RSET command to assign a value to a field variable. A regular assignment statement, or an INPUT statement, disassociates the field variable from its corresponding width in the file buffer.

3. All field variables are designed to store string values. To store numeric values efficiently in a field variable, a program should use the string conversion functions MKI\$, MKS\$, and MKD\$. The CVI, CVS, and CVD functions change such values back into numbers.

Writing a record to a random-access file: The PUT# statement

The PUT# statement writes the contents of the record buffer to a random-access file. Its format is:

PUT *#fileNumber, recordNumber*

where *recordNumber* is a specified record position in the file and *fileNumber* is the number associated with an open random-access file.

Before using PUT#, a program must use LSET or RSET to assign specific values to each field variable in the record buffer. A PUT# statement then writes the entire record to a specified record in the file. For example, the following sequence assigns values to four fields of an employee's record and then writes the information as the tenth record of the file:

```
LSET lastName$ = "Smith"
LSET firstName$ = "Robin"
LSET dateHired$ = DATE$
LSET position$ = "Office Mgr"
PUT #1, 10
```

Caution: If the program has read some other record from a file just before performing this write operation, the field values from the former record are still in the buffer. To avoid writing the old values to the new record, assign a new string value to every field variable. To erase a former field value without storing a new value, assign an empty string value to the field variable. Any blank fields are written to the file as strings of spaces, and anything originally present is overwritten. (This technique is used in the *Employee* program.)

In summary, these are the steps for writing a record to a random-access file, assuming the program has already opened the file and issued a FIELD statement to specify field widths:

1.   Use MKI$, MKS$, or MKD$ to convert any numeric field value to a string before storing the value in a field variable.

2.   Use LSET or RSET to assign values to the designated field variables in the record buffer.

3.   Use PUT# to write the record currently in the record buffer to a specific location in the file.

You can use this process either to write a completely new record to a file or to revise the contents of a record currently stored in the file. Examples of both procedures are in the *Employee* program.

Both sequential files and random-access files use the same CLOSE statement. In review, the format for closing one or more open files is:

CLOSE *#fileNumber(s)*

where *fileNumber(s)* is a list of one or more numbers (separated by commas) that indicates open files. For example, the following statement closes two files, #1 and #3:

```
CLOSE #1, #3
```

After these files are closed, the program can use the numbers 1 and 3 for other files. A file number is associated with a specific filename only while it's open. To close all open files, enter the CLOSE statement with no arguments.

You have seen how to use the QuickBASIC commands and functions to handle random-access files. Now it is time to use them with the *Employee* program.

A SAMPLE RUN OF THE *EMPLOYEE* PROGRAM

Employee is a menu-driven program; the program's recurring menu is shown in Figure 7-1. This menu offers four options that deal with individual records in the employee database, and one option that works with the entire database:

- The *Examine an employee's record* option displays a specified employee's record.

- The *Add a new employee* option conducts an input dialog to obtain field information for a new employee record. When the dialog is complete, the program writes the record into the file.

- The *Change an employee's record* option lets you change certain fields of information in an employee's record. Specifically, you can enter new values for the employee's department, job title, and salary.

- The *Record a departure* option records the departure of an employee from the company. The employee's record is modified but not deleted from the file.

- The *Print a list of employees* option prints a table of employee records, arranged in alphabetic order. Depending on your instructions, the program can either include or omit the records of employees who have left the firm.

Because the menu reappears after each operation, you can work with as many employee records as you want during a session. The final option on the menu is *Quit,* which terminates the program.

The *Employee* program actually creates and maintains two different files on disk. The database itself is stored in a random-access file named *EMP.DAT.* Each time you add a new record to the database or

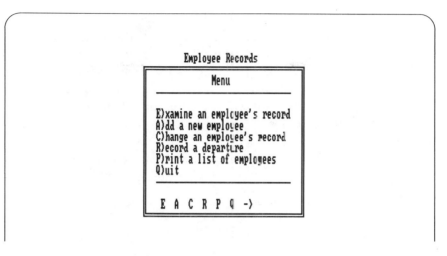

Figure 7-1. *The main menu for the* Employee *program.*

revise the contents of a current record, *Employee* writes the information to this database file. Records in this file are stored in chronological order; that is, each new record is placed at the end of the file.

In addition, *Employee* creates an *index file,* stored in a sequential file named *EMP.NDX.* Although you see no explicit evidence that this index file exists when running the program, the program would be unable to locate employee records without it. The file contains two items of information for each employee:

1. The employee's name

2. The employee's record number in the database

When the program is run, it first reads this index into the computer's memory. As it manipulates the records, the program always sorts this index alphabetically by the name entries. Each time you add a new record to the database, the program also adds the new employee's name and record number to the index and then re-sorts the index. Finally, when you quit, the program saves the current index on disk again, where it can be found at the beginning of the next performance.

When you request an option that requires the use of a record currently stored in the database, the *Employee* program first asks for the employee's name. The program then searches for this name in the

alphabetized index. If the name is in the index, the program gets the
employee's record number from the index, reads that record from the
database file, and displays the record on the screen. This occurs so
quickly that you are unaware of the search taking place.

In short, an employee's name is the key to locating a given record
in the database. For this reason, whenever you choose one of the first
four options in the menu, the program will always begin by asking you
for a name.

Here is a sample of the dialog that takes place when you choose
the *Examine an employee's record* option:

```
Enter the employee's name:
----- --- ---------- -----


Last name   --> Moltry
First name --> Robert
```

In response to this input, the program searches for the Robert Moltry
entry in the employee index of the database, retrieves the employee's
record number, reads the corresponding record from the database,
and displays the record on the screen. Figure 7-2 shows the resulting
record display.

```
Name:        Robert Moltry
Soc. Sec. #: 345-67-8901
Date hired:  05-16-1983
Department:  Accounting
Job Title:   Bookkeeper
Salary:      ***$32,000 per year
```

Figure 7-2.   *The* Examine an employee's record
display.

If you enter an employee name that does not exist in the index,
the *Employee* program displays the message shown in Figure 7-3.

```
Enter the employee's name:
----- --- ---------- -----


Last name   --) Moltry
First name  --) Richard

This name is not in the employee file.
```

Figure 7-3. *The resulting display if an employee is not in the index.*

When you select the *Add a new employee* option, the *Employee* program elicits all the necessary field information for a new employee record. Figure 7-4 (on the next page) shows an example of this dialog. The program asks for only seven items of information, even though the record structure contains nine fields. The two remaining fields contain dates: the date hired and the date of departure from the firm. The program saves the current date on the system clock as the field entry for the date hired. The date of departure is, of course, left blank until the employee actually leaves the firm.

Notice how the program asks for the employee's salary. After you enter the salary figure, the program prompts you to enter the period of time for which this salary applies—either hourly, monthly, or annually. In response to this prompt, you press one of three keys: *H, M,* or *A.* When the program later displays an employee record on the screen, this field is combined with the salary figure in display lines such as the following:

```
Salary:      ***$11.50 per hour

Salary:      ***$1,750 per month

Salary:      ***$32,000 per year
```

After you enter all the fields of information for which the *Add a new employee* option prompts, the following confirmation question appears on the screen:

```
Save this record? (Y or N) ->
```

```
              Enter information for new employee
              ----- ----------- --- --- --------


              Last name    --> Breuner
              First name   --> Patricia
              Soc. Sec. # --> 765-43-2109
              Department   --> Sales
              Position     --> Salesperson
              Salary       --> 1500
              H)ourly,
              M)onthly, or
              A)nnual      --> M

              Save this record? (Y or N) -> Y




                                      Press <Enter> to continue.
```

Figure 7-4. *The display and sample entry for the*
Add a new employee *option.*

You can now examine the field information you entered to be sure everything is correct. Press *Y* to save the record. If you have made a mistake in the input process, press *N* to abandon the record. In this case, the program does not write the record to the database file.

The *Add a new employee* option does not let you enter a new record with an employee name that already exists in the file. The program's indexing system relies on having distinct names for every employee. For this reason, the program searches through the index as soon as you enter an employee name in the *Add a new employee* option dialog. If the name already exists, the program displays the following message on the screen:

```
This name is already in the employee file.
```

If two employees have the same first and last names, you must distinguish between them. You can, for example, include a middle initial or abbreviate one of the first names.

The *Change an employee's record* option begins by eliciting the name of the employee whose record you wish to revise. After it locates the employee's record, the program then displays a secondary menu. Figure 7-5 shows the menu for Donald Denver. This menu serves two purposes: It displays current information from the employee's file, and it lets you select the field or fields you want to change. You can enter new values for the employee's department, job title, and/or salary. In each case, the program conducts a short dialog to facilitate the entry of the new field value or values.

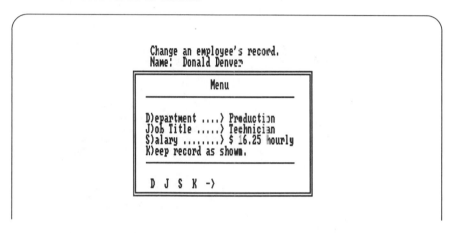

```
Change an employee's record.
Name:  Donald Denver

                   Menu
        ───────────────────────────
        D)epartment ....) Production
        J)ob Title .....) Technician
        S)alary ........) $ 16.25 hourly
        K)eep record as shown.


         D  J  S  K  -)
```

Figure 7-5. *The display for the* Change an employee's record *option.*

For example, the following dialog would occur if you chose *Salary* and entered a new salary of $17.50 per hour:

```
New Salary      --> 17.50
H)ourly, M)onthly, A)nnually --> H
```

After you complete this dialog, the *Change an employee's record* menu reappears and displays the information you entered. After you make all the necessary changes, press *K* to *Keep record as shown.*

The *Employee* program then writes the new version of the record—with any changes you have made—to the database file.

The *Record a departure* option modifies a departing employee's record in two ways:

1.   The word "DEPARTED" is stored in the department field of the record (*dept$*).

2.   The current date is stored in the departure date field (*depDate$*).

As always, the program first asks you for the name of the employee. Then it displays the employee's entire record so that you can be sure you are modifying the correct record.

Figure 7-6 shows the screen display for a departing employee. As you can see, the program displays the following question below the record itself:

```
Is this the employee who is leaving? (Y or N) ->
```

```
                    Name:          Arthur Hines
                    Soc. Sec. #: 901-23-4567
                    Date hired:  04-09-1984
                    Department:  Personnel
                    Job Title:   Personnel Mgr.
                    Salary:         ***$37,500 per year

                    Is this the employee who is leaving? (Y or N) -> Y

                    *** The departure has been recorded. ***




                                              Press <Enter> to continue.
```

Figure 7-6. *The dialog for the* Record a departure *option.*

If you press *Y,* the program modifies the record and displays this message:

```
*** The departure has been recorded. ***
```

However, if you press *N,* the program takes no action on the record and displays this message:

```
No change in this employee's status.
```

The record display for an employee who has left the company is different from the usual display. For example, Figure 7-7 shows the display produced by the *Examine an employee's record* option for a former employee. Notice that the departure date appears at the bottom of the record, below this message:

```
*** No longer an employee ***
```

```
Name:        Arthur Hines
Soc. Sec. #: 901-23-4567
Date hired:  04-09-1984
Job Title:   Personnel Mgr.
Salary:      ***$37,500 per year

*** No longer an employee ***

Date left:   11-08-1986




                              Press <Enter> to continue.
```

Figure 7-7. *The record display for a former employee.*

The *Print a list of employees* option

Finally, the main menu's *Print a list of employees* option sends a table of employee records to the printer. The program also arranges the table in alphabetic order. When you select this option, the program first asks you the following question:

```
Do you want to include
former employees
in the printed list? (Y or N) ->
```

Depending on your answer, the program prints either the entire database or only the records of current employees.

Before printing the table, the program pauses to let you turn on the printer and position the paper properly. The following message appears on the screen:

```
Press the space bar
when the printer is ready.
```

When you press the space bar, the printing begins. Figure 7-8 shows a sample printed employee table that includes former employees. Notice that the program inserts a double asterisk to the left of the record of any former employee.

```
        Last Name        First       Soc.Sec.#   Job Title        Current Salary
        ---------        -----       ---------   ---------        --------------

        Atkins           Jacqueline  234-56-7890 Vice President   ***$38,000 /yr
        Bradford         Alice       876-54-3210 Artist           ***$13.25 /hr
        Breuner          Patricia    765-43-2109 Salesperson      ***$1,500 /mo
        Carlson          Emmy        890-12-3456 Staff Attorney   ***$45,000 /yr
        Denver           Donald      567-89-0123 Technician       ***$16.25 /hr
     ** Hines            Arthur      901-23-4567 Personnel Mgr.   ***$37,500 /yr
     ** Holt             Douglas     543-21-0987 Sales Assistant  ***$11.50 /hr
        Jackson          Jaime       876-54-3210 Sales Mgr.       ***$2,100 /mo
        Kelly            Lynne       765-43-2109 Advertising Mgr  ***$28,000 /yr
        Larson           Richard     678-90-1234 Artist           ***$14.50 /hr
        Moltry           Robert      345-67-8901 Bookkeeper       ***$32,000 /yr
     ** Oliver           Michael     789-01-2345 Secretary        ****$8.75 /hr
        Quinn            Paris       654-32-1098 Secretary        ***$1,350 /mo
        Wilson           Terry       987-65-4321 Clerk            ****$8.25 /hr
        Young            Sara        123-45-6789 President         ***$45,000 /yr
     ** Zim              Patricia    456-78-9012 Office Manager   ***$1,950 /mo


     ** Former employee.
```

Figure 7-8. *A printed list of current and former employees.*

Now we can turn to the listing of the *Employee* program and examine the techniques it uses to manage the database. Although the program is a modest example of a database application, the techniques will work effectively in programs that perform more sophisticated operations and deal with more complex record structures.

Figure 7-9 presents a structure chart for the program, showing the major calls made at each subprogram level.

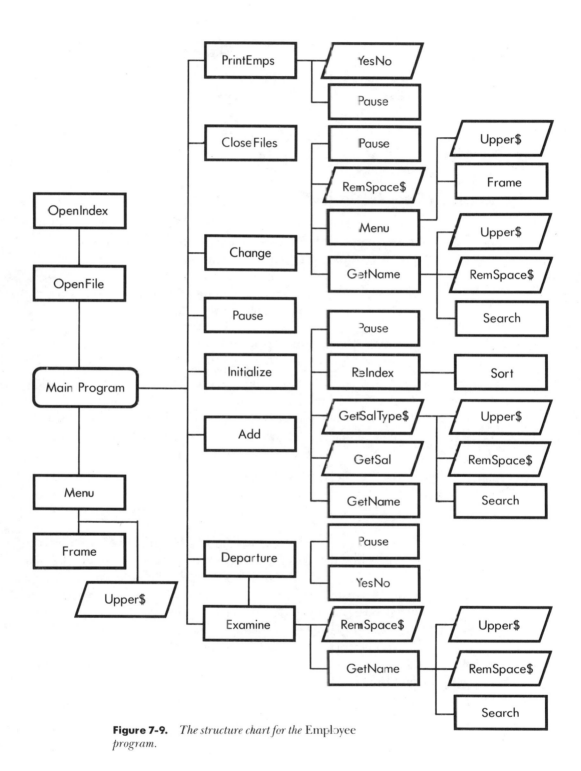

Figure 7-9. *The structure chart for the Employee program.*

INSIDE THE *EMPLOYEE* PROGRAM

The complete listing of the *Employee* program appears in Figure 7-10. As we examine the listing, we will concentrate on two aspects of database programming:

1.   Using QuickBASIC's random-access file commands

2.   Developing a technique for indexing a database

The global variable declarations area

The *Employee* program begins with the dimensioning of two static arrays, *employeeMenu$* and *changeMenu$*. These arrays hold the contents of the program's two menus, which are initialized in the *Initialize* subprogram, discussed later in the chapter.

Next, a COMMON SHARED statement establishes an important group of global variables. Among these variables are:

●   *totEmpRecords%*, which always contains the number of records currently in the database.

●   Two, one-dimensional index arrays: *empRecIndex%*, an integer array that contains the employee record numbers, and *empNameIndex$*, a string array that contains the employee names. (Notice that these are both dynamic arrays: As new records are added to the file, their lengths will change.)

●   All nine field variables that define the structure of the records. (As we have seen, field variables must be declared global to be available to subprogram units throughout the program.)

As always, the Boolean variables *true%* and *false%* are both declared and initialized to the Boolean values of −1 (true) and 0 (false). In addition, the Boolean variable *neverExisted%* is declared in the COMMON SHARED statement. This global variable is assigned in the *Examine* subprogram and used in the *Departure* subprogram to determine if the employee name in question ever existed in the database.

Another global variable that plays a minor role throughout the program is *indent%*, which stores the TAB position at which the program displays information on the screen. A few lines after the COMMON SHARED statement, it is assigned a value of 25.

```
'       EMPLOYEE.BAS
'       The Employee program manages a database of information about
'           a company's employees.  The program keeps two files on disk:
'
'           EMP.DAT is the database itself (a random-access file).
'           EMP.NDX is an index into the database (a sequential file).
'
'       Employee builds the index automatically.  The index is required
'           for locating individual employee records in the database.

'---------------------| Global Variable Declarations |----------------------


       DIM employeeMenu$(6), changeMenu$(4)
       COMMON SHARED employeeMenu$(), totEmpRecords%, empRecIndex%(1), _
          empNameIndex$(1), indent%, lastName$, firstName$, socialSecurity$, _
          hireDate$, dept$, position$, salary$, salaryType$, depDate$, _
          lastTemp$, firstTemp$, changeMenu$(), d$, j$, s$, _
          true%, false%, neverExisted%

'       ---- Initialize Boolean variables true% and false%
       true% = -1
       false% = 0

'       ---- Initialize indent% for later output formatting use.
       indent% = 25

'--------------------------| Function Area |---------------------------------


'       ---- Read in and compile BASIC user-defined functions.
       REM $INCLUDE : 'UPPER.BAS'
       REM $INCLUDE : 'YESNO.BAS'


'       The RemSpace$ function removes all spaces from the string it receives
'           as an argument.  RemSpace$ is used to create the name entries for
'           the index, and to prepare field items for display on the screen.

DEF FN RemSpace$(completeName$)
       STATIC temp$, chTemp$, i%
       temp$ = ""

       FOR i% = 1 to LEN(completeName$)
          chTemp$ = MID$(completeName$, i%, 1)
          IF (chTemp$ <> " ") THEN
               temp$ = temp$ + chTemp$
          END IF
       NEXT i%

       FN RemSpace$ = temp$
END DEF


'       The GetSal function elicits a numeric input value for the current
'           employee's salary.  To avoid QuickBASIC's "?Redo from start" error
'           message, GetSal initially stores the input value in a string
'           variable, and only accepts the value if it can be successfully
'           converted to a number.
```

RemSpace

Figure 7-10. *The* Employee *program.*   *(more . . .)*

The main program area

After the function area, which we will discuss on a function by function basis, the main program area begins with a call to the *Initialize* subprogram.

This routine simply assigns strings of the option choices to the two menu arrays. The array *employeeMenu$* represents the main menu, and *changeMenu$* represents the secondary menu displayed by the *Change an employee's record* option.

The *OpenFile* subprogram

To open the database file and the index file, the main program next calls the *OpenFile* subprogram. This routine uses the OPEN command to open *EMP.DAT* as a random-access file, assigns the file a file number of 1, and establishes the record length as 91. The FIELD command then creates a record structure of nine field variables.

You have seen how to use the built-in LOF function to determine the number of employee records in the newly opened file. The following statement assigns this initial value to the *totEmpRecords%* variable:

```
totEmpRecords% = LOF(1) / 91
```

The *OpenIndex* subprogram

Finally, assuming the database file is not empty, *OpenFile* calls the *OpenIndex* subprogram to open *EMP.NDX*, the index file:

```
IF (totEmpRecords% <> 0) THEN CALL OpenIndex
```

If *EMP.DAT* exists but *EMP.NDX* does not, a message specifying this is displayed and program execution halts.

The program stores the index in two arrays: *empRecIndex%* for the record numbers, and *empNameIndex$* for the employee names. The first task of the *OpenIndex* routine is to establish the initial dimensions of these two index arrays. Each array contains one element for every employee record in the file:

```
REDIM empRecIndex%(totEmpRecords%), empNameIndex$(totEmpRecords%)
```

```
DEF FN GetSal                                                          GetSal
    STATIC salary, sal$, currentX%, currentY%

    currentX% = POS(0)
    currentY% = CSRLIN

    salary = 0
    WHILE salary = 0
        INPUT "Salary       --> ", sal$
        salary = VAL(sal$)
        IF (salary = 0) THEN
            LOCATE currentY%, currentX%
            PRINT SPACE$(LEN(sal$) + 16)
            LOCATE currentY%, currentX%
        END IF
    WEND

    FN GetSal = salary
END DEF


'   The GetSalType$ function accepts a single-letter keystroke indicating
'   the term of the current employee's salary:  hourly (H), monthly (M),
'   or annual (A).  The function rejects any invalid keystrokes.

DEF FN GetSalType$                                                     GetSalType
    STATIC sType$
    sType$ = ""

    WHILE sType$ = ""
        sType$ = INKEY$
        IF INSTR("HMAhma",sType$) = 0 THEN
            BEEP
            sType$ = ""
        END IF
    WEND

    sType$ = FN Upper$(sType$)
    PRINT sType$
    FN GetSalType$ = sType$
END DEF

'---------------------------| Main Program Area |---------------------------


'   ---- Build the menu arrays, and open the two files.
    CALL Initialize
    CALL OpenFile

'   ---- Display the main menu on the screen, and call an appropriate
'        subprogram to respond to each menu choice.
    WHILE choice% <> 6
        LOCATE 2,32: PRINT "Employee Records"
        CALL Menu(employeeMenu$(), choice%)

        IF (choice% = 1 AND totEmpRecords% <> 0) THEN
            CALL Examine(dummy%)
            CALL Pause
        ELSEIF (choice% = 2) THEN
            CALL Add
```

Figure 7-10. *The* Employee *program (continued).*   *(more...)*

Next, the routine sets an error trap (in case *EMP.NDX* doesn't exist); then it opens the index file and prepares to read it as a sequential file:

```
ON ERROR GOTO Terminate
OPEN "EMP.NDX" FOR INPUT AS #2
ON ERROR GOTO 0
```

Notice that the index receives a file number of 2, since two files are now open.

If an error does occur, the following routine, listed directly below the *OpenIndex* subprogram, is called:

```
Terminate:
    CLS
    PRINT "EMP.DAT exists but EMP.NDX does not."
    PRINT "Program execution halted."
RESUME Finish
```

After an appropriate message is printed, the *Employee* program branches to the alphanumeric label *Finish*, located before the END statement in the main program. You must either enter the employee list again or modify the *Employee* program to create a new index file from the existing database. (See suggestion #1 in the *Conclusion* section of this chapter for details.)

After error handling is disabled with the *ON ERROR GOTO 0* statement, an INPUT# statement within a FOR...NEXT loop reads each entry of the index file into the two index arrays:

```
FOR i% = 1 TO totEmpRecords%
    INPUT#2, empRecIndex%(i%), empNameIndex$(i%)
NEXT i%
```

Then, since the index is held in memory until you quit the program, the index file is closed:

```
CLOSE #2
```

With control returned to the main program section, the stage is now set for the database operations to begin. Within a WHILE...WEND loop, the program calls the *Menu* subprogram repeatedly to display the main menu and elicit your menu choice:

```
WHILE choice% <> 6
    LOCATE 2,32: PRINT "Employee Records"
    CALL Menu(employeeMenu$(), choice%)
```

```
            ELSEIF (choice% = 3 AND totEmpRecords% <> 0) THEN
                CALL Change
            ELSEIF (choice% = 4 AND totEmpRecords% <> 0) THEN
                CALL Departure
            ELSEIF (choice% = 5 AND totEmpRecords% <> 0) THEN
                CALL PrintEmps
            END IF
      WEND

'     ---- Close the database file and save the index.
      CALL CloseFiles

'     ---- The Finish label is used by an error-handling routine found in the
'          GetSal function.
Finish:
      END


      '--------------------------| Subprogram Area |--------------------------


'     ---- Read in and compile BASIC subprograms.
      REM $INCLUDE : 'FRAME.BAS'
      REM $INCLUDE : 'MENU.BAS'
      REM $INCLUDE : 'SORT.BAS'
      REM $INCLUDE : 'SEARCH.BAS'


'     The Initialize subprogram assigns values to the two arrays that the
'          program uses for storing menu choices.  The first array,
'          employeeMenu$, contains the main menu strings.  The second array,
'          changeMenu$, stores the choices that are displayed when the
'          user invokes the Change option from the main menu.

SUB Initialize STATIC
      FOR i% = 1 TO 6
          READ employeeMenu$(i%)
      NEXT i%

      DATA examine an employee's record
      DATA add a new employee
      DATA change an employee's record
      DATA record a departure
      DATA print a list of employees
      DATA quit

      d$ = "Department ....> "
      j$ = "Job Title .....> "
      s$ = "Salary ........> "
      changeMenu$(4) = "Keep record as shown."
END SUB


'     The OpenFile subprogram opens the main database file, and establishes
'          its field variables.  Note that these variables are declared
'          global with the COMMON SHARED statement in the main program area.

SUB OpenFile STATIC
      OPEN "EMP.DAT" FOR RANDOM AS #1 LEN = 91
```

> Initialize

> OpenFile

Figure 7-10. *The* Employee *program (continued).*   *(more...)*

291

The looping continues until you choose the sixth menu option, *Quit*. For each menu choice other than *Quit*, an IF…THEN…ELSE structure calls the appropriate subprogram: *Examine* displays an individual employee record; *Add* adds a new record to the file; *Change* modifies the contents of a record; *Departure* records the departure of an employee; and *PrintEmps* prints a table of records.

Note the list of $INCLUDE metacommands located near the beginning of the function area and the subprogram area. The *Employee* program uses six of the subprograms and functions that we developed in Chapters 2 and 3, including *Sort, Search, Upper$, Frame, Menu,* and *YesNo*. If you linked a user library containing these routines to the *Employee* program when you initially started QuickBASIC, as we discussed in Chapter 3, you need not include a reference to any of the routines here. Since the current version of the program uses $INCLUDE metacommands, however, these routines must all be stored in the current directory.

The *Add* subprogram

Examining the activities of the *Add* subprogram and the various other routines that it, in turn, calls gives an overall picture of the *Employee* program's indexing system. In particular, we will see how the program builds the database index and how individual entries that go into the index are formatted. We will also see how the program uses the *Sort* and *Search* routines to manage the index.

The *GetName* subprogram

The *Add* routine first displays a title on the screen and then immediately makes a call to the *GetName* subprogram (listed directly after *Add*). The *Examine* and *Change* subprograms also call *GetName*. The routine prompts for the name fields for the record that is to be added (or, in other contexts, prompts for the record that is to be examined). *GetName* then searches the index to see if the name exists in the file.

The call to *GetName* includes two variable arguments, both passed by reference. *GetName* uses these two variables to pass two items of information—an integer and a string value—back to the calling subprogram. *Add* makes the following call:

```
CALL GetName(inFile%, newName$)
```

```
        FIELD #1, 15 AS lastName$, _         ' Last name
               10 AS firstName$, _           ' first name
               11 AS socialSecurity$, _      ' social security number
               10 AS hireDate$, _            ' date hired
               15 AS dept$, _                ' department (or "departed")
               15 AS position$, _            ' position
               4  AS salary$, _              ' current salary
               1  AS salaryType$, _          ' salary type (hr, mo, yr)
               10 AS depDate$                ' date of departure from firm

'    ---- The LOF function is used to calculate the number of records in
'         the employee file.
        totEmpRecords% = LOF(1) / 91

'    ---- If the database file is not empty, open the index file.
        IF (totEmpRecords% <> 0) THEN CALL OpenIndex
END SUB


'    The OpenIndex subprogram opens the index file, named EMP.NDX, and
'         reads the contents of the file into two arrays:  totEmpRecords%
'         holds the record number for each employee, and empNameIndex$
'         holds the employee names.

SUB OpenIndex STATIC
'    ---- Since the size of the index will change each time an employee is
'         added to the file, use the REDIM statement to set the current
'         dimensions of the two arrays.

        REDIM empRecIndex%(totEmpRecords%), empNameIndex$(totEmpRecords%)

'    ---- If there is a problem opening the file EMP.NDX, jump to Terminate.
        ON ERROR GOTO Terminate
        OPEN "EMP.NDX" FOR INPUT AS #2
        ON ERROR GOTO 0

        FOR i% = 1 TO totEmpRecords%
            INPUT#2, empRecIndex%(i%), empNameIndex$(i%)
        NEXT i%

'    ---- Until the end of the current program performance the index will
'         be held in memory.  Close the index file for the moment.
        CLOSE #2
END SUB

'    ---- If called, the Terminate error-handling routine prints some
'         explanatory shutdown messages and jumps to Finish in the main
'         program.

Terminate:
        CLS
        PRINT "EMP.DAT exists but EMP.NDX does not."
        PRINT "Program execution halted."
RESUME Finish


'    The Pause subprogram creates a pause in the action of the program, so
'         that the user can examine a screenful of information.  The user
'         presses the Enter key to continue the program (any key will work).
```

OpenIndex

Figure 7-10. *The* Employee *program (continued).*   *(more . . .)*

The string value *newName$* is the employee name itself, specially for-matted for the index file. (We will examine this format shortly.) The in-teger value, *inFile%*, indicates whether or not the name is in the index:

- A value of 0 indicates that the name is not in the file.

- An integer value greater than 0 is the actual record number of the name.

To produce the string value for the index, *GetName* first prompts you for the employee's last name and first name and then stores the in-put values in the global variables *lastTemp$* and *firstTemp$*:

```
PRINT TAB(indent%);: INPUT "Last name    --> ", lastTemp$
PRINT TAB(indent%);: INPUT "First name   --> ", firstTemp$
```

The index entry is a concatenation of these two values, with all spaces removed by the *RemSpace$* user-defined function and all letters con-verted to uppercase by the *Upper$* user-defined function. Let's see what kind of string results from this process. Suppose you want to up-date information for *Joseph La Monte*; you enter the following two name fields in response to the input prompts:

```
Last name    --> La Monte
First name   --> Joseph
```

Concatenating these two strings, removing the space, and capitalizing the letters produces the following string:

```
LAMONTEJOSEPH
```

This standardized string is the entry that the *GetName* subprogram searches for in the index.

After the concatenation and capitalization is stored in the *target$* variable, the *Search* subprogram, which was loaded into the *Employee* program at compile time with a $INCLUDE statement, begins a search of the employee index if at least one employee record exists:

```
IF (totEmpRecords% <> 0) THEN
    CALL Search(empRecIndex%(), recordNum%, _
        empNameIndex$(), target$)
END IF
```

We originally discussed the *Search* subprogram in Chapter 3. In the *Employee* program, the routine searches the *empNameIndex$* array and tries to match the string stored in *target$*. If *Search*

```
SUB Pause STATIC                                                         Pause
    LOCATE 25,50
    PRINT "Press <Enter> to continue.";
    character$ = ""
    WHILE character$ = ""
        character$ = INKEY$
    WEND
    CLS
END SUB


'   The Add subprogram controls the process of adding a new employee to
'       the database.

SUB Add STATIC                                                           Add
    PRINT: PRINT: PRINT: PRINT
    PRINT TAB(indent%) "Enter information for new employee"
    PRINT TAB(indent%) "----- ----------- --- --- --------"

'   ---- GetName elicits the name of the employee.
    CALL GetName(inFile%, newName$)

'   ---- Do not allow duplicates of the same name.
    IF inFile% THEN
        PRINT
        PRINT TAB(indent%) "This name is already in the employee file."
    ELSE

'   ---- Elicit additional employee information.
        PRINT TAB(indent%);
        INPUT "Soc. Sec. # --> ", ssTemp$
        PRINT TAB(indent%);
        INPUT "Department  --> ", deptTemp$
        PRINT TAB(indent%);
        INPUT "Position    --> ", posiTemp$
        PRINT TAB(indent%);
        salTemp = FN GetSal
        PRINT TAB(indent%) "H)ourly,"
        PRINT TAB(indent%) "M)onthly, or"
        PRINT TAB(indent%) "A)nnual     --> ";
        typeTemp$ = FN GetSalType$

'   ---- Assign the data to the field variables.
        LSET lastName$ = lastTemp$
        LSET firstName$ = firstTemp$
        LSET socialSecurity$ = ssTemp$
        LSET hireDate$ = DATE$
        LSET dept$ = deptTemp$
        LSET position$ = posiTemp$
        LSET salary$ = MKS$(salTemp)
        LSET salaryType$ = typeTemp$

        PRINT
        PRINT TAB(indent%);

'   ---- Allow the user to abandon the new record for any reason
'       (for example, if an input error has occurred).  Otherwise,
'       save the record in the employee file.
```

Figure 7-10.   *The* Employee *program (continued).*   *(more . . .)*

finds the string, it returns the corresponding record number—from the array *empRecIndex%*—to the variable *recordNum%*. If it does not find the string, it returns a value of 0 to *recordNum%*.

The value of *recordNum%* is then passed to the *inFile%* argument in the *Add* subprogram. In the following passage, *Add* uses *inFile%* as a Boolean variable in which any nonzero number represents true and the number 0 represents false:

```
IF inFile% THEN
    PRINT
    PRINT TAB(indent%) "This name is already in the employee file."
ELSE
    [elicit additional new employee information]
```

In other words, if *inFile%* is any number other than 0—meaning that the input name is in the database index—the *Add* subprogram calls the *Pause* subprogram and ends. This is the means by which *Add* prevents the entry of duplicate names.

However, if *inFile%* contains a value of 0, *Add* proceeds with the ELSE condition and prompts for the remaining fields of data for the new employee record. For reasons that we discussed earlier, these values are all stored in temporary variables rather than directly in the field variables. For example:

```
INPUT "Soc. Sec. # --> ", ssTemp$
INPUT "Department   --> ", deptTemp$
```

The *GetSal* and *GetSalType$* user-defined functions

Add elicits values for the salary and the salary type with the *GetSal* and *GetSalType$* user-defined functions. The *GetSal* function accepts a valid numeric value for the salary. Designed to avoid QuickBASIC's *?Redo from start* error message, *GetSal* first accepts the value as a string, and then uses the VAL function to convert the string to a number. The input process is repeated if the number is zero. (Similar numeric-input functions appear in the *Mortgage* program that was presented in Chapter 4.) *Add* stores the numeric result of *GetSal* in the *salTemp* variable:

```
salTemp = FN GetSal
```

```
        IF (FN YesNo("Save this record?")) THEN
            totEmpRecords% = totEmpRecords% + 1
            PUT#1, totEmpRecords%
            CALL ReIndex(newName$)
        END IF
    END IF

    CALL Pause
END SUB


'   The GetName subprogram elicits the name of the employee that the
'       program will subsequently search for in the database.  GetName
'       passes two values back to the caller:  recordNum% is the record
'       number (or 0, if the record was not found); and target$ is the
'       indexed employee name.

SUB GetName (recordNum%, target$) STATIC
    PRINT: PRINT
    PRINT TAB(indent%);: INPUT "Last name   --> ", lastTemp$
    PRINT TAB(indent%);: INPUT "First name  --> ", firstTemp$
    target$ = FN RemSpace$(lastTemp$ + firstTemp$)
    target$ = FN Upper$(target$)

    IF (totEmpRecords% <> 0) THEN
        CALL Search(empRecIndex%(), recordNum%, empNameIndex$(), target$)
    END IF
END SUB


'   The ReIndex subprogram rebuilds the index after each new employee
'       is added to the database.

SUB ReIndex (empName$) STATIC
'   ---- Begin by copying the current index to two temporary arrays:
'        recTemp% and nameTemp$.
    IF (totEmpRecords% > 1) THEN
        oldTotal% = totEmpRecords% - 1
        REDIM recTemp%(oldTotal%), nameTemp$(oldTotal%)

        FOR i% = 1 TO oldTotal%
            recTemp%(i%) = empRecIndex%(i%)
            nameTemp$(i%) = empNameIndex$(i%)
        NEXT i%
    END IF

'   ---- Now redimension the index arrays to the new required length.
'        (This process also erases all data from the arrays, which is why
'        the program has to make temporary copies first.)

    REDIM empRecIndex%(totEmpRecords%), empNameIndex$(totEmpRecords%)

'   ---- Finally, copy the index entries back into the index arrays, and
'        also store the new entry at the end of the index.
    IF (totEmpRecords% > 1) THEN
        FOR i% = 1 to oldTotal%
            empRecIndex%(i%) = recTemp%(i%)
            empNameIndex$(i%) = nametemp$(i%)
        NEXT i%
    END IF
```

GetName

ReIndex

Figure 7-10. *The* Employee *program (continued).*   *(more...)*

The *GetSalType$* function accepts one of three letters from the keyboard: *H,* for an hourly salary; *M,* for a monthly salary; or *A,* for an annual salary. The value that the user inputs is stored in *typeTemp$*:

```
typeTemp$ = FN GetSalType$
```

After *Add* receives input values for all of the required fields, a series of LSET statements assigns the values to the field variables:

```
LSET lastName$ = lastTemp$
LSET firstName$ = firstTemp$
LSET socialSecurity$ = ssTemp$
LSET hireDate$ = DATE$
LSET dept$ = deptTemp$
LSET position$ = posiTemp$
LSET salary$ = MKS$(salTemp)
LSET salaryType$ = typeTemp$
```

Notice that the program uses the built-in DATE$ function to read the current date from the system calendar; the program assigns this date to the *hireDate$* field when the record is created. The program also uses the MKS$ function to convert *salTemp* (a single-precision number) into a four-byte string value that is stored in the *salary$* field.

Finally, after all the field values are loaded into the record buffer, the *Add* subprogram is ready to write the record to the database file. Before doing so, however, the subprogram calls the external *YesNo* function to prompt the user to confirm the operation:

```
IF (FN YesNo("Save this record?")) THEN
```

YesNo, you will recall, elicits a yes-or-no response from the user. If you confirm that you want to save the record, *Add* increments the number of records in the database by 1:

```
totEmpRecords% = totEmpRecords% + 1
```

The current record is then written at the end of the database file:

```
PUT#1, totEmpRecords%
```

This statement uses the current value of *totEmpRecords%* as the record number for the new record.

The *Add* subprogram's final procedures consist of adding an entry to the index for the new record and then re-sorting the index. Both operations are performed by the *ReIndex* subprogram. *Add* calls this

```
    empRecIndex%(totEmpRecords%) = totEmpRecords%
    empNameIndex$(totEnpRecords%) = empName$

'   ---- Re-sort the index, now that it has been rebuilt.
    CALL Sort(empRecIndex%(), empNameIndex$())
END SUB


'   The Examine subprogram displays a specified employee record
'       on the screen.

SUB Examine(number%) STATIC
    PRINT: PRINT: PRINT: PRINT
    PRINT TAB(indent%) "Enter the employee's name:"
    PRINT TAB(indent%) "----- --- ---------- -----"
    CALL GetName(number%, searchName$)

    neverExisted% = false%
    IF (number% = 0) THEN

'   ---- If the name is not in the employee list, print an appropriate
'        message and set the global Boolean variable neverExisted% to
'        true%.  This value is used in the Departure subprogram.
        PRINT
        PRINT TAB(indent%) "This name is not in the employee file."
        neverExisted% = true%
    ELSE
        CLS
        GET #1, number%
        PRINT: PRINT: PRINT
        PRINT: PRINT: PRINT
        PRINT TAB(indent%) "Name:          ";
        PRINT FN RemSpace$(firstName$) " " lastName$
        PRINT TAB(indent%) "Soc. Sec. #: " socialSecurity$
        PRINT TAB(indent%) "Date hired:  " hireDate$

        IF (LEFT$(dept$, 8) <> "DEPARTED") THEN
            PRINT TAB(indent%) "Department: " dept$
        END IF
        PRINT TAB(indent%) "Job Title:   " position$
        PRINT TAB(indent%) "Salary:      ";

        IF (salaryType$ = "H") THEN
            PRINT USING "**$###.## per hour"; CVS(salary$)
        ELSEIF (salaryType$ = "M") THEN
            PRINT USING "**$#,#### per month"; CVS(salary$)
        ELSE
            PRINT USING "**$#,##### per year"; CVS(salary$)
        END IF

'   ---- If the employee no longer works for the firm, supply an extra
'        note in the record display.
        IF (LEFT$(dept$, 8) = "DEPARTED") THEN
            PRINT
            PRINT TAB(indent%) "*** No longer an employee ***"
            PRINT
            PRINT TAB(indent%) "Date left:   " depDate$
        END IF
    END IF
END SUB
```

Figure 7-10. *The* Employee *program (continued).*   *(more...)*

routine and passes the formatted string (such as "LAMONTEJOSEPH") that was originally created by the *GetName* subprogram. This value is stored in the *newName$* argument variable:

```
CALL ReIndex(newName$)
```

The *ReIndex* subprogram

The *ReIndex* subprogram executes the following steps:

1. It makes temporary copies of the two index arrays. The copy of *empRecIndex%* is stored in an array named *recTemp%*, and the copy of *empNameIndex$* goes into *nameTemp$*.

2. It uses the REDIM statement to establish the new dimensions of the index arrays. (Each array is one element longer than the previous array.)

3. It transfers the temporary copy of the index into the newly dimensioned index arrays.

4. It stores the index entry for the new record at the end of each index array.

5. It sorts the index.

ReIndex must make a temporary copy of the index at the beginning of this process, because the two index arrays lose all their values when they are redimensioned by the REDIM statement.

The lengths of the two temporary arrays are established at the beginning of the *ReIndex* routine. The global variable *totEmpRecords%*, already incremented by the *Add* subprogram, represents the new length of the database. The lengths of the temporary arrays are set at 1 less than this value:

```
oldTotal% = totEmpRecords% - 1
REDIM recTemp%(oldTotal%), nameTemp$(oldTotal%)
```

A FOR...NEXT loop copies the index into these temporary arrays:

```
FOR i% = 1 TO oldTotal%
    recTemp%(i%) = empRecIndex%(i%)
    nameTemp$(i%) = empNameIndex$(i%)
NEXT i%
```

```
'   The Change subprogram elicits revisions for a given employee record.
'       Change uses Menu to offer the choices.

SUB Change STATIC
    PRINT: PRINT: PRINT: PRINT
    PRINT TAB(indent%) "Enter the employee's name:"
    PRINT TAB(indent%) "----- --- ---------- -----"
    CALL GetName(number%, dummy$)
    IF (number% = 0) THEN
        PRINT
        PRINT TAB(indent%) "This name is not in the employee file."
        CALL Pause
    ELSE
        CLS
        GET #1, number%
        change% = 0
        WHILE (change% <> 4)
            PRINT TAB(indent%) "Change an employee's record."
            PRINT TAB(indent%) "Name:  ";
            PRINT FN RemSpace$(firstName$) " " lastName$

            changeMenu$(1) = d$ + FN RemSpace$(dept$)
            changeMenu$(2) = j$ + FN RemSpace$(position$)

            IF (salaryType$ = "H") THEN
                sal$ = " hourly"
            ELSEIF salaryType$ = "M" THEN
                sal$ = " monthly"
            ELSE
                sal$ = " annually"
            END IF

            sal$ = "$" + STR$(CVS(salary$)) + sal$
            changeMenu$(3) = s$ + sal$
            CALL Menu(changeMenu$(), change%)

            PRINT: PRINT: PRINT: PRINT
            PRINT TAB(indent%);
            IF (change% = 1) THEN
                INPUT "New department --> ", tempDept$
                LSET dept$ = tempDept$
            ELSEIF (change% = 2) THEN
                INPUT "New job title --> ", tempPos$
                LSET position$ = tempPos$
            ELSEIF (change% = 3) THEN
                PRINT "New ";
                salTemp = FN GetSal
                LSET salary$ = MKS$(salTemp)
                PRINT TAB(indent%);
                PRINT "H)ourly, M)onthly, A)nnually --> ";
                sType$ = FN GetSalType$
                LSET salaryType$ = sType$
                CALL Pause
            END IF
            CLS
        WEND
        PUT #1, number%
    END IF
END SUB
```

Figure 7-10. *The* Employee *program (continued).*   *(more...)*

Next, to accommodate the new record, the two index arrays are redimensioned to a length that is one element longer than their previous length:

```
REDIM empRecIndex%(totEmpRecords%), empNameIndex$(totEmpRecords%)
```

Because this statement actually redimensions both arrays as new and larger arrays, all the elements of *empRecIndex%* are reset to zero and all the elements of *empNameIndex$* are reset as empty (null) strings. Another FOR...NEXT loop copies the index back into these larger arrays from the temporary arrays if at least one record is in the database:

```
IF (totEmpRecords > 1) THEN
    FOR i% = 1 to oldTotal%
        empRecIndex%(i%) = recTemp%(i%)
        empNameIndex$(i%) = nameTemp$(i%)
    NEXT i%
END IF
```

The last element of each array receives the index entry for the new record. The *empRecIndex%* array receives the record number from *totEmpRecords%*:

```
empRecIndex%(totEmpRecords%) = totEmpRecords%
```

The *empNameIndex$* array receives the formatted employee name entry from the *ReIndex* subprogram's string parameter variable, *empName$*:

```
empNameIndex$(totEmpRecords%) = empName$
```

Finally, a simple call to the *Sort* subprogram rearranges the index in alphabetic order according to the employee names:

```
CALL Sort(empRecIndex%(), empNameIndex$())
```

Recall from Chapter 3 that the *Sort* routine implements a fast Shell sort. Thanks to this routine, the reindexing process performed by *ReIndex* is quick, even if the employee database grows to several thousand records.

The *Examine* subprogram

Examine is a relatively simple subprogram that displays a record on the screen. It begins by calling *GetName* to elicit the employee name for the desired record:

```
CALL GetName(number%, searchName$)
```

```
'   The Departure subprogram revises an employee record to indicate that
'       the employee has left the firm.  Specifically, the word "DEPARTED"
'       is stored in the dept$ field, and the depDate$ field receives the
'       current date.

SUB Departure STATIC
    CALL Examine(which%)
    PRINT: PRINT: PRINT TAB(indent%);

'   ---- Continue if a valid record exists in the database.
    IF NOT neverExisted% THEN
        IF (LEFT$(dept$, 8) <> "DEPARTED") THEN
            IF (FN YesNo("Is this the employee who is leaving?")) THEN
                LSET dept$ = "DEPARTED"
                LSET depDate$ = DATE$
                PRINT
                PRINT TAB(indent%) "*** The departure has been recorded. ***"

                PUT #1, which%

'   ---- Clear the depDate$ field.
                LSET depDate$ = ""
            ELSE
                PRINT
                PRINT TAB(indent%) "No change in this employee's status."
            END IF
        ELSE
            PRINT
            PRINT TAB(indent%) "This employee has already left."
        END IF
    END IF
    CALL Pause
END SUB


'   The PrintEmps subprogram prints a table of employees.  The subprogram
'       offers the user the option of printing or omitting former employees.

SUB PrintEmps STATIC
    PRINT: PRINT: PRINT
    PRINT TAB(indent%) "Do you want to include
    PRINT TAB(indent%) "former employees "
    prompt$ = "in the printed list?"
    PRINT TAB(indent%);
    former% = FN YesNo(prompt$)

    PRINT
    PRINT TAB(indent%) "Press the space bar "
    PRINT TAB(indent%) "when the printer is ready."

    character$ = ""
    WHILE (character$ <> " ")
        character$ = INKEY$
    WEND

    LPRINT "   Last Name         First      Soc.Sec.#   Job Title";
    LPRINT "        Current Salary"
    LPRINT "   ---------         -----      ---------   ---------";
    LPRINT "        --------------"
    LPRINT
```

Departure

PrintEmps

Figure 7-10. *The* Employee *program (continued).*   *(more . . .)*

QUICKBASIC

As we have seen, *GetName* passes back a value of 0 to *number%* if the record is not found in the index. In this case, *Examine* displays an appropriate message and sets the Boolean variable *neverExisted%* to *true%*:

```
IF (number% = 0) THEN
    PRINT
    PRINT TAB(indent%) "This name is not in the employee file."
    neverExisted% = true$
```

NeverExisted% is a global variable used to prevent the *Departure* subprogram from attempting to change the departure status of a record not in the database.

If the record is located, *Examine* loads the record from the database file into the field variables:

```
ELSE
    CLS
    GET #1, number%
```

After the GET# statement, the program can access the record values from the field variables. For example, the following statements display an employee's name:

```
PRINT TAB(indent%) "Name:          ";
PRINT FN RemSpace$(firstName$) " " lastName$
```

Notice the use of the *RemSpace$* function to remove the spaces from the end of the *firstName$* field. This is necessary because, as we learned earlier, an LSET statement "pads" field values with spaces in order to fill out the width of the field.

The *Examine* subprogram uses an IF...THEN...ELSE structure to display the salary and the salary type. The structure contains three different PRINT USING commands:

```
IF (salaryType$ = "H") THEN
    PRINT USING "**$###.## per hour"; CVS(salary$)
ELSEIF (salaryType$ = "M") THEN
    PRINT USING "**$#,#### per month"; CVS(salary$)
ELSE
    PRINT USING "**$#,##### per year"; CVS(salary$)
END IF
```

```
    FOR i% = 1 TO totEmpRecords%
        GET #1, empRecIndex%(i%)
        gone% = (LEFT$(dept$, 8) = "DEPARTED")

        IF (gone% IMP former%) THEN
            IF gone% THEN LPRINT "** "; ELSE LPRINT "    ";

            LPRINT lastName$ " " firstName$ " " _
                socialSecurity$ " " position$;

            IF (salaryType$ = "H") THEN
                LPRINT USING " **$###.## /hr"; CVS(salary$)
            ELSEIF (salaryType$ = "M") THEN
                LPRINT USING " **$#,#### /mo"; CVS(salary$)
            ELSE
                LPRINT USING " **$#,##### /yr"; CVS(salary$)
            END IF
        END IF
    NEXT i%

    IF former% THEN
        LPRINT: LPRINT: LPRINT
        LPRINT "** Former employee."
    END IF

    CALL Pause
END SUB


'   The CloseFiles subprogram closes the database file, and then saves
'       the current updated index in the file EMP.NDX.

SUB CloseFiles STATIC
    CLOSE #1

    IF (totEmpRecords% > 0) THEN
        OPEN "EMP.NDX" FOR OUTPUT AS #1

        FOR i% = 1 TO totEmpRecords%
            WRITE #1, empRecIndex%(i%), empNameIndex$(i%)
        NEXT i%

        CLOSE #1
    END IF
END SUB
```

CloseFiles

Figure 7-10. *The* Employee *program (continued).*

Note how this segment employs the CVS function to convert the string in the *salary$* field to a printable number.

Finally, the *Examine* subprogram ends with a special section that deals with former employees. We have seen that the *Record* option stores the word *DEPARTED* in the record of an employee who has left the firm. If *Examine* finds this value, the routine displays an appropriate message, along with the date of departure:

```
IF (LEFT$(dept$, 8) = "DEPARTED") THEN
    PRINT
    PRINT TAB(indent%) "*** No longer an employee ***"
    PRINT
    PRINT TAB(indent%) "Date left:    " depDate$
END IF
```

The *Change* subprogram

The *Change* subprogram displays the secondary menu shown in Figure 7-5 and prompts the user to enter changes to one or more of the following fields of an employee record: the department, job title, and salary. Like the *Add* and *Examine* subprograms, *Change* calls *GetName* to prompt for the target record's name. If the name is located, *Change* adds menu option strings to the array *changeMenu$*. The first three elements of this array receive prompt strings that include the current values of the three relevant fields. When the menu array is ready, *Change* calls the *Menu* subprogram to display the menu on the screen:

```
CALL Menu(changeMenu$(), change%)
```

The subsequent action depends on the user's menu choices. An IF...THEN...ELSE block conducts the appropriate input dialog to elicit the new field values. Thanks to a controlling WHILE...WEND loop, the menu reappears after each input dialog, until you choose the fourth option, *Keep record as shown.* When the changes are complete, the *Change* subprogram writes the revised record back to its original location in the database file:

```
PUT#1, number%
```

The *Departure* subprogram

The *Departure* subprogram alters the record of a departing employee. You can see in Figure 7-6 that this routine first gets an employee's name and then displays the target record on the screen and asks the user to confirm that the record shown is the one for the departing employee. The *Departure* subprogram then calls the *Examine* routine to display the record:

```
CALL Examine(which%)
```

Examine passes back the number of the target record to the argument variable *which%*.

If you confirm that this is the correct record, the routine stores the word *DEPARTED* in the department field and the current date in the departure date field:

```
IF (FN YesNo("Is this the employee who is leaving?")) THEN
    LSET dept$ = "DEPARTED"
    LSET depDate$ = DATE$
```

The program then writes the revised record back to its original location in the database file:

```
PUT #1, which%
```

Departure is the only routine in the program that assigns a value to the *depDate$* field. Other routines leave the field blank. To avoid sending an incorrect departure date to the next new record, *Departure* "erases" the field from the buffer after revising the current record:

```
LSET depDate$ = ""
```

This statement simply assigns an empty string to the field variable.

Notice that the main action of the *Departure* subprogram is structured within three nested IF...THEN...ELSE decisions. The outer decision uses the Boolean variable *neverExisted%* to determine if the target record exists in the database. The middle decision checks to see if the target record already represents a former employee. The inner decision gives you the opportunity to cancel the record revision.

The *PrintEmps* subprogram

PrintEmps prints a table of records from the employee database. The subprogram first asks you whether or not to include former employees in the table. The *YesNo* function retrieves the answer to this question, and then stores the Boolean result in the variable *former%*:

```
former% = FN YesNo(prompt$)
```

A WHILE...WEND loop then creates a pause until you press the space bar. This gives you time to prepare the printer:

```
character$ = ""
WHILE (character$ <> " ")
    character$ = INKEY$
WEND
```

PrintEmps then issues a series of LPRINT statements that sends lines of information to the printer, starting with the headings for the table. The records themselves are printed within a FOR...NEXT loop. At the beginning of each loop iteration, a GET# statement reads one record from the database file:

```
FOR i% = 1 TO totEmpRecords%
    GET #1, empRecIndex%(i%)
```

This FOR...NEXT loop takes the record numbers one by one from the *empRecIndex%* array. Since the records are stored in alphabetic order in the index, the resulting table is also in alphabetic order.

To determine whether or not to print a given record, the program tests to see if the record represents a former employee. The employee's status is stored in the Boolean variable *gone%*:

```
gone% = (LEFT$(dept$, 8) = "DEPARTED")
```

The variables *gone%* and *former%* determine if a given record will be printed:

```
IF (gone% IMP former%) THEN
    [print employee record]
```

This IF statement uses the logical operator IMP to decide the outcome. If *gone%* is true (this is a former employee) and *former%* is false (you do not want to include former employees in the table), then the IMP expression returns a value of false and the record is not printed. All other logical combinations of *gone%* and *former%* produce a value of true and print the record.

The *CloseFiles* subprogram

The last subprogram in the listing, *CloseFiles,* is called at the end of the main program section to close the database file and save the current index. It first closes the database file (*EMP.DAT*), which is file #1:

```
CLOSE #1
```

Then, assuming the database file contains at least one record, the routine opens the sequential file *EMP.NDX* and prepares to overwrite it with the newest version of the index:

```
OPEN "EMP.NDX" FOR OUTPUT AS #1
```

A FOR…NEXT loop writes the current index to the file from the index arrays *empRecIndex%* and *empNameIndex$*:

```
FOR i% = 1 TO totEmpRecords%
    WRITE #1, empRecIndex%(i%), empNameIndex$(i%)
NEXT i%
```

Finally, the routine closes the index file:

```
CLOSE #1
```

The next time it is run, the program finds an index file that is updated and correctly describes the status of the database.

CONCLUSION

If you would like to continue working with the *Employee* program, here are a few suggestions for programming exercises:

1. Enhance the error-handling routine that takes over when the program cannot locate the index file, *EMP.NDX*. (Sometimes computer users inadvertently erase important files; this error routine would restore the database if the index were lost.) The routine should open the database file (*EMP.DAT*) and read the name fields of each record. As the routine progresses, it should store the names in the *empNameIndex$* array and the record numbers in the *empRecIndex%* array. After sorting the new index, the *Employee* program should resume as usual.

2. Devise a subprogram that removes former employees from the database. One approach is to divide *EMP.DAT* into two files: *EMPFORM.DAT* for storing former employees, and *EMPCUR.DAT* for storing current employees. When the process is complete, the original *EMP.DAT* can be deleted (or renamed as a backup file, *EMP.BAK*) and *EMPCUR.DAT* can be renamed *EMP.DAT*. You might also develop a separate set of subprograms to let the user access a database of former employees.

3. Create other indexes for accessing the records in the file. For example, one index might arrange the records by department and then by employee name within each department. (Each element in the string array of the index should contain a concatenation of the department name first, followed by an employee name.) Using such an index, the program could produce a printed table in which employees are listed by department.

4. Write a utility program designed to expand the field structure of the database. For example, such a utility might add fields for the employee's birth date and family status. To implement the new database structure, the utility should begin by creating an entirely new database with the necessary record length and field structure. Then, by opening the new database and *EMP.DAT* simultaneously, the current field information from each record of *EMP.DAT* can be copied to the new database. Finally, the process should include an input dialog to elicit the new field values for each employee.

Structured Decisions in QuickBASIC: *A Game of Twenty-one*

So far in this book we have concentrated on "serious" applications—those involving financial, business, and database programs. Now let's move to something lighter, a program that plays the popular card game known as *Twenty-one* or *Blackjack*.

Twenty-one is a relatively simple gambling game that uses a full deck of 52 cards. In this computerized version, the computer is the dealer, and you—sitting at the keyboard—are the player. You begin each round by placing a bet, an amount that you will ultimately either win or lose unless the round ends in a draw.

The action is fast and seductive, and you can continue playing as long as you wish. By design, the odds are always in the dealer's favor. (Happily, this computer-based game offers a striking advantage over real-life gambling: If you find yourself losing too dramatically, you can always wander away from the table. When you end the game, the computer conveniently forgets about your losses.)

Simple though the game is, the *Twenty-one* program itself is rich in complex and challenging algorithms. We studied some of these algorithms in Chapter 3 when we examined the *Shuffle* subprogram and saw how to set up a digital deck of cards. *Shuffle* appears in the *Twenty-one* program, along with some other routines developed in Chapter 3.

The action of *Twenty-one* depends on three sorts of events and conditions: first, the random shuffle of the deck; second, the decisions you make as you play your own hand; and third, the fixed rules that determine how the dealer responds. The program must be prepared to handle a variety of outcomes. During each round, the program deals and displays the cards, and keeps a "count" of the two hands—yours and the dealer's. Given the cards contained in the two hands, the program must also determine the available playing options for any turn of the game and then control the action accordingly.

The *Twenty-one* program provides an excellent way to explore QuickBASIC's versatile IF...THEN...ELSE structure. You have already seen some examples of the decision structure in previous chapters; in this chapter, IF...THEN...ELSE is the main focus. Let's begin with a quick review of the syntax of this structure.

THE IF...THEN...ELSE STRUCTURE

The IF...THEN...ELSE structure has the following syntax:

IF *condition1* **THEN**
> *[block of statements that will be performed if* condition1 *is true]*

ELSEIF *condition2* **THEN**
> *[block of statements that will be performed if* condition2 *is true (you may include additional ELSEIF blocks in the structure)]*

ELSE
> *[block of statements that will be*
> *performed if none of the previous*
> *conditions is true]*

END IF

The major elements are an IF statement, optional ELSEIF and ELSE clauses, and an END IF statement. As you examine this syntax, keep in mind the following characteristics:

- The conditions in the IF statement and the ELSEIF clause may be any expressions that QuickBASIC can evaluate as true or false (these are often called *logical* expressions).

- The IF statement and the ELSEIF and ELSE clauses are each followed by a block of program statements. QuickBASIC evaluates the conditions of the IF statement and the ELSEIF clauses in the order in which they appear and performs the block of statements corresponding to the first condition that results in a true value.

- The ELSE block is performed if none of the IF or ELSEIF condition expressions evaluate to true. The ELSE clause is optional; if you do not include it, and all the previous conditions are false, no action is performed.

- You may optionally include multiple ELSEIF clauses, each with its own conditional expression and corresponding block of statements.

- At most, only one block of statements in the structure is performed, even if more than one of the IF or ELSEIF conditions evaluates to true. As soon as QuickBASIC encounters one true condition, it ignores the remaining clauses.

- You can nest IF...THEN...ELSE structures within other structures, creating the potential for complex patterns of decision-making.

- To build conditional expressions, you can use the six relational operators ($=$, $<>$, $>$, $<$, $>=$, $<=$) and the six logical (or Boolean) operators. The most commonly used logical operators are AND, OR, and NOT; the other three are XOR (exclusive OR), EQV (equivalence), and IMP (implication).

● As discussed in Chapter 4, QuickBASIC evaluates conditional expressions to one of any two numeric values: − 1 for true, 0 for false. Knowing this, you can create special numeric variables that by design always contain one of these two values; you can use such "Boolean" variables to keep track of important conditions that change during the course of a program. These variables, once established, can take the place of other forms of conditional expressions in IF statements and ELSEIF clauses.

Now let's review the rules of Twenty-one and discuss the kinds of decisions the program must make to conduct the game.

DECISIONS IN THE TWENTY-ONE PROGRAM

Your goal in each round is to accumulate a hand with a count that is as close as possible to 21, but not more than 21. Count the cards in your hand as follows:

● Face cards (Jack, Queen, King) of any suit count 10.

● Aces count either 11 or 1, whichever works to your advantage in reaching, but not exceeding, 21.

● The number cards (2 through 10) are worth their face value.

A round begins when the dealer deals two cards each to you and to himself. The dealer places his own first card face down on the table, and the second face up so that you can see it. You examine your two cards and evaluate your hand. (Meanwhile, the dealer evaluates his hand.) If either hand contains a "natural" 21—that is, an ace plus a face card or a 10—the round ends immediately. If the natural is yours, you win twice your bet; if the natural is the dealer's, you lose your bet. (Occasionally, both hands are naturals, in which case the round ends in a draw.)

If neither hand is a natural, you play first in the round. You must decide whether to "hit" (take another card) or "stay" (play with your current hand). If you indicate that you want to hit, the dealer gives you another card from the top of the deck. You can continue hitting (receiving additional cards) until your count either reaches or exceeds 21.

If you go over 21—a "bust"—you lose the round. The dealer does not play his hand or expose the face-down card. You lose your bet immediately.

If, however, you elect to stay at a point where your hand has a count of 21 or less, the dealer must take a turn. A fixed set of rules determines when the dealer will hit or stay:

- The dealer hits at a count of 16 or less and stays at a count of 17 or more.

- In a "soft" count of 17 or more—that is, in a hand that contains an ace plus a card worth 6 or more—the dealer does not have the option of counting the ace as 1 and hitting again. The ace counts as 11, and the dealer must stay.

If the dealer busts, you win the round and your bet. Otherwise, the count of your hand is compared with the dealer's. The hand that has the higher count wins. If the hands are equal, the round finishes in a draw.

Now let's look at a couple of screens from our *Twenty-one* program.

Figure 8-1 shows how the program turns your computer's display screen into the playing table. The player's hand is on the left; the dealer's hand is on the right. Imagine that you are playing this round. Since you have three cards, you have already hit once. Your count is still less than 21.

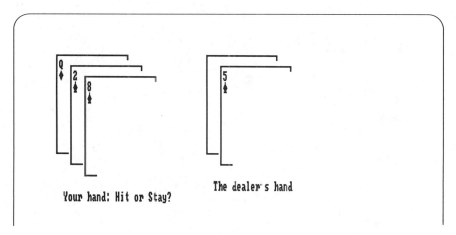

Figure 8-1. *The* Twenty-one *program's "playing table."*

The program asks:

`Your hand: Hit or Stay?`

A flashing cursor at the end of the question indicates that the program is waiting for you to respond. Press *H* to hit, or *S* to stay. (Pressing any other key produces no response.)

Notice that the dealer's hand is displayed according to the rules: The first card is hidden, face down; the second is face up. You may want to base your hit-or-stay strategy partly on what you can deduce from the dealer's up card.

Figure 8-2 shows another screen later in the same round. You can see that you decided to stay with your three-card hand. The dealer then began taking more cards, following the prescribed hit-or-stay rules. The dealer's final hit resulted in a bust. When the dealer busts, you win regardless of your count. The program displays your winnings at the bottom of the screen.

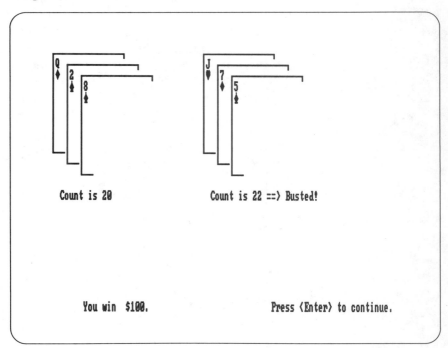

Figure 8-2. *A round of Twenty-one.*

The screen also shows the following message in the lower-right corner:

```
Press <Enter> to continue.
```

To begin a new round, press Enter. You start the next round by placing a bet, after which the program deals two new hands. Figure 8-3 shows the screen in which the program requests your bet. (The program produces only two screens: this one and the actual playing table. Simplicity is always an important design element in game programs.)

```
Twenty-one
==========

    The computer is the dealer.
    You currently have:     $350

Place your bet.
----------------
    The house betting limits are:
      -) minimum bet --  $10
      -) maximum bet -- $100
    (Press (Enter) for maximum bet.)
    (Press (Q) to Quit.)

         ==)
```

Figure 8-3. *The screen for inputting your bet.*

After seeing these screens, you can easily list the major decision-making processes that must take place in the program. During the play itself, the first important decisions occur as soon as the two initial hands are dealt. The program evaluates both hands and proceeds as follows:

- If one of the hands is a natural 21, the round is over. Display the player's win or loss.

- If both hands are naturals, the round is over and ends in a draw.

- If neither hand is a natural, display the *Hit or Stand?* prompt below the player's cards.

If neither hand is a natural, the player decides whether to hit or stand. The program proceeds as follows:

- If the player presses *H* (*hit*), draw a card from the top of the deck and redisplay the player's hand along with the new card. Determine the player's new count.

  — If the new count is more than 21, the player busts and the round is over. Display the player's loss at the bottom of the screen.
  — If the player's count is less than 21, display the *Hit or Stay?* prompt again and wait for the player's next instruction.
  — If the player's count is exactly 21, display the message *Twenty-one!* and begin the dealer's play.

- If the player presses *S* (*stay*), display the player's final count on the screen and then begin the dealer's play.

Unless the player has busted, it is the dealer's turn. The program "turns over" the dealer's hidden card, displaying both cards along with the current count of the dealer's hand. The ensuing decision process is as follows:

- If the dealer's count is less than 16, display the message *Dealer hits*. Also display *Press <Enter> to continue* at the bottom of the screen. (To carry out each turn in the dealer's play, the program requires the player to press Enter. The player can thus examine each new card the dealer draws and prevent the game from moving too quickly.) When the player presses Enter, deal another card into the dealer's hand. Display the new hand and count.

  — If the new count is still less than 17, display *Dealer hits* again.
  — If the new count is 17 or more, display the message *Dealer stays*. (If the hand is soft—that is, if it contains an ace—count the ace as 11 as long as the total count is between 17 and 21, inclusive. However, if a soft hand would become a bust if the ace were counted as 11, count the card as 1. The dealer thus hits again if the total count is still less than 17.)

When both the player's and dealer's hands have been played, determine the winner and display the results of the round:

- If the player's count and the dealer's count are equal, display the message *A draw. . .* at the bottom of the screen. (The player's current assets do not change.)

- If the player has busted, or if the dealer's hand is greater than the player's hand (as long as the dealer has not busted), display a message such as *You lose $100* and deduct the amount of the bet from the player's current assets.

- If the dealer has busted, or if the player's count is greater than the dealer's count, display a message such as *You win $100* and add the amount of the bet to the player's current assets.

- If the player's hand has only two cards and a count of 21 (hence a natural), display a message such as *You win $200* and add twice the amount of the bet to the player's current assets. (However, if the dealer's hand is also a natural, end the game as a draw.)

These are the major decisions that determine how the program works. Many less obvious, but often essential, decisions occur during the program's carefully designed "input and output" processes: accepting keyboard instructions from the player and preparing the two display screens.

Finally, the program must track the status of the deck. A "pointer" variable identifies the location of the current "top" of the deck. When the entire 52-card deck has been dealt, the program reshuffles all the cards not currently displayed. These duties require some rather careful planning, which you will see when you study the program listing.

SAMPLE ROUNDS OF THE *TWENTY-ONE* PROGRAM

Figures 8-4 through 8-11 (on the following pages) show screens produced by the *Twenty-one* program. As you examine them, keep in mind the following two basic design goals:

- Keyboard input should be fast, easy, and obvious. Placing a bet, specifying a hit or a stay, and requesting an additional round should require as few keystrokes as possible so that the input process does not interfere with the pace of the game.

- The presentation of the game on the screen should be visual, not verbal. The player should be allowed to concentrate on the cards. Therefore, the display of the two hands must be simple but clear. Furthermore, the program should avoid distracting the player with excessive written instructions or messages.

The "user-interface" issues of screen design and keyboard input are essential in *any* programming project. In a game program these issues determine whether or not the game is attractive, enjoyable, appropriately paced, and successful.

Figure 8-3 shows the screen that precedes each round. This screen introduces the program and tells you, the player, how much money you have. When you start the game, the program gives you $250. The bet range is from $10 to $100, and at the end of each round the program adjusts your current assets. You can go into debt to the dealer. If your dollar holdings fall below zero, the program tells you, for example:

```
You owe the house:   $1,250.
(The house extends credit.)
```

The house extends unlimited credit!

The program next displays the house betting limits and asks for your bet. You may simply press Enter to bet the maximum amount, which is $100.

At this time you may also quit the program by entering a lower- or uppercase *Q*.

If you enter any other nonnumeric value or a number outside the allowable betting range, the program redisplays the arrow prompt, for another input value.

After you place your bet, the screen becomes the card table, and the program deals the beginning hands of two cards each, as you can see in Figure 8-4. If neither hand is a natural 21, you must indicate whether you want to hit or stay.

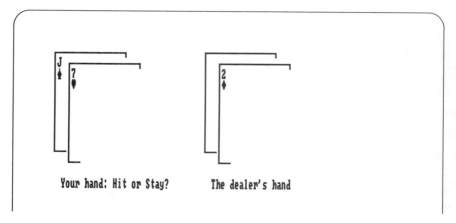

Figure 8-4.   *The initial deal in a round of Twenty-one.*

A word or two on playing strategy: Your decision to hit or stay will probably be based primarily on the count of your own hand. If the count is 11 or less, you should certainly hit; no single card that you could receive would put you over 21. If the count is 17 or more, you should give serious thought to staying. The chances of a bust are high if you take another card, and you know that the dealer stays on a count of 17 or more.

A count of 12, 13, 14, 15, or 16 presents a more difficult decision. If you are a serious player, you might take a number of factors into account: the value of the dealer's up card (that is, the card that is displayed); your mental record of the cards that have been dealt since the last shuffle; and your instinct for the percentages. Many books are available on the strategy and the mathematics of Twenty-one or Blackjack. But since playing strategy is not our main concern, let's look quickly at the remaining sample rounds.

Figure 8-5 shows a round that has ended in a draw: The two hands have equal counts. You neither win nor lose.

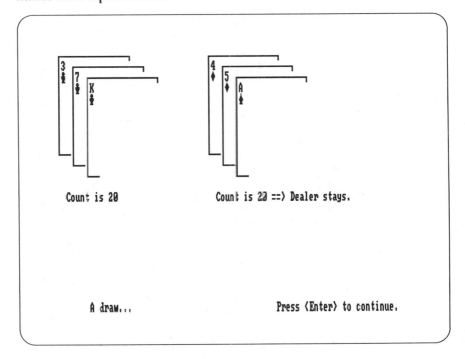

Figure 8-5. *A round ending in a draw.*

Figures 8-6, 8-7, and 8-8 show various ways in which you can win a round. In Figure 8-6 your initial deal is a natural, and you therefore win twice your bet. In Figure 8-7 you have taken additional cards, and your count is 21. Given the rules, the dealer has been forced to stay on a count that is less than yours; so you win. (Note that your winnings are not doubled for just any count of 21—only for a natural.) Finally, Figure 8-8 shows a round in which the dealer has busted; again, you win, regardless of your count.

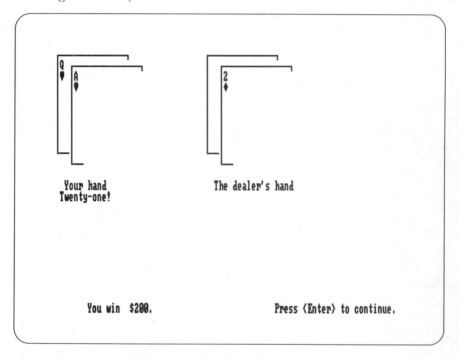

Figure 8-6. *A "natural" Twenty-one (the player wins double the bet).*

Figures 8-9 and 8-10 show two rounds in which you have lost. In the first, the dealer accumulated a higher count than you. In the second, you busted on the third card. Notice the message displayed below your hand:

```
Count is 26 ==> Busted!
```

(To rub it in a little, the computer also beeps at you when you bust.) The dealer does not take a turn when you bust, but automatically collects your bet. This is the dealer's most important advantage in the

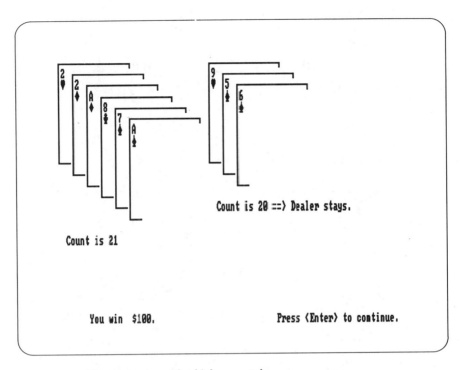

Count is 20 ==> Dealer stays.

Count is 21

You win $100.   Press <Enter> to continue.

Figure 8-7. *The player wins with a higher count than the dealer.*

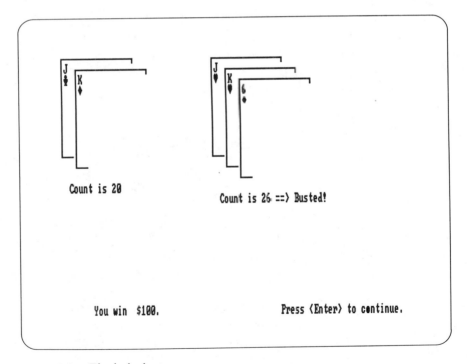

Count is 20

Count is 26 ==> Busted!

You win $100.   Press <Enter> to continue.

Figure 8-8. *The dealer busts.*

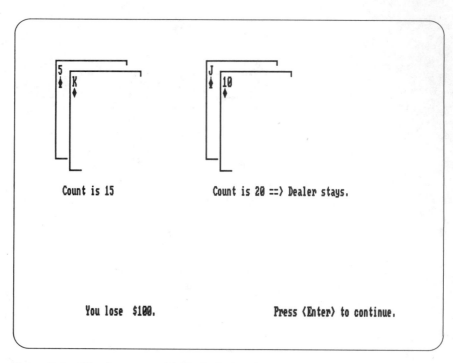

Figure 8-9. *The player stays with 15, the dealer wins with 20.*

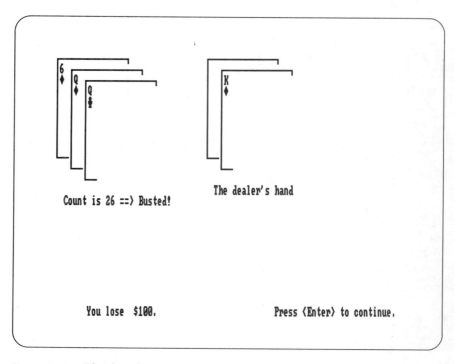

Figure 8-10. *The player busts.*

design of the game: If he played after your bust, he might well bust also, perhaps with a count identical to yours. But by ending the round on your bust, he avoids the risk of ending in a draw or busting himself.

Figure 8-11, the last of our sample screens, shows the message that appears when the program is reshuffling the cards. The cards currently on the table are not included in the shuffle. In this example, three cards are on the table, so the reshuffling message appears as:

```
Reshuffling 49 cards...
```

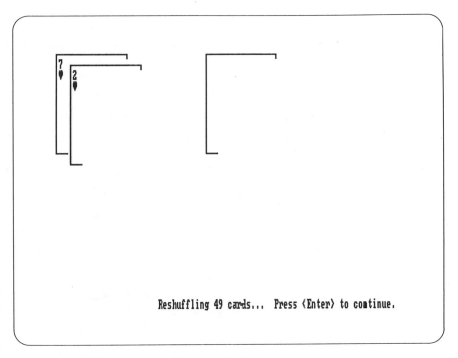

Figure 8-11. *The screen displayed when the deck is being reshuffled.*

The program intentionally interrupts the game for reshuffling so that you know you will subsequently be working with a newly shuffled deck; this fact may enter into your playing strategy. (Reshuffling takes less than a second. After you see the message, press Enter to continue.)

Now that we know what the program does, let's begin exploring in detail the decisions that it makes throughout the game. Figure 8-12 (on the next page) shows the structure of the program. Refer to this chart for overall organization as we focus on individual routines.

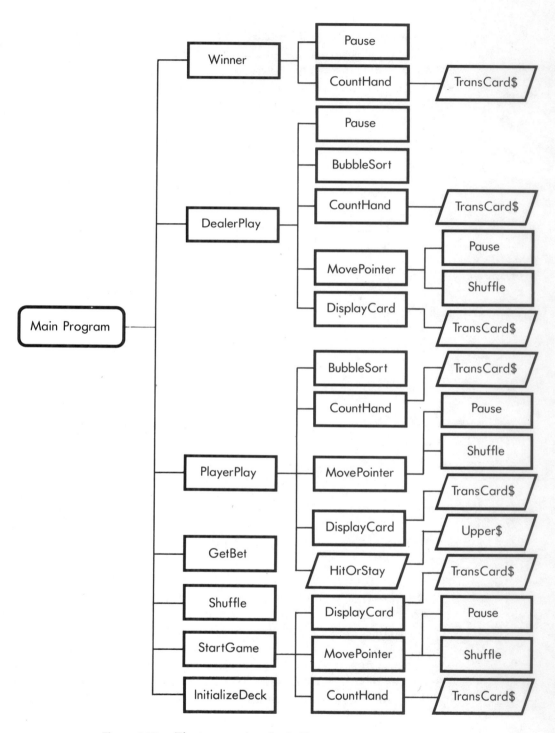

Figure 8-12. *The structure chart for the* Twenty-one
program.

INSIDE THE *TWENTY-ONE* PROGRAM

The program listing appears in Figure 8-13. First, we will study the global variable declarations area and the main program area, and then we will examine the subprograms in the order in which they are performed.

```
'   BJACK.BAS
'   Plays the game of 21 (or Blackjack).  The computer is always
'       the dealer, and the person at the keyboard is the player.
'       No "splitting" of pairs is allowed, nor is "doubling down" of
'       bets allowed. The player begins with $250, and may place bets
'       that range from $10 to $100.

'--------------------| Global Variable Declarations |--------------------


    OPTION BASE 1
    DIM rank$(13), deck%(52), playerHand%(11), dealerHand%(11)

    COMMON SHARED rank$(), deck%(), playerHand%(), dealerHand%(), _
        nextCard%, currentHoldings%, betAmount%, playerCards%, _
        dealerCards%, true%, false%

'   ---- Set the player's initial gambling sum to $250.
    currentHoldings% = 250

'   ---- Initialize Boolean variables true% and false%.
    true% = -1
    false% = 0


'--------------------------| Function Area |--------------------------


'   ---- Read in and compile BASIC user-defined function.
    REM  $INCLUDE : 'UPPER.BAS'


'   The TransCard$ function translates a number from 1 to 52 into a
'       two-character string representing the suit and rank of the
'       corresponding card.
DEF FN TransCard$(cardNumber%)
    suit$ = CHR$(((cardNumber% - 1) \ 13) + 3)
    rnk$ = rank$((((cardNumber% - 1) MOD 13) + 1)
    FN TransCard$ = suit$ + rnk$
END DEF


'   The HitOrStay function asks the player if he or she wants to "hit"
'       (take another card), or "stay" (play with the current hand).
'       HitOrStay returns a value of true if the player wants to stay.
DEF FN HitOrStay
    LOCATE playerCards% + 12, 5
    answer$ = ""
    PRINT "Your hand: Hit or Stay? ";
```

TransCard

HitOrStay

Figure 8-13. *The* Twenty-one *program.*   *(more...)*

The global variable declarations area

In previous chapters we have seen how global variables, used judiciously, can simplify the structure of a program. Using the COMMON SHARED statement to declare a small and deliberately selected group of variables as global can be a great advantage in a large program. Accordingly, the *Twenty-one* program uses a short list of global arrays and variables that store information about the deck and the two hands:

```
COMMON SHARED rank$(), deck%(), playerHand%(), dealerHand%(), _
    nextCard%, currentHoldings%, betAmount%, playerCards%, _
    dealerCards%, true%, false%
```

These variables are used often throughout the program. By declaring them global we avoid having to pass them back and forth as arguments to the subprograms. The following table explains how the program uses each of these variables:

rank$	An array of characters representing the 13 card ranks.
deck%	An array of integers representing the 52 cards in the deck.
playerHand% and *dealerHand%*	Arrays of integers representing the cards in the player's hand and the dealer's hand, respectively.
nextCard%	A pointer variable, which always contains the position of the current top card in the *deck%* array.
currentHoldings%	An integer representing the player's current dollar assets.
betAmount%	The amount of the bet for the current round.
playerCards% and *dealerCards%*	The number of cards currently held in the player's hand and the dealer's hand, respectively.

The program's four global arrays—*rank$*, *deck%*, *playerHand%*, and *dealerHand%*—all have static dimensions and therefore must be defined *before* the COMMON SHARED statement:

```
DIM rank$(13), deck%(52), playerHand%(11), dealerHand%(11)
```

The array *rank$* is designed to hold the 13 symbols for the cards' ranks, and the array *deck%* holds integers representing the 52 cards. The hand arrays, *playerHand%* and *dealerHand%*, have dimensions of 11—the largest possible hand that could yield a count of 21—but the odds against ever accumulating so large a hand are enormous. A hand rarely contains more than 5 or 6 cards at a time.

```
        WHILE (answer$ = "") OR (INSTR("HS", answer$) = 0)
            LOCATE ,, 1
            answer$ = INKEY$
            answer$ = FN Upper$(answer$)
        WEND
        LOCATE playerCards% + 12, 5: PRINT SPACE$(25);
        FN HitOrStay = (answer$ = "S")
    END DEF

'-------------------------| Main Program Area |----------------------------


        LOCATE ,, 1

'     ---- Initialize the deck, and shuffle it.
        CALL InitializeDeck
        nextCard% = 1
        CALL Shuffle(deck%())

'     ---- The play:  For each round, get a bet, deal two cards each to the
'           player and the dealer, and draw more cards if appropriate.
'           Declare the result of the round.

        gameOver% = false%
        WHILE NOT gameOver%
            CALL GetBet (gameOver%)

            IF NOT gameOver% THEN
                CALL StartGame (roundOver%)
                IF NOT roundOver% THEN
                    CALL PlayerPlay (busted%)
                    IF NOT busted% THEN
                        CALL DealerPlay
                    END IF
                END IF
                CALL Winner
            END IF
        WEND

        END

'-------------------------| Subprogram Area |----------------------------


'     ---- Read in and compile BASIC subprogram.
        REM  $INCLUDE : 'SHUFFLE.BAS'


'     The InitializeDeck subprogram initializes the rank$ and deck% arrays.

    SUB InitializeDeck STATIC
        FOR i% = 1 TO 13
            READ rank$(i%)
        NEXT i%

        DATA 2, 3, 4, 5, 6, 7, 8, 9, T, J, Q, K, A

        FOR i% = 1 to 52
            deck%(i%) = i%
        NEXT i%
    END SUB
```

`InitializeDeck`

Figure 8-13. *The* Twenty-one *program (continued).*   *(more...)*

Since none of these arrays require the "zeroth" element, the following OPTION BASE statement starts them all out at an element of 1:

```
OPTION BASE 1
```

Initializations take place next in the global variable declaration area. First, the player's initial betting allowance is set to $250:

```
currentHoldings% = 250
```

Finally, the Boolean variables *true%* and *false%* are initialized to contain the logical values of −1 (true) and 0 (false).

```
true% = -1
false% = 0
```

The main program area

The main program area begins by initializing and shuffling the deck of cards. The program first calls the *InitializeDeck* subprogram to initialize the rank and deck arrays. This routine reads the 13 ranks from a DATA statement:

```
FOR i% = 1 TO 13
    READ rank$(i%)
NEXT i%
DATA 2, 3, 4, 5, 6, 7, 8, 9, T, J, Q, K, A
```

The integers 1–52 represent the cards in the deck:

```
FOR i% = 1 to 52
    deck%(i%) = i%
NEXT i%
```

(You'll see how to use these two important arrays as we progress through the various subprograms. You'll also learn how the program translates the integers 1–52 into the ranks and suits of individual cards.) When *InitializeDeck* completes its two tasks, the main program section takes control again and sets the deck pointer, *nextCard%,* at the top of the deck:

```
nextCard% = 1
```

Finally, the program shuffles the entire deck for the first time:

```
CALL Shuffle(deck%())
```

```
'    The GetBet subprogram announces the player's current holdings (or
'        indebtedness), and invites the player to place a bet.

SUB GetBet (quit%) STATIC
    lowBet% = 10
    highBet% = 100
    PRINT: PRINT: PRINT
    PRINT "        Twenty-one"
    PRINT "        =========="
    PRINT
    PRINT "           The computer is the dealer."
    PRINT "           ";
    IF (currentHoldings% >= 0) THEN
        PRINT USING "You currently have: $$#,####'"; currentHoldings%
    ELSE
        PRINT USING "You owe the house: $$#,###"; ABS(currentHoldings%)
        PRINT "           (The house extends credit.)"
    END IF

    PRINT
    PRINT "        Place your bet."
    PRINT "        ---------------"
    PRINT "           The house betting limits are:"
    PRINT USING "               ->  minimum bet -- $$###"; lowBet%
    PRINT USING "               ->  maximum bet -- $$###"; highBet%
    PRINT "           (Press <Enter> for maximum bet.)"
    PRINT "           (Press <Q> to Quit.)"
    PRINT

'    ---- Read the bet amount as a string value, betString$.  If betString$
'         is empty, assume that the player wants to bet the maximum amount.
'         If betString$ is "Q", Quit the program.
    ok% = false%
    WHILE NOT ok%
        PRINT "                     ";
        INPUT "==> ", betString$
        IF betString$ = "" THEN
            betAmount% = highBet%
            ok% = true%
            quit% = false%
        ELSEIF (betString$ = "Q") OR (betString$ = "q") THEN
            ok% = true%
            quit% = true%
        ELSE
            betAmount% = VAL(betString$)
            ok% = (betAmount% >= lowBet%) AND (betAmount% <= highBet%)
            quit% = false%
        END IF
    WEND
    CLS
END SUB


'    The StartGame subprogram deals the first two cards to the player and
'        the dealer, and determines if anyone has 21 at the outset.  If so,
'        StartGame sends a Boolean value of true back to the main program
'        in the win% variable.

SUB StartGame (win%) STATIC
    playerCards% = 0 : dealerCards% = 0
```

GetBet

StartGame

Figure 8-13. *The* Twenty-one *program (continued).* *(more...)*

331

The *Shuffle* subprogram (discussed in Chapter 3) is read into the program listing at compile time by a $INCLUDE metacommand at the top of the subprogram area.

```
REM $INCLUDE : 'SHUFFLE.BAS'
```

The *Shuffle* subprogram, you'll recall, rearranges the elements of an array into a random order.

When all these initialization tasks are complete, the game can begin. A single WHILE...WEND loop, with a sequence of nested IF statements, conducts the broad action of the game by repeatedly calling on the following five main subprograms:

- *GetBet* finds out if the player wants to play another round, and if so elicits the player's bet.

- *StartGame* deals the first two cards to each hand and checks for naturals.

- *PlayerPlay* controls the player's turn at hitting or staying and monitors the count of the player's hand.

- *DealerPlay* conducts the dealer's turn.

- *Winner* determines who has won and adjusts the player's money.

The *GetBet, StartGame,* and *PlayerPlay* subprograms

Three of these subprograms, *GetBet, StartGame,* and *PlayerPlay,* pass Boolean values back to the main program to indicate various conditions of the game. The program uses these values to decide exactly how each round should proceed. These are the first big decisions of the program, so let's examine them carefully.

First, before any round begins, *GetBet* must find out if the player wants to quit. If the player indicates this (by pressing the letter *Q*), a value of true is sent back to the *gameOver%* variable in the main program:

```
CALL GetBet (gameOver%)
```

If *gameOver%* is true, the player has chosen to quit the game. No further action takes place, and the controlling WHILE...WEND structure in the main program section ultimately terminates its looping:

```
WHILE NOT gameOver%
```

```
        FOR i% = 1 TO 2
            playerHand%(i%) = deck%(nextCard%)
            CALL DisplayCard (i% + 1, i% * 3, playerHand%(i%), true%)
            playerCards% = playerCards% + 1
            CALL MovePointer

            dealerHand%(i%) = deck%(nextCard%)
            CALL DisplayCard (i% + 1, 32 + i% * 3, dealerHand%(i%), 1 - i%)
            dealerCards% = dealerCards% + 1
            CALL MovePointer
        NEXT i%

        LOCATE 14,5: PRINT "Your hand"
        LOCATE 14,37: PRINT "The dealer's hand"

'       ---- Count the hands.
        CALL CountHand(playerHand%(), 2, playerTotal%)
        CALL CountHand(dealerHand%(), 2, dealerTotal%)

'       ---- Analyze the situation, and display the value of each hand if
'            appropriate.  (The dealer's hand will not be displayed if the
'            player gets a 21.)
        IF (dealerTotal% = 21) OR (playerTotal% = 21) THEN
            win% = true%

            IF (dealerTotal% = 21) THEN
                CALL DisplayCard(2 , 35, dealerHand%(1), true%)
                LOCATE 15,40
                PRINT "Twenty-one!"
            END IF

            LOCATE 15,4
            IF (playerTotal% = 21) THEN
                PRINT "Twenty-one!"
            ELSE
                PRINT "Count is: " playerTotal%
            END IF
        ELSE
            win% = false%
        END IF
END SUB


'   The MovePointer subprogram increments the nextCard% variable.  When
'       nextCard% goes past 52, this routine shuffles all the cards that
'       aren't currently on the table.

SUB MovePointer STATIC
    nextCard% = nextCard% + 1

    IF (nextCard% > 52) THEN
        tableCards% = playerCards% + dealerCards%
        usedCards% = 52 - tableCards%
        LOCATE 25,25: PRINT "Reshuffling" usedCards% "cards...";

'       ---- The tempDeck% array will contain all those cards that are not
'            in a current hand.
        REDIM tempDeck%(usedCards%)

        FOR i% = 1 TO usedCards%
            tempDeck%(i%) = deck%(i%)
        NEXT i%
```

Figure 8-13. *The* Twenty-one *program (continued).*   *(more...)*

MovePointer

On the other hand, if the player chose not to quit, the program immediately calls on *StartGame* to deal the initial hands:

```
IF NOT gameOver% THEN
    CALL StartGame (roundOver%)
```

StartGame duly counts the value of each hand, checking for naturals. If either hand has a natural 21, the round ends. In this case *StartGame* passes a value of true back to the main program in the variable *roundOver%*. The value true means that neither *PlayerPlay* nor *DealerPlay* needs to be performed this round, since no further cards are dealt when a round starts out with a natural.

But if *roundOver%* is false, the program must begin offering additional cards to the player. This is *PlayerPlay's* job:

```
IF NOT roundOver% THEN
    CALL PlayerPlay (busted%)
```

PlayerPlay repeatedly gives the player the choice between hitting or staying until one of three events occurs: the player elects to stay with the current cards; the player reaches a count of exactly 21; or the player busts. In the last case, *PlayerPlay* passes a value of true to the argument variable *busted%*, and the program skips the dealer's play.

On the other hand, if *busted%* is false, meaning that the player has stayed with a count of 21 or less, the dealer must play:

```
IF NOT busted% THEN
    CALL DealerPlay
```

These three decisions are carefully organized to ensure that the right sequence of subprograms is called to meet the requirements of a given round. The key to this is progressive nesting of the IF...THEN statements. Let's review the entire sequence:

```
CALL GetBet (gameOver%)
IF NOT gameOver% THEN
    CALL StartGame (roundOver%)
    IF NOT roundOver% THEN
        CALL PlayerPlay (busted%)
        IF NOT busted% THEN
            CALL DealerPlay
        END IF
    END IF
    CALL Winner
END IF
```

```
'    ---- Shuffle the tempDeck% array.
        CALL Shuffle(tempDeck%())
'    ---- For the next shuffle, keep a record of the cards that are on the
'        table.  (In effect, put these cards on the bottom of the deck.)
        FOR i% = 1 TO tableCards%
            deck%(i%) = deck%(usedCards% + i%)
        NEXT i%

'    ---- Fill up the rest of the deck with the newly shuffled cards.
        FOR i% = 1 to usedCards%
            deck%(tableCards% + i%) = tempDeck%(i%)
        NEXT i%

'    ---- The nextCard% variable should point to the top of the newly
'        shuffled cards.
        nextCard% = tableCards% + 1
        CALL Pause
        LOCATE 25,25: PRINT SPACE$(54);
    END IF
END SUB


'    The PlayerPlay subprogram gives the player a chance to take more cards.
'        If the player's hand goes over 21, PlayerPlay returns a value of
'        true in the variable over21%.

SUB PlayerPlay (over21%) STATIC
    over21% = false%
    done% = false%

'    ---- Continue until the player is done or the hand goes over 21.
    WHILE NOT (over21% OR done%)
        done% = FN HitOrStay
        IF NOT done% THEN

'    ---- Deal the player another card.
            playerCards% = playerCards% + 1
            playerHand%(playerCards%) = deck%(nextCard%)

'    ---- Redisplay the hand with the new card (sort cards by suit).
            CALL BubbleSort(playerHand%(), playerCards%)
            FOR i% = 1 to playerCards%
                CALL DisplayCard(i% + 1, i% * 3, playerHand%(i%), true%)
            NEXT i%
            CALL MovePointer

'    ---- Analyze the new hand count.
            CALL CountHand(playerHand%(), playerCards%, playerTotal%)
            IF (playerTotal% > 21) THEN
                over21% = true%
                LOCATE playerCards% + 12, 5
                PRINT "Count is" playerTotal% "==> Busted!"
                BEEP
            ELSEIF (playerTotal% = 21) THEN
                done% = true%
            END IF
        ELSE
            CALL CountHand(playerHand%(), playerCards%, playerTotal%)
        END IF
    WEND
```

Figure 8-13. *The* Twenty-one *program (continued).*   *(more...)*

The ELSE and ELSEIF clauses would not have worked successfully for this sequence. In contrast to decision structures we will look at later, the program here is not attempting to choose one of several alternative courses, but rather is deciding at each turn whether or not to take the next step. Each decision is based on the result of the previous step.

In all well-structured programs the main program section is a kind of outline of the entire action. Master the logic of the main program, and you will understand how the program flows. Of course, there are many more details to explore; in the sections that follow, we will examine the highlights of the subprograms, starting with *GetBet*.

Place your bet: The *GetBet* subprogram

The *GetBet* subprogram first initializes *lowBet%* and *highBet%* with the minimum bet amount ($10) and the maximum bet amount ($100) allowed:

```
lowBet% = 10
highBet% = 100
```

GetBet next prints some introductory information including the program title, the player's current cash balance, and the house betting limits. The cash balance is determined by a simple IF...THEN...ELSE block that utilizes the global integer variable *currentHoldings%*. If *currentHoldings%* has a value greater than or equal to zero, *currentHoldings%* is printed together with some descriptive text by a PRINT USING statement. If *currentHoldings%* has a negative value, the debt is expressed as a dollar value owed to the house by PRINT USING and ABS, QuickBASIC's absolute value function. The IF...THEN...ELSE block appears like this:

```
IF (currentHoldings% >= 0) THEN
    PRINT USING "You currently have: $$#,####"; currentHoldings%
ELSE
    PRINT USING "You owe the house: $$#,###"; ABS(currentHoldings%)
    PRINT "        (The house extends credit.)"
END IF
```

GetBet next uses the local variables *lowBet%* and *highBet%* and a series of PRINT statements to display the betting limits and prompt the

```
        IF done% THEN
            LOCATE playerCards% + 12, 5
            PRINT "Count is" playerTotal%
        END IF
END SUB


'   The Pause subprogram suspends the program until the player is ready to
'       continue.  Pause places a message in the lower-right corner of the
'       screen, and waits for the player to press the Enter key (any key
'       will work).

SUB Pause STATIC
    LOCATE 25,50: PRINT "Press <Enter> to continue.";
    character$ = ""
    WHILE character$ = ""
        character$ = INKEY$
    WEND
END SUB


'   The DealerPlay subprogram draws more cards for the dealer's hand until
'       the count is 17 or over.

SUB DealerPlay STATIC
'   ---- Begin by displaying the dealer's hidden card.
    CALL DisplayCard(2, 35, dealerHand%(1), true%)

'   ---- Count the hand.
    CALL CountHand(dealerHand%(), dealerCards%, dealerTotal%)

'   ---- The dealer must stay at 17 or greater, no matter what the player's
'       count is.
    WHILE dealerTotal% < 17

'   ---- Deal the dealer another card.
        LOCATE 11 + dealerCards%, 37: PRINT SPACE$(30)
        LOCATE 12 + dealerCards%, 37
        PRINT "Count is" dealerTotal% "==> Dealer hits."
        CALL Pause
        dealerCards% = dealerCards% + 1
        dealerHand%(dealerCards%) = deck%(nextCard%)
        CALL BubbleSort(dealerHand%(), dealerCards%)

'   ---- Display the dealer's cards, sorted by suit.
        FOR i% = 1 to dealerCards%
            verticalPos% = i% + 1
            horizontalPos% = 32 + i% * 3
            CALL DisplayCard(verticalPos%, horizontalPos%, _
                dealerHand%(i%), true%)
        NEXT i%
        CALL MovePointer
        CALL CountHand(dealerHand%(), dealerCards%, dealerTotal%)
    WEND
```

Figure 8-13. *The* Twenty-one *program (continued).*   *(more...)*

337

player for the wager. Notice the text of the following PRINT statements within that series of statements:

```
PRINT "        (Press <Enter> for maximum bet.)"
PRINT "        (Press <Q> to Quit.)"
```

The player has three choices at this point: enter a value between 10 and 100, press the Enter key to select a bet of 100 to be entered by default, or enter the letter Q to exit the program. The *GetBet* subroutine processes these choices with an IF...THEN...ELSE block operating inside a WHILE...WEND loop.

  If the player presses Enter, an empty string is assigned to *betString$*; in this case, *GetBet* assigns the maximum bet to *betAmount%*:

```
IF betString$ = "" THEN
    betAmount% = highBet%
```

  If an upper- or lowercase Q is entered, the Boolean variables *ok%* and *quit%* are set to *true%*. The *ok%* variable is used as the logical expression in the WHILE...WEND loop. Setting it to *true%* means that a valid response was received from the user and that dialog with the player is no longer necessary. The *quit%* variable is returned to the main program when the *GetBet* subprogram has been completed:

```
SUB GetBet (quit%) STATIC
```

When *quit%* is returned with a true value, program execution ends.

  If the player enters a numeric bet amount from the keyboard, the VAL function converts *betString$* to its numeric equivalent:

```
ELSE
    betAmount% = VAL(betString$)
```

If *betString$* is a string value that cannot be converted to a number, VAL returns a value of 0. To be sure that *betAmount%* is inside the legal numeric range (from *lowBet%* to *highBet%*), the result of a compound conditional expression is assigned to the Boolean variable *ok%*:

```
ok% = (betAmount% >= lowBet%) AND (betAmount% <= highBet%)
```

To make sure the player's input amount is valid, the WHILE...WEND loop repeats the input process until *ok%* is true:

```
WHILE NOT ok%
```

  When *GetBet* has accepted a valid bet, the *StartGame* subprogram takes over and sets up the playing table with two initial hands.

```
'    ---- Display the appropriate card count information.
     LOCATE 11 + dealerCards%, 37: PRINT SPACE$(30)
     LOCATE 12 + dealerCards%, 37
     IF (dealerTotal% > 21) THEN
         PRINT "Count is" dealerTotal% "==> Busted!" + SPACE$(8)
     ELSE
         PRINT "Count is" dealerTotal% "==> Dealer stays."
     END IF
END SUB


'    The Winner subprogram announces whether the player has won or lost,
'        and adds the bet amount to---or subtracts it from---the player's
'        current holdings.

SUB Winner STATIC
     CALL CountHand(playerHand%(), playerCards%, playerTotal%)
     CALL CountHand(dealerHand%(), dealerCards%, dealerTotal%)

'    ---- If the counts of the two hands are equal, the round is a draw.
     IF (playerTotal% = dealerTotal%) THEN
         difference% = 0

'    ---- If the player has busted, or has a lower count than the dealer,
'        the player loses.
     ELSEIF (playerTotal% > 21) OR _
         (playerTotal% < dealerTotal% AND dealerTotal% < 22) THEN
         difference% = -1 * betAmount%
     ELSE

'    ---- If the player had 21 after the initial deal (of 2 cards)
'        then the player earns twice the bet.
         IF (playerTotal% = 21) AND (playerCards% = 2) THEN
             difference% = 2 * betAmount%

'    ---- Otherwise, the player simply earns the bet itself.
         ELSE
             difference% = betAmount%
         END IF
     END IF

'    ---- Add difference% (a negative or positive amount) to the player's
'        current worth, currentHoldings%.
     currentHoldings% = currentHoldings% + difference%

'    ---- Announce the result of the round.
     LOCATE 25, 10
     IF (difference% = 0) THEN
         PRINT "A draw... ";
     ELSEIF (difference% < 0) THEN
         PRINT USING "You lose $$###."; -1 * difference%;
     ELSE
         PRINT USING "You win $$###."; difference%;
     END IF

     CALL Pause
     CLS
END SUB
```

Winner

Figure 8-13. *The* Twenty-one *program (continued).*   *(more...)*

Dealing the cards: The *StartGame* subprogram

StartGame conducts the program's card-dealing procedure, variations of which occur in two other major subprograms: *PlayerPlay* and *DealerPlay.* The procedure requires several steps each time a card is dealt either to the player or to the dealer. The steps are:

1. Assign the current top card in the deck to the next available element of the appropriate hand array (*playerHand%* or *dealerHand%*).

2. Display the newly dealt card on the screen. (The *DisplayCard* subprogram does this.)

3. Increase the number of cards in the hand by 1. (This value is stored in *playerCards%* or *dealerCards%*.)

4. Move the deck pointer, *nextCard%*, forward by one card. (The *MovePointer* subprogram does this and also reshuffles the deck whenever necessary.)

5. Compute the new count of the hand that has just received a card. (The *CountHand* subprogram does this.)

As you can see, the process is complex enough to require three different subprograms—*DisplayCard, MovePointer,* and *CountHand.* We will look at each one of these routines a little later, but first let's see exactly how *StartGame* uses them.

A FOR...NEXT loop deals out the first two cards to each hand; each iteration of the loop deals one card to the player and then one card to the dealer:

```
FOR i% = 1 TO 2
```

The player gets the first card. Since *nextCard%* points to the current top of the deck, the expression *deck%(nextCard%)* always supplies the next card to be dealt:

```
playerHand%(i%) = deck%(nextCard%)
```

Keep in mind that *deck%, playerHand%,* and *dealerHand%* are all arrays of integers. The card being dealt to *playerHand%* in this assignment statement is represented by a number in the range of 1 to 52. Thanks to the *Shuffle* subprogram, those 52 numbers are currently arranged in a random order inside *deck%*.

```
'    The CountHand subprogram counts the value of a hand, and returns the
'       value of the count in the total% parameter.  The other parameters
'       are hand%, an array of card numbers, and number%, the number
'       of cards in the hand.

SUB CountHand(hand%(1), number%, total%) STATIC
    total% = 0
    aces% = 0

'    ---- Tens, Jacks, Queens, and Kings are worth ten.  The ace is worth
'         eleven unless the player's hand is over 21.  Other cards are
'         worth their face value.
    FOR i% = 1 to number%
        cardRank$ = RIGHT$(FN TransCard$(hand%(i%)), 1)
        IF (INSTR("TJQK", cardRank$) <> 0) THEN
            cardValue% = 10
        ELSEIF (cardRank$ = "A") THEN
            cardValue% = 11
            aces% = aces% + 1
        ELSE
            cardValue% = VAL(cardRank$)
        END IF
        total% = total% + cardValue%
    NEXT i%

'    ---- If total% is over 21, and if the hand contains aces, count one
'         or more aces as 1 rather than 11.
    WHILE (total% > 21) AND (aces% > 0)
        total% = total% - 10
        aces% = aces% - 1
    WEND
END SUB


'    The DisplayCard subprogram displays one card on the screen.  The
'       subprogram has four parameters:  verticalPos% and horizontalPos%
'       are the line and column locations of the upper-left corner of the
'       card display; card% is the card's number (from 1 to 52); and show%
'       is a Boolean value indicating whether the card is to be displayed
'       face up or face down.

SUB DisplayCard (verticalPos%, horizontalPos%, card%, show%) STATIC
'    ---- Begin by drawing the outline of the card.
    topEdge$ = CHR$(218) + STRING$(14,196) + CHR$(191)
    LOCATE verticalPos%, horizontalPos%: PRINT topEdge$

    FOR i% = verticalPos% + 1 to verticalPos% + 8
        LOCATE i%, horizontalPos%: PRINT CHR$(179)
    NEXT i%

    LOCATE verticalPos% + 9, horizontalPos%: PRINT CHR$(192) + STRING$(2,196)

'    ---- If the card is face up (show% is true), display the card's suit and
'         value.  Use the TransCard$ function to determine these from the
'         card's number.
    IF show% THEN

'    ---- Prepare a two-character string containing symbols for the card's
'         suit and value.
        card$ = FN TransCard$(card%)
```

CountHand

DisplayCard

Figure 8-13. *The Twenty-one program (continued).*   *(more...)*

The *DisplayCard* subprogram has the complex task of displaying a single card on the screen. Its parameter list is declared as follows:

```
SUB DisplayCard(verticalPos%, horizontalPos%, card%, show%) STATIC
```

The first two parameters, *verticalPos%* and *horizontalPos%*, indicate the location on the screen where *DisplayCard* places the upper-left corner of the card. The third parameter, *card%*, is a number in the range of 1 to 52 representing the card that is to be displayed, and the final parameter, *show%*, is a Boolean value that indicates whether the card is to be displayed face up (true) or face down (false). If *DisplayCard* receives a value of false for *show%*, the routine draws only the outline of the card and does not display rank and suit.

Here is how *StartGame* calls *DisplayCard* for displaying the cards dealt to the player's hand and the dealer's hand:

```
CALL DisplayCard (i% + 1, i% * 3, playerHand%(i%), true%)
CALL DisplayCard (i% + 1, 32 + i% * 3, dealerHand%(i%), 1 - i%)
```

The arguments sent to *verticalPos%* and *horizontalPos%* are computed from the loop index, *i%*. Single elements of the two hand arrays— *playerHand%(i%)* and *dealerHand%(i%)*—are the arguments sent to the *card%* parameters. For the player's hand, an argument of *true%* is always sent to the *show%* parameter, since both of the player's cards are face up. For the dealer's hand, however, the expression $1 - i\%$ produces a Boolean value of false for the first card and true for the second card, resulting in one card face down and one face up.

After a card is displayed, the variable that keeps count of the number of cards in a given hand (*playerCards%* or *dealerCards%*) must be increased by 1; for example:

```
playerCards% = playerCards% + 1
```

Likewise, the deck pointer, *nextCard%*, must be incremented by 1 so that a subsequently dealt card is the next one in the deck; the *MovePointer* subprogram, which takes no arguments, does this:

```
CALL MovePointer
```

Each newly dealt card results in a new count for the hand that receives it, so the final step in dealing a card is to recount the value

```
'    ---- Print the suit.
     LOCATE verticalPos% + 2, horizontalPos% + 1: PRINT LEFT$(card$,1)

'    ---- If the card value in the card$ string is "T", print "10";
'         otherwise print the value followed by a space.
     LOCATE verticalPos% + 1, horizontalPos% + 1
     IF RIGHT$(card$,1) = "T" THEN
         PRINT "10"
     ELSE
         PRINT RIGHT$(card$,1) + " "
     END IF

    END IF
END SUB


'   The BubbleSort subprogram is a bubble sort routine.  It is used to
'   rearrange the cards in a hand before the hand is displayed on the
'   screen.  Since a hand seldom has more than five or six cards, a
'   bubble sort is just as efficient as any of the more sophisticated
'   sorting routines.

SUB BubbleSort (array%(1), number%) STATIC
    FOR i% = 1 TO (number% - 1)
        FOR j% = (i% + 1) TO number%
            IF (array%(i%) > array%(j%)) THEN SWAP array%(i%), array%(j%)
        NEXT j%
    NEXT i%
END SUB
```

`BubbleSort`

Figure 8-13. *The* Twenty-one *program (continued).*

of the hand. The *StartGame* subprogram only needs to count the hands once, after each hand has received two cards. The *CountHand* subprogram, which counts the hands, receives three parameters:

```
SUB CountHand(hand%(1), number%, total%) STATIC
```

The first parameter is an array containing the hand that is to be counted, and the second is the number of cards in the hand. The third parameter, *total%,* is a variable in which *CountHand* can pass the computed count back to the calling subprogram.

Consider the two calls that *StartGame* makes to *CountHand*:

```
CALL CountHand(playerHand%(), 2, playerTotal%)
CALL CountHand(dealerHand%(), 2, dealerTotal%)
```

After these calls are performed, the variables *playerTotal%* and *dealerTotal%* contain the correct counts for the player's hand and the dealer's hand, respectively.

With the initial two hands duly dealt and counted, *StartGame* can analyze the current situation and decide if the round should continue.

The important question at this point is: Does one (or do both) of the hands have a natural count of 21? This question is answered and acted upon by the following IF...THEN...ELSE structure:

```
IF (dealerTotal% = 21) OR (playerTotal% = 21) THEN
    win% = true%
    IF (dealerTotal% = 21) THEN
        [display the dealer's hidden card and print
         a "Twenty-one!" message under the dealer's cards]
    IF (playerTotal% = 21) THEN
        [print a "Twenty-one!" message under the player's cards]
    ELSE
        [print the card count under the player's cards]
ELSE
    win% = false%
```

One task of this decision structure is to assign an appropriate value to the Boolean variable *win%*—*true%* if a natural has occurred, *false%* if not. This value is then passed back to the main program to indicate the status of the round.

If the dealer's hand contains a natural 21, another call to *DisplayCard* shows the dealer's hidden card:

```
CALL DisplayCard(2, 35, dealerHand%(1), true%)
```

Then a pair of nested IF...THEN...ELSE structures decide what message to display beneath each hand—*Twenty-one!* for the natural hand or the count for the losing hand. The dealer's hand is the exception to this rule. If the player has a 21 and the dealer does not, the dealer's hand is not shown. If the player has been taking note of the dealer's cards to figure the odds, this prevents the player from getting a free peek. (Also, if the player busts before the dealer plays, the dealer's cards are not displayed.)

After these decisions are made, *StartGame* relinquishes control to the main program section, potentially for calls to the *PlayerPlay* and *DealerPlay* subprograms. Before we study those routines, let's look at the three ubiquitous subprograms that are responsible for displaying a card (*DisplayCard*), incrementing the deck pointer (*MovePointer*), and counting a hand (*CountHand*).

Displaying a card on the screen: The *DisplayCard* subprogram

Recall that *DisplayCard* receives its four parameter values in the following variables:

```
SUB DisplayCard(verticalPos%, horizontalPos%, card%, show%) STATIC
```

- *verticalPos%* and *horizontalPos%* represent the screen coordinates where the card will be displayed: the row number and the column number

- *card%* receives the card number (an integer in the range 1 to 52)

- *show%* receives the Boolean value that indicates if the card's suit and rank should be displayed

The subprogram first draws the outline of the card at the correct position. To do so, it uses the CHR$ function to gain access to five of the graphics characters available in the extended character set:

- CHR$(218)—the upper-left corner character

- CHR$(191)—the upper-right corner character

- CHR$(192)—the lower-left corner character

- CHR$(196)—the horizontal line character

- CHR$(179)—the vertical line character

The technique for drawing the card outlines is the same as in similar routines discussed in Chapters 2 and 5. The LOCATE statement places the cursor at the correct position for a given character, and PRINT displays the character itself, supplied by the CHR$ function.

The STRING$ function can produce a horizontal line of identical characters. For example, the following expression produces a string that becomes the card's top edge:

```
topEdge$ = CHR$(218) + STRING$(14,196) + CHR$(191)
```

A vertical line, however, has to be displayed character by character, within a FOR...NEXT loop:

```
FOR i% = verticalPos% + 1 to verticalPos% + 8
    LOCATE i%, horizontalPos%: PRINT CHR$(179)
NEXT i%
```

Every element of the display is calculated from the starting point coordinates of *verticalPos%* and *horizontalPos%*.

When the outline is on the screen, *DisplayCard* next displays the card's suit and rank, but only if the *show%* parameter has received a Boolean value of true:

```
IF show% THEN
```

DisplayCard first converts the card integer, *card%*, to a card string, *card$*. (QuickBASIC recognizes *card%* and *card$* as two distinct variables, one an integer and the other a string.)

The *Twenty-one* program contains a convenient user-defined function named *TransCard$* that supplies the rank and suit of a card, given a card number in the range of 1 to 52. The function receives the card number in the variable *cardNumber%* and uses two rather complex arithmetic expressions to produce a suit number and a rank number from *cardNumber%*.

Using integer division, the following expression effectively divides the deck into four equal groups of 13 cards and yields suit numbers of 3, 4, 5, or 6:

```
((cardNumber% - 1) \ 13) + 3
```

Conveniently, the version of the ASCII code for the IBM PC contains four card suit characters:

- CHR$(3) is the heart.
- CHR$(4) is the diamond.
- CHR$(5) is the club.
- CHR$(6) is the spade.

Hence, the following statement assigns one of these four characters to the string variable *suit$*:

```
suit$ = CHR$(((cardNumber% - 1) \ 13) + 3)
```

To produce a rank number (the card number within the suit), *TransCard$* employs the MOD operation. The effect is to divide the deck into 13 groups of four cards each and to yield rank numbers from 1 to 13:

```
((cardNumber% - 1) MOD 13) + 1
```

Recall that the *InitializeDeck* subprogram sets up an array called *rank$*, which stores symbols for the 13 card ranks. So the following statement assigns one of these characters to the variable *rnk$*:

```
rnk$ = rank$(((cardNumber% -1) MOD 13) + 1)
```

In short, *TransCard$* returns a two-character string. The first character is the suit symbol, and the second character is the rank symbol corresponding to the *cardNumber%*:

```
FN TransCard$ = suit$ + rnk$
```

DisplayCard calls on this function to produce the card string from a card number:

```
card$ = FN TransCard$(card%)
```

It then uses the LEFT$ function to access the suit symbol for display in the card:

```
LOCATE verticalPos% + 2, horizontalPos% + 1: PRINT LEFT$(card$,1)
```

We should be able to use a nearly identical pair of statements, using the RIGHT$ function, to display the rank symbol. There are two problems with this, however. To assign each rank a single-character symbol, the *rank$* array uses the symbol *T* to represent the 10 card. But the *DisplayCard* subprogram needs to display *10* rather than *T*. Furthermore, since new cards are often redisplayed over the previous positions of other cards, *DisplayCard* needs a way to erase completely the two-character *10* symbol from the screen before placing a one-character rank symbol in its place. These two troublesome details are taken care of by the following simple IF...THEN...ELSE block:

```
IF RIGHT$(card$,1) = "T" THEN
    PRINT "10"
ELSE
    PRINT RIGHT$(card$,1) + " "
END IF
```

A space is included to the right of any single-character rank symbol, in case the previously displayed rank was the two-character string *10*.

As always, planning a complex screen display seems to require more attention to detail than almost any other programming task. But careful effort produces satisfying results.

Keeping track of the deck: The *MovePointer* subprogram

MovePointer always begins by performing the essential task of incrementing the deck pointer:

```
nextCard% = nextCard% + 1
```

Only the value of the pointer is changed. The *nextCard%* variable keeps track of the next card that should be dealt from the array. In other words, no changes are actually made in the *deck%* array between one deal and the next—using this pointer variable is much more efficient than rearranging the deck each time.

As long as *nextCard%* contains a value of 52 or less—actually pointing to a card in the deck—the *MovePointer* subprogram need take no further action. However, each time *nextCard%* goes past 52, the deck has to be reshuffled. This is the important decision that *MovePointer* makes:

```
IF (nextCard% > 52) THEN
    [reshuffle all the cards not currently on the table]
END IF
```

Unlike the initial shuffle of the entire deck, which takes place when the program is first run, reshuffling requires careful manipulation. Cards that are currently displayed on the screen (the table) must be left out of the shuffle; furthermore, a record of these same cards must be kept at an appropriate position in the deck so that they will be included in the next shuffle.

If a reshuffling is required, then, the first step is to count the number of cards on the table for the current round (*tableCards%*—the player's cards plus the dealer's cards), and the number that have been used for previous rounds since the last shuffle (*usedCards%*):

```
tableCards% = playerCards% + dealerCards%
usedCards% = 52 - tableCards%
```

MovePointer also displays a message at the bottom of the screen, announcing the reshuffle and the number of cards that are being shuffled:

```
LOCATE 25,25: PRINT "Reshuffling" usedCards% "cards...";
```

The next step is to create a dynamic deck array (*tempDeck%*) to temporarily store the cards to be shuffled. Since this array may have a different size each time the deck is shuffled, a REDIM statement is required for specifying the array's dimension:

```
REDIM tempDeck%(usedCards%)
```

If four cards are currently on the table, the used cards, which need to be reshuffled, are from *deck%(1)* to *deck(48)*; the routine assigns these cards to *tempDeck%*:

```
FOR i% = 1 TO usedCards%
    tempDeck%(i%) = deck%(i%)
NEXT i%
```

Then *MovePointer* calls the *Shuffle* subprogram to reshuffle the cards in *tempDeck%*:

```
CALL Shuffle(tempDeck%())
```

Recall from Chapter 3 that *Shuffle* receives the array in the parameter variable named *shuffledArray%*. The routine uses the UBOUND function to determine the size of the array it has received:

```
length% = UBOUND(shuffledArray%)
```

To shuffle *shuffledArray%*, *Shuffle* swaps random pairs of elements down the length of the array:

```
FOR card% = 1 TO length%
    randomCard% = INT(RND * length%) + 1
    SWAP shuffledArray%(card%), shuffledArray%(randomCard%)
NEXT card%
```

(For a more detailed review of *Shuffle*, see Chapter 3.)

When *tempDeck%* is shuffled, *MovePointer* has to reassemble the *deck%* array. First, the cards currently on the table are placed at the top of the array, where they remain unused until the next shuffle:

```
FOR i% = 1 TO tableCards%
    deck%(i%) = deck%(usedCards% + i%)
NEXT i%
```

Then the newly shuffled cards are copied from *tempDeck%* to *deck%*:

```
FOR i% = 1 to usedCards%
    deck%(tableCards% + i%) = tempDeck%(i%)
NEXT i%
```

The new effective position for the "top of the deck" starts at the first of the newly shuffled cards:

```
nextCard% = tableCards% + 1
```

The *Pause* subprogram

With this, the reshuffling process is complete. *MovePointer* calls on the *Pause* subprogram to create a pause in the action so the player may see the reshuffling message:

```
CALL Pause
```

Pause places the *Press <Enter> to continue* message on the screen. After displaying the message, the routine waits for the player to press the Enter key before sending control back to the calling subprogram. (Actually, the player can press any key to exit *Pause,* but it's a good user-interface technique to specify a key.)

Computing the value of a hand: The *CountHand* subprogram

CountHand has a list of three parameters:

```
SUB CountHand(hand%(1), number%, total%) STATIC
```

The *hand%* array receives the hand to be counted; *number%* is the number of cards in *hand%*; and *total%* is the variable that *CountHand* uses to pass the computed total back to the calling program.

CountHand actually has two tasks: (1) to count the cards according to the prescribed value of each rank, and (2) to adjust the count if the hand contains aces that should be valued at 1 instead of 11.

The routine begins by initializing two counting variables—*total%* (the total count) and *aces%* (the number of aces in the hand)—to zero:

```
total% = 0
aces% = 0
```

Then, in a FOR...NEXT loop that moves card by card through the entire hand, the routine accumulates the total count into the variable *total%*. Let's see how this is done.

The first step is to find the rank symbol of a given card and store the character in the variable *cardRank$*. The rank is the second of the two characters in the string returned by the *TransCard$* function:

```
cardRank$ = RIGHT$(FN TransCard$(hand%(i%)), 1)
```

An IF...THEN...ELSE structure examines this character and assigns its corresponding numeric value to the variable *cardValue%*:

```
IF (INSTR("TJQK", cardRank$) <> 0) THEN
    cardValue% = 10
ELSEIF (cardRank$ = "A") THEN
    cardValue% = 11
    aces% = aces% + 1
ELSE
    cardValue% = VAL(cardRank$)
END IF
```

Three different possibilities are expressed in this decision structure:

1. The IF statement: If *cardRank$* is one of the four characters in the string *TJQK*, the rank's value is 10. (The INSTR function returns a value of 0 if *cardRank$* is *not* in *TJQK*.)

2. The ELSEIF clause: If the value of *cardRank$* is *A*—representing an ace—the rank's value is set at 11, at least initially, and the number of aces in the hand is increased by 1.

3. The ELSE clause: Otherwise, *cardRank$* must be a digit from 2 to 9, and the rank's value is simply VAL (*cardRank$*).

When the rank's value is thus determined for a given card, the routine adds *cardValue%* to the current value of *total%* before moving to the next card:

```
total% = total% + cardValue%
```

When all the cards have been counted, *CountHand* may need to reevaluate any aces in the hand. Here is the rule: If the hand contains one or more aces *and* the current count of the hand is greater than 21, then aces are devalued one at a time, from 11 down to 1, until the total count is 21 or less or until the hand runs out of aces. This set of conditions translates into a simple WHILE...WEND loop structure in the final four lines of the subprogram:

```
WHILE (total% > 21) AND (aces% > 0)
    total% = total% - 10
    aces% = aces% - 1
WEND
```

The *CountHand, MovePointer,* and *DisplayCard* subprograms are the game's real workhorse routines. All three are called upon virtually every time a card is dealt. Now that we have seen what they do and how they are organized, we can continue following the main activities of the program. *PlayerPlay* is the next subprogram to be performed; then, *DealerPlay,* and finally, *Winner.*

Conducting the player's turn: The *PlayerPlay* subprogram

During the player's turn the *PlayerPlay* subprogram must constantly monitor three conditions; if any one of these conditions becomes true, the player's turn is over:

- The count of the player's hand exceeds 21.

- The player's hand reaches exactly 21.

- The player indicates that he or she wishes to stay with the count of the current hand.

To keep track of the current status of these conditions, the subprogram creates two Boolean variables, *over21%* and *done%*, both of which are assigned initial values of *false%*:

```
over21% = false%
done% = false%
```

The main action of the player's turn takes place within a controlling WHILE...WEND loop, which repeatedly offers the player the chance to hit or stay. The looping stops when either one of the Boolean variables is assigned a value of *true%*:

```
WHILE NOT (over21% OR done%)
```

Notice the importance of the parentheses in the WHILE condition. Another way to write the same condition is:

```
WHILE (NOT over21%) AND (NOT done%)
```

The *HitOrStay* function

The first statement inside this WHILE...WEND loop makes a call to a user-defined function named *HitOrStay* and assigns the resulting Boolean value to the variable *done%*:

```
done% = FN HitOrStay
```

The *HitOrStay* function is similar to the *YesNo* function presented in Chapter 3. Both functions display a prompt on the screen, accept one of two possible single-keystroke responses, and then return a Boolean value of true or false to indicate which response was received.

HitOrStay elicits the player's choice between "hitting" (taking another card) or "staying" (stopping with the cards currently in hand). The function places the hit-or-stay prompt below the player's hand:

```
PRINT "Your hand: Hit or Stay? ";
```

The INKEY$ function is then used (from inside a WHILE...WEND loop) to get the user's keystroke, and the user-defined function *Upper$* (discussed in Chapter 2) converts the letter response to uppercase:

```
answer$ = INKEY$
answer$ = FN Upper$(answer$)
```

The looping ends when *answer$* contains either an *H* or an *S*. The *HitOrStay* function returns a value of true to indicate a stay and a value of false to indicate a hit:

```
FN HitOrStay = (answer$ = "S")
```

This statement may seem unusual in format; in performing it, QuickBASIC first evaluates the logical expression *ans$ = S* to true or false and returns that value as the result of *HitOrStay*.

The next action of the *PlayerPlay* subprogram depends directly on the value that *HitOrStay* has assigned to the *done%* variable:

```
IF NOT done% THEN
    [deal the player another card, redisplay
     the hand with the new card, and analyze
     the new count]
ELSE
    [count the current hand]
END IF
```

If *done%* is false, the player gets another card. The routine increments the value of *playerCards%* by 1 and deals the next card in the deck to the player's hand:

```
playerCards% = playerCards% + 1
playerHand%(playerCards%) = deck%(nextCard%)
```

PlayerPlay next takes the extra step of sorting the hand before redisplaying the cards. As a result, the hand that subsequently appears on the screen is arranged by suits (hearts, diamonds, clubs, spades), and within each suit the cards appear in order of rank (2 up to ace). The *Twenty-one* program contains its own sorting routine, *BubbleSort*, written specifically for the task of rearranging the hands.

The *BubbleSort* subprogram

The *BubbleSort* subprogram implements a simple algorithm called a *bubble sort.* Although the bubble sort is easier to write and to understand than the Shell sort that we developed in Chapter 3, it is also a slower method for sorting long lists of items. However, an array representing a hand of cards in *Twenty-one* seldom has more than five or six elements. For small arrays, the speed of the bubble sort is competitive with that of the more sophisticated sorting algorithms.

The principle of the bubble sort is to compare each array element with every element below it; whenever a pair of elements is out of order, they are swapped. The comparisons occur within a pair of nested FOR...NEXT loops, and the following IF...THEN statement performs a swap whenever necessary:

```
IF (array%(i%) > array%(j%)) THEN SWAP array%(i%), array%(j%)
```

The effect of this sort on a given hand is to restore the original order of the cards, as they appeared in the *deck%* array before the first shuffle. A call to *BubbleSort* takes two arguments: an array representing a hand and an integer representing the number of cards in the hand. Here is how *PlayerPlay* sorts the player's hand:

```
CALL BubbleSort(playerHand%(), playerCards%)
```

After the sort, *PlayerPlay* makes calls to three familiar subprograms to display the cards on the screen (*DisplayCard*), increment the deck pointer (*MovePointer*), and finally to count the current value of the hand (*CountHand*). Given the new count, *playerTotal%*, the following IF...THEN structure checks for a bust or a value of exactly 21:

```
IF (playerTotal% > 21) THEN
    over21% = true%
    [display the count and the message
    "Busted!" on the screen, and sound a beep]
ELSEIF (playertotal% = 21) THEN
    done% = true%
END IF
```

This structure works with the two Boolean variables, *over21%* and *done%*. If the count is greater than 21, *over21%* is assigned a value of *true%*. If the count is 21 exactly, *done%* is assigned a value of *true%*. Since this structure has no ELSE clause, a count less than 21 results in no action.

When one of these variables finally becomes true, the lengthy WHILE...WEND loop in *PlayerPlay* stops. The final step of the subprogram is to display the player's final count, but only if *done%* has been assigned a value of *true%* (meaning either that the player has stayed or the count of the hand is exactly 21):

```
IF done% THEN
    [display the player's count]
END IF
```

PlayerPlay passes the value of *over21%* back to the main program to indicate whether or not the player has busted. If a bust has not occurred (*over21%* is false), the program next calls the *DealerPlay* subprogram to give the dealer a turn.

Conducting the dealer's turn: the *DealerPlay* subprogram

The *DealerPlay* subprogram starts out by turning up the dealer's hidden card and evaluating the two-card hand:

```
CALL DisplayCard(2, 35, dealerHand%(1), true%)
CALL CountHand(dealerHand%(), dealerCards%, dealerTotal%)
```

Recall the rule that determines the subsequent action: the dealer stays with a count of 17 or higher and hits with a count below 17. Given the calculated count, *dealerTotal%,* a WHILE...WEND loop takes control of the action:

```
WHILE dealerTotal% < 17
    [deal another card to the dealer's hand]
WEND
```

The statements performed inside this WHILE...WEND loop are similar to the card-dealing sequence in the *PlayerPlay* subprogram. The *Pause* subprogram waits for the player's keystroke before the action continues. When a key is pressed, *DealerPlay* increases the number of cards in the dealer's hand (*dealerCards%*) by 1 and assigns the next card in the deck to the hand array (*dealerHand%*). The *BubbleSort* subprogram sorts the hand. *DisplayCard* shows each card on the screen. *MovePointer* increments *nextCard%*, the deck pointer. And finally, *CountHand* computes a new count of the hand, adding on the newly dealt card.

The WHILE...WEND loop continues until the count is 17 or more. Recall that the *CountHand* subprogram follows the rules for handling aces in the dealer's hand: If the count will otherwise exceed 21, any aces in the hand may be devalued to 1; otherwise aces are worth 11.

Finally, at the end of the subprogram, the following IF...THEN...ELSE structure chooses one of two messages to display on the screen:

```
IF (dealerTotal% > 21) THEN
    PRINT "Count is" dealerTotal% "==> Busted!" + SPACE$(8)
ELSE
    PRINT "Count is" dealerTotal% "==> Dealer stays."
END IF
```

After both the player and the dealer have taken their turns, the action of the round is over except for determining who has won. This final task belongs to the *Winner* subprogram.

Declaring the winner: The *Winner* subprogram

The *Winner* subprogram has two tasks: finding out how much money the player has won or lost in the last round and displaying an appropriate message on the screen. *Winner* does this within a series of IF...THEN...ELSE decisions.

To start, the subprogram makes two calls to *CountHand* to compute the final counts of the player's and dealer's hands. These two values are stored in *playerTotal%* and *dealerTotal%*. The first decision structure then looks to see if the game has ended in a draw:

```
IF (playerTotal% = dealerTotal%) THEN
    difference% = 0
```

The variable *difference%* stores the amount of money the player has won or lost during this round; for a draw, the player's current assets (or debts!) do not change.

On the other hand, if the player has busted or if the dealer's count is greater than the player's count, then the player loses the bet. Recall that the bet is stored in the global variable *betAmount%*:

```
ELSEIF (playerTotal% > 21) OR _
    (playerTotal% < dealerTotal% AND dealerTotal% < 22) THEN
    difference% = -1 * betAmount%
```

This ELSEIF clause has a compound conditional expression. If the following expression is true, the player has busted:

```
playerTotal% > 21
```

If the following is true, the dealer has a better hand than the player:

```
playerTotal% < dealerTotal% AND dealerTotal% < 22
```

This expression also checks to be sure the dealer has not busted.

The player wins twice the bet for a natural (exactly 2 cards, with a count of 21) or the bet itself for a hand that is superior to the dealer's. A nested IF...THEN...ELSE structure checks for these possibilities:

```
ELSE
    IF (playerTotal% = 21) AND (playerCards% = 2) THEN
        difference% = 2 * betAmount%
    ELSE
        difference% = betAmount%
    END IF
END IF
```

The nesting is not actually necessary, since the following revision, with an additional ELSEIF clause, results in the same decision:

```
ELSEIF (playerTotal% = 21) AND (playerCards% = 2) THEN
    difference% = 2 * betAmount%
ELSE
    difference% = betAmount%
END IF
```

The nested version, however, results in clearer, more readable code by isolating the statements that deal with a winning round for the player. But the choice between the two versions is a matter of personal preference.

A final decision structure in the *Winner* subprogram uses the value of *difference%* to select one of three possible concluding messages:

```
IF (difference% = 0) THEN
    PRINT "A draw... ";
ELSEIF (difference% < 0) THEN
    PRINT USING "You lose $$###."; -1 * difference%;
ELSE
    PRINT USING "You win $$###."; difference%;
END IF
```

Winner next calls on *Pause* to wait for a keystroke that will end the round:

```
CALL Pause
CLS
```

At this point the screen is cleared and control returns to the main program, possibly for another round of the game.

CONCLUSION

In the process of designing and writing almost any game program, two general problems concern the programmer:

1.   Creating carefully structured decisions that successfully moni-tor—and act upon—all the controlling conditions in the game.

2.   Designing a good user-interface (that is, attractive screen dis-plays and efficient keyboard input techniques) that creates an ap-propriate atmosphere and pace for the game.

The *Twenty-one* program illustrates both these problems and pre-sents individual approaches to solving them. If you are interested in working on a game program of your own, you may prefer to start by revising this one. Here is an opportunity for a programming exercise: Two traditional playing options are not permitted in the simplified version of Twenty-one played by this program. The options are *splitting pairs* and *doubling down*:

- *Splitting pairs.* A player who receives (in the initial deal) a pair of cards with the same rank may elect to split the pair into two hands and then play each hand separately. The player's previously specified bet applies twice, once to each hand.

- *Doubling down.* Upon examining the initial hand of two cards, a player may elect to double the bet. In exchange for this privilege, the player must take one—and only one—more card, for a total of three cards in the hand.

Now that you are familiar with Twenty-one and this program, you might want to try implementing one or both of these optional features. Like all the QuickBASIC programs in this book, the *Twenty-one* program is structured into a hierarchy of many small, self-contained subprograms. If you expand the program, you can use this structure to your advantage.

INDEX

A page number in italics indicates a
    figure on that page.

Symbols

! (suffix for single-precision variables),
    86–87, 88
(suffix for double-precision variables),
    86, 88–89
$ (suffix for string variables), 92–94
$DYNAMIC metacommand, 9
$INCLUDE metacommand, 9, 47–50
$STATIC metacommand, 9
% (suffix for integer variables), 86
* operation, 89
+ operation, 89
,A option in BASICA, 13
− operation, 89
/ operation, 89
?Redo from start error message. *See*
    Redo from start error message
\ operation, 90
^ operation, 89

A

ABS, 336
Accuracy
    in dollar-and-cent operations, 114
    double-precision numbers, 88
    single-precision numbers, 87
addition, 89
Alphabetic case conversion, 38–40
Alphanumeric labels, 8
Alt key, 12
AND, 95, 110, 313, 338, 352
Arguments
    array arguments, 28–29
    passed by reference, 7, 24, 26–27, 58,
        292
    passed by value, 7, 24, 27–28

Arrays
    DIM to define data type of, 140–41
    dynamic *v* static, 328
    elements passed as arguments, 28–29
    general description, 139
    global *v* local, 142–43
    indexing with, 300–302
    OPTION BASE with, 140
    passed as arguments, 28–29
    REDIM to define, 143
    static *v* dynamic, 8, 141–42, 286
    subscripts in, 139, 140, 143
    Twenty-one program, 340–44
    variable names for, 140
    zeroth element, 141
ASC, 221
ASCII, 92–93, 95
    alphabetic case conversion, 39–40
    characters in string functions, 92–93,
        95
    code number displayed, 221
    creating a program file from
        BASICA, 13
    graphics characters, 30, 144–47,
        345–46
    printable characters, 149
Auto Save command (File menu), 13

B

BASICA
    creating an ASCII program file
        from, 13
    global variables in, 33–34
    interpreter, 2–6
    LPRINT statement, 250
    program example, *33*
    user-defined functions in, 36–37
    WRITE# statement, 190
BCOM20.LIB, 21

DOUGLAS HERGERT

A native Californian, Douglas Hergert received a bachelor's degree in English and French from Washington University, St. Louis, Missouri, in 1974. After graduation, he spent five years in the Peace Corps, teaching English in Afghanistan and Senegal. Doug is the author of more than a dozen books, including the best-selling **COMMAND PERFORMANCE: dBASE III, COMMAND PERFORMANCE: MICROSOFT EXCEL**, and **MICROSOFT EXCEL WITH MACROS**, all published by Microsoft Press.

The manuscript for this book was prepared and submitted to Microsoft Press in electronic form. Text files were processed and formatted using Microsoft Word.

Cover design by Greg Hickman
Interior text design by Microsoft Press
Principal typographer: Ruth Pettis
Principal production artist: Rick Bourgoin

The high-resolution screen displays were created using the COMPAQ Portable 286, and were printed on the Hewlett Packard LaserJet Plus and by ImageSet Corporation.

Text composition by Microsoft Press in Baskerville with display in Futura Bold, using the CCI composition system and the Mergenthaler Linotron 202 digital phototypesetter.